Mastering
Data Warehouse
Aggregates

D1616207

Mastering
Data Warehouse
Aggregates
Solutions for Star
Schema Performance

Christopher Adamson

WILEY

Wiley Publishing, Inc.

Mastering Data Warehouse Aggregates: Solutions for Star Schema Performance
Published by
Wiley Publishing, Inc.
10475 Crosspoint Boulevard
Indianapolis, IN 46256
www.wiley.com

ISBN-13: 978-0-471-77709-0
ISBN-10: 0-471-77709-9

Manufactured in the United States of America

10 9 8 7 6 5 4 3 2 1

1MA/SQ/QW/QW/IN

Library of Congress Cataloging-in-Publication Data

Adamson, Christopher, 1967–
  Mastering data warehouse aggregates: solutions for star schema performance / Christopher Adamson.
    p. cm.
  Includes index.
  ISBN-13: 978-0-471-77709-0 (pbk.)
  ISBN-10: 0-471-77709-9 (pbk.)
  1. Data warehousing. I. Title.
QA76.9.D37A333 2006
005.74—dc22

                    2006011219

For Wayne H. Adamson

1929–2003

Through those whose lives you touched,
your spirit of love endures.

About the Author

Christopher Adamson is a data warehousing consultant and founder of Oakton Software LLC. An expert in star schema design, he has managed and executed data warehouse implementations in a variety of industries. His customers have included Fortune 500 companies, large and small businesses, government agencies, and data warehousing tool vendors. Mr. Adamson also teaches dimensional modeling and is a co-author of *Data Warehouse Design Solutions* (also from Wiley). He can be contacted through his website, www .ChrisAdamson.net.

Credits

Executive Editor
Robert Elliott

Development Editor
Brian Herrmann

Technical Editor
Jim Hadley

Copy Editor
Nancy Rapoport

Editorial Manager
Mary Beth Wakefield

Production Manager
Tim Tate

**Vice President and Executive
  Group Publisher**
Richard Swadley

**Vice President and Executive
  Publisher**
Joseph B. Wikert

Project Coordinator
Michael Kruzil

**Graphics and Production
  Specialists**
Jennifer Click
Denny Hager
Stephanie D. Jumper
Heather Ryan

Quality Control Technicians
John Greenough
Brian H. Walls

Proofreading and Indexing
Techbooks

Contents

Foreword

In 1998 I wrote the foreword for Chris Adamson and Mike Venerable's book *Data Warehouse Design Solutions* (Wiley, 1998). Over the intervening eight years I have been delighted to track that book, as it has stayed high in the list of data warehouse best sellers, even through today. Chris and Mike had identified a set of data warehouse design challenges and were able to speak very effectively in that book to the community of data warehouse designers.

Viewed in the right perspective, the mission of data warehousing has not changed at all since 1998! In that foreword, I wrote that the data warehouse must be driven from business analysis needs, must be a mirror of management's urgent priorities, and must be a presentation facility that is understandable and fast. All of these perspectives have held true through today. While our databases have exploded in size, and the database content has become much more operational, the original description of the data warehouse rings true. If anything, the data warehouse, in its role as the platform for all forms of business intelligence, has become much more important than it was in 1998.

At the same time that the reach of the data warehouse has penetrated to every worker's desktop, we have all been swept along by the development of the Internet, and particularly search engines like Google. This parallel revolution, surprisingly, has sent data warehousing and business intelligence a powerful and simple message. As the saying goes, "The medium is the message." In this case, Google's message is:

You can search the entire contents of the Internet in less than a second.

The message to data warehousing is:

You should expect instantaneous results from your data warehouse queries.

To be perfectly frank, data warehousing and business intelligence have so far made only partial progress toward instantaneous performance. Our databases are more complicated than Google's documents, and our queries are more complex. *But*, we have some powerful tools that can be used to get us much closer to the goal of instantaneous performance.

Those of us who, like Chris and the Kimball Group, have long recognized that the class of data warehouse designs known as dimensional models offers a systematic opportunity for a huge performance boost, above and beyond database indexes, hardware RAM, faster processors, or parallelism. In fact, this additional performance opportunity, known as *aggregates*, when used correctly, can trump all the other performance techniques!

The idea behind aggregates is very simple. Always start with the most atomic, transaction-grained data available from the original source systems. Place that atomic data in full view of the end users in a dimensional format. Of course, if you stop there, you will have performance problems because many queries will do a huge amount of I/O no matter how much hardware you throw at the problem. Now aggregates come to the rescue. You systematically create a set of physically stored, pre-calculated summary records that are predictable common queries, or parts of queries posed by the end users. These summary records are the aggregates.

Aggregates, when used correctly, can provide performance improvements of a hundred or even a thousand times. No other technology is capable of such gains.

This book is all about aggregates. Chris explains how they rely on the dimensional approach, which aggregates to build, how to build them, and how to maintain them. He also shows in detail how Oracle's materialized views and IBM's materialized query tables are perfect examples of aggregates used effectively.

I was delighted to see Chris return to being an author after his wonderful first book. His only excuse for waiting eight years was that he was "busy building data warehouses." I'll accept that excuse! Now we can apply Chris's insights into making our data warehouse and business intelligence systems a big step closer to being instantaneous.

Ralph Kimball
Founder, Kimball Group
Boulder Creek, California

Acknowledgments

Thank you to everyone who read my first book, *Data Warehouse Design Solutions*, which I wrote with Mike Venerable. The positive feedback we received from around the world was unexpected, and most appreciated. Without your warm reception, I doubt that the current volume would have come to pass.

This book would not have been possible without Ralph Kimball. The value of his contribution to the data warehousing world cannot be understated. He has established a practical and powerful approach to data warehousing and provided terminology and principles for dimensional modeling that are used throughout the industry. I am deeply grateful for Ralph's continued support and encouragement, without which neither this nor my previous book would have been written.

I thank everyone at Wiley who contributed to this effort. Bob Elliott was a pleasure to work with and provided constructive criticism that was instrumental in shaping this book. Brian Herrmann made the writing process as painless as possible. I also thank the anonymous reviewers of my original outline, whose comments made this a better book.

Thanks also to Jim Hadley, who put in long hours reviewing drafts of this book. Through his detailed comments and advice, he made a substantial contribution to this effort. His continuing encouragement got me through several rough spots.

I am grateful to the customers and colleagues with whom I have worked over the years. The opportunity to learn from one another enriches us all. In particular, I thank three people as yet unmentioned. Mike Venerable has offered me opportunities that have shaped my career, along with guidance and advice that have helped me grow in numerous dimensions. Greg Jones's work managing data warehouse projects has profoundly influenced my own perspective, as is evident in Chapter 7. And Randall Porter has always been a welcome source of professional guidance, which was offered over many breakfasts during the writing of this book.

A very special thank you to my wife, Gladys, and sons, Justin and Carter, whose support and encouragement gave me the resolve I needed to complete this project. I also received support from my mother, sister, in-laws, and sisters-in-law. I could not have done this without all of you.

Introduction

In the battle to improve data warehouse performance, no weapon is more powerful and efficient than the aggregate table. A well-planned set of aggregates can have an extraordinary impact on the overall throughput of the data warehouse. After you ensure that the database is properly designed, configured, and tuned, any measures taken to address data warehouse performance should begin with aggregates.

Yet many businesses continue to ignore aggregates, turning instead to proprietary hardware products, converting to specialized databases, or implementing complex caching architectures. These solutions carry high price tags for acquisition and implementation and often require specialized skills to maintain. This book aims to fill the knowledge gap that has led businesses down this expensive and risky path.

In these pages, you will find tools and techniques you can use to bring stunning performance gains to *your* data warehouse. This book develops a set of best practices for the selection, design, construction, and use of aggregate tables. It explores how these techniques can be incorporated into projects, studies advanced design considerations, and covers how aggregates affect other aspects of the data warehouse lifecycle.

Intended Audience

This book is intended for *you*, the data warehouse practitioner with an interest in improving query performance. You may serve any one of a number of roles in the data warehouse environment, including:

- Business analyst
- Star schema designer
- Report developer
- ETL developer
- Project manager
- Database administrator
- Data administrator
- I.T. director
- Chief information officer
- Power user

Regardless of your role or current level of knowledge, the best practices in this book will help you and your team achieve astounding increases in data warehouse performance, without requiring an investment in exotic technologies.

It will be assumed that you have a very basic familiarity with relational database technology, understanding the concepts of tables, columns, and joins. Occasional examples of SQL code will be provided, and they will be fully explained in the accompanying text.

For those new to data warehousing, the background necessary to understand the examples will be provided along the way. For example, an overview of the star schema is presented in Chapter 1. The Extract Transform Load (ETL) process for the data warehouse is described in Chapter 5. The high-level data mart implementation process is described in Chapter 7.

About This Book

This book assumes a star schema approach to data warehousing. The necessary background is provided for readers new to this approach. It also considers implications of snowflake designs and, to a lesser extent, schemas in third normal form (3NF).

The design principles and best practices developed in each chapter make no assumptions about specific software products in the data warehouse. This tool-agnostic perspective is periodically supplemented with specific advice for users of Oracle's materialized views and IBM DB/2's materialized query tables.

Star Schema Approach

The techniques presented in this book are intended for data warehouses that are designed according to the principles of *dimensional modeling*, more popularly known as the *star schema approach*. Popularized by Ralph Kimball in the 1990s, the dimensional model is now widely accepted as the optimal method to organize information for analytic consumption.

Ralph Kimball and Margy Ross provide a comprehensive treatment of dimensional modeling in *The Data Warehouse Toolkit, Second Edition* (Wiley, 2002). The seminal work on the subject, their book is required reading for any student of data warehousing. The best practices in this book build on the foundation provided by Kimball and Ross and are described using terminology established by *The Toolkit*.

If you are not familiar with the star schema approach to data warehouse design, Chapter 1 provides an overview of the basic principles necessary to understand the examples in this book.

Snowflakes and 3NF Designs

Although this book focuses on the star schema, it does not ignore other approaches to schema design. From time to time, this book will examine the impact of a *snowflake design* on principles established throughout the book. For example, implications of a snowflake schema for aggregate design are explored in Chapters 2 and 3, and discussed more fully in Chapter 8.

In addition, Chapter 8 will look at how dimensional aggregates can service a *third normal form* schema design. Because of the complex relationships between the tables of a normalized schema, dimensional aggregates can have a tremendous impact. Of course, this is really the impact of the dimensional model itself. Best practices would suggest beginning with the most granular design possible, which is not really an aggregate at all. Still, a dimensional perspective can be used to augment query performance in such an environment.

Tool Independence

This book makes no assumptions regarding the presence of specific software products in your data warehouse architecture. Many commercial products offer features to assist in the implementation of aggregate tables. Each implementation is different; each has its own benefits and drawbacks; all are constantly changing.

Regardless of the tools used to build and navigate aggregates, you will need to address the same major tasks. You must choose which aggregates to implement; the aggregates must be designed; the aggregates must be built; a process must be established to ensure they are refreshed, or loaded, on a regular basis; the warehouse must be configured so that application queries are redirected to the aggregates.

This book provides a set of principles and best practices to guide you through these common tasks.

You can also use the principles in this book to guide the selection of specific technologies. For example, one component that you may need to add to your data warehouse architecture is the *aggregate navigator*. Chapter 4 develops a set of requirements for the aggregate navigator function. Three styles of commercial implementations are identified and evaluated against these requirements. You can use these requirements to evaluate your current technology options, as described in Chapter 7. They will remain valid even as specific products change and evolve.

Materialized Views and Materialized Query Tables

Specific database features from Oracle (materialized views) and IBM's DB/2 (materialized query tables) can be used to load and maintain aggregate tables as well as provide aggregate navigation services.

Throughout this book, the impact of using these technologies to build and navigate dimensional aggregates is explored. After establishing principles and best practices, we consider the implications of using these products. What is potentially gained or lost? How can you modify your process to accommodate the products' strengths and weaknesses? This is information that cannot be gleaned from a syntax reference manual.

Keep in mind that these products continue to evolve. Over time, their capabilities can be expected to expand and change. If you use these products, it behooves you to study their capabilities closely, compare them with the requirements of dimensional aggregation, test their application, and identify relevant implications. In fact, this is advised for users of *any* tool in Chapter 7.

MATERIALIZED VIEWS AND MATERIALIZED QUERY TABLES

The tool-agnostic principles and techniques in this book are periodically supplemented with a look at the impact of Oracle's *materialized views* and IBM DB/2's *materialized query tables*.

TOPIC	CHAPTER	DESCRIPTION
Aggregate Design	Chapter 3	Schema designers targeting these technologies should model the hierarchies implicit within a dimension table, and the relationships among their attributes. This information should be included in design documentation, along with defining queries for each aggregate table.
Aggregate Use	Chapter 4	Chapter 4 describes the use of materialized views and materialized query tables to provide query rewrite capabilities. It also shows how these technologies are used to implement aggregate fact tables, virtual aggregate dimension tables, and pre-joined aggregates.
Aggregate Refresh	Chapter 5	Materialized views and materialized query tables do not eliminate the need to manage the refresh of aggregates. It is also necessary to coordinate the refresh mechanism with the query rewrite mechanism.
Aggregate Construction	Chapter 6	It is not necessary to build an ETL process to load a materialized view or materialized query table. Once their refresh is configured, the database will take care of this job. But some adjustments to the base schema's ETL process may improve the overall performance of the aggregates.

Purpose of Each Chapter

This book is organized into chapters that address the major activities involved in the implementation of star schema aggregates. After establishing some fundamentals, chapters are dedicated to aggregate selection, design, usage, and construction. The remaining chapters address the organization of these activities into project plans, explore advanced design considerations, and address other impacts on the data warehouse.

Chapter 1: Fundamentals of Aggregates

This chapter establishes a foundation on which the rest of the book will build. It introduces the *star schema*, *aggregate tables*, and the *aggregate navigator*. Even if you are already familiar with these concepts, you should read Chapter 1. It establishes guiding principles for the development of *invisible aggregates*, which have zero impact on production applications. These principles will shape the best practices developed through the rest of the book. This chapter also introduces several forms of summarization that are not invisible to applications but may provide useful performance benefits.

Chapter 2: Choosing Aggregates

Chapter 2 takes on the difficult process of determining which aggregates should be built. You will learn how to identify and describe potential aggregates and determine the appropriate combination for implementation. This will require balancing the performance of potential aggregates with their potential usage and available resources. A variety of techniques will prove useful in identifying high-value aggregate tables.

Chapter 3: Designing Aggregates

The design of aggregate tables requires the same rigor as that of the base schema. Chapter 3 lays out a detailed set of principles for the design of dimensional aggregates. Best practices are identified and explained in detail, and a concrete set of deliverables is developed for the design process. Common pitfalls that can disrupt accuracy or ease of use are fully explored.

Chapter 4: Using Aggregates

In the most successful implementations, aggregate tables are invisible to users and applications. The job of the aggregate navigator is to redirect all queries to the best performing summaries. Chapter 4 develops a set of requirements for the aggregate navigator and uses them to evaluate three common styles of solutions. It explores two specific technologies in detail—Oracle's materialized views and IBM DB/2's materialized query tables—and provides practical advice for working without an aggregate navigator.

Chapter 5: ETL Part 1: Incorporating Aggregates

This book dedicates two chapters to the process of building aggregate tables. Chapter 5 describes how the base schema is loaded and how aggregates are integrated into that process. You will learn when it makes sense to design an incremental load for aggregate tables, and when you are better off dropping and rebuilding them each time the base schema is updated. For data warehouses loaded during batch windows, this chapter outlines several benefits of loading aggregates after the base schema. The ETL process will be required to interact with the aggregate navigator, or to take the entire data warehouse offline during the load. Data warehouses loaded in real-time require a different strategy for the maintenance of aggregates; specific techniques are discussed to minimize the impact of aggregates on this process.

Database features such as materialized views or materialized query tables may automate the construction process but are subject to the same requirements. As Chapter 5 shows, they must be configured to remain synchronized with the base schema, and designers must still choose between drop-and-rebuild and incremental load.

Chapter 6: ETL Part 2: Loading Aggregates

The second of two chapters on ETL, Chapter 6 describes the specific tasks required to load aggregate tables. Best practices are provided for identifying changed data in the base schema, constructing aggregate dimensions and their surrogate keys, and building aggregate fact tables. Pre-joined aggregates are also considered, along with complications that can arise from the presence of type 1 attributes.

The best practices in this chapter apply whether the load is developed using an ETL tool, or hand-coded. Database features such as materialized views or materialized query tables eliminate the need to design load routines, but may benefit from some adjustment to the schema design.

Chapter 7: Aggregates and Your Project

Aggregates should always be designed and implemented as part of a project. Chapter 7 provides a standard set of tasks and deliverables that can be used to add aggregates to existing schema, or to incorporate aggregates into the scope of a larger data warehouse development project. Major project phases are covered, including strategy, design, construction, testing, and deployment. The ongoing maintenance of aggregates is discussed, tying specific responsibilities to established data warehousing roles.

Chapter 8: Advanced Aggregate Design

This chapter outlines numerous advanced techniques for star schema design and fully analyzes the implications of each technique on aggregation. Design topics include:

- The periodic snapshot
- The accumulating snapshot
- Two kinds of factless fact tables
- Three kinds of bridge tables
- The transaction dimension
- Families of core and custom schemas

Chapter 8 also looks at how the techniques in this book can be adapted for snowflake schemas and third normal form designs.

Chapter 9: Related Topics

This final chapter collects several remaining topics that are influenced by aggregates:

- *The archive process* must be extended to involve aggregate tables. Some common misconceptions are discussed, and often-overlooked opportunities are highlighted.
- *Security requirements* may call for special care in implementing aggregates, which may also prove part of the solution.
- *Derived tables* are summarizations of base schema data that are not invisible. They include merged fact tables, sliced fact tables, and pivoted fact tables. Standard invisible aggregates may further summarize derived tables.
- *Deploying summary data before detail* can present new challenges, particularly if unanticipated. This chapter concludes by providing alternative techniques to deal with this unusual problem.

Glossary

Important terms used throughout this book are collected and defined in the glossary. You may find it useful to refer to these definitions as you read this book, particularly if you choose to read the chapters out of sequence.

Mastering
Data Warehouse
Aggregates

CHAPTER

1

Fundamentals of Aggregates

A decade ago, Ralph Kimball described aggregate tables as "the single most dramatic way to improve performance in a large data warehouse." Writing in *DBMS Magazine* ("Aggregate Navigation with (Almost) No Metadata," August 1996), Kimball continued:

Aggregates can have a very significant effect on performance, in some cases speeding queries by a factor of one hundred or even one thousand. No other means exist to harvest such spectacular gains.

This statement rings as true today as it did ten years ago. Since then, advances in hardware and software have dramatically improved the capacity and performance of the data warehouse. Aggregates *compound* the effect of these improvements, providing performance gains that fully harness capabilities of the underlying technologies.

And the pressure to improve data warehouse performance is as strong as ever. As the baseline performance of underlying technologies has improved, warehouse developers have responded by storing and analyzing larger and more granular volumes of data. At the same time, warehouse systems have been opened to larger numbers of users, internal and external, who have come to expect instantaneous access to information.

This book empowers *you* to address these pressures. Using aggregate tables, you can achieve an extraordinary improvement in the speed of *your* data warehouse. And you can do it today, without making expensive upgrades to hardware, converting to a new database platform, or investing in exotic and proprietary technologies.

Although aggregates can have a powerful impact on data warehouse performance, they can also be misused. If not managed carefully, they can cause confusion, impose inordinate maintenance requirements, consume massive amounts of storage, and even provide inaccurate results. By following the best practices developed in this book, you can avoid these outcomes and maximize the positive impact of aggregates.

The introduction of aggregate tables to the data warehouse will touch every aspect of the data warehouse lifecycle. A set of best practices governs their selection, design, construction, and usage. They will influence data warehouse planning, project scope, maintenance requirements, and even the archive process. Before exploring each of these topics, it is necessary to establish some fundamental principles and vocabulary.

This chapter establishes the foundation on which the rest of the book builds. It introduces the *star schema*, *aggregate tables*, and the *aggregate navigator*. Guiding principles are established for the development of *invisible aggregates*, which have zero impact on production applications—other than performance, of course. Last, this chapter explores several other forms of summarization that are not invisible to applications, but may also provide useful performance benefits.

Star Schema Basics

A star schema is a set of tables in a relational database that has been designed according to the principles of *dimensional modeling*. Ralph Kimball popularized this approach to data warehouse design in the 1990s. Through his work and writings, Kimball established standard terminology and best practices that are now used around the world to design and build data warehouse systems. With coauthor Margy Ross, he provides a detailed treatment of these principles in *The Data Warehouse Toolkit, Second Edition* (Wiley, 2002).

To follow the examples throughout this book, you must understand the fundamental principles of dimensional modeling. In particular, the reader must have a basic grasp of the following concepts:

- The differences between data warehouse systems and operational systems
- How facts and dimensions support the measurement of a business process
- The tables of a star schema (fact tables and dimension tables) and their purposes

- The purpose of surrogate keys in dimension tables
- The grain of a fact table
- The additivity of facts
- How a star schema is queried
- Drilling across multiple fact tables
- Conformed dimensions and the warehouse bus
- The basic architecture of a data warehouse, including ETL software and BI software

If you are familiar with these topics, you may wish to skip to the section "Invisible Aggregates," later in this chapter.

For everyone else, this section will bring you up-to-speed. Although not a substitute for Kimball and Ross's book, this overview provides the background needed to understand the examples throughout this book. I encourage *all* readers to read *The Toolkit* for more immersion in the principles of dimensional modeling, particularly anyone involved in the design of the dimensional data warehouse.

Data warehouse designers will also benefit from reading *Data Warehouse Design Solutions*, by Chris Adamson and Mike Venerable (Wiley, 1998). This book explores the application of these principles in the service of specific business objectives and covers standard business processes in a wide variety of industries.

Operational Systems and the Data Warehouse

Data warehouse systems and operational systems have fundamentally different purposes. An operational system supports the *execution* of business process, while the data warehouse supports the *evaluation* of the process. Their distinct purposes are reflected in contrasting usage profiles, which in turn suggest that different principles will guide their design. The principles of dimensional modeling are specifically adapted to the unique requirements of the warehouse system.

Operational Systems

An operational system directly supports the *execution* of business processes. By capturing detail about significant events or transactions, it constructs a record of the activity. A sales system, for example, captures information about orders, shipments, and returns; a human resources system captures information about the hiring and promotion of employees; an accounting system captures information about the management of the financial assets and liabilities of the business. Capturing the detail surrounding these activities is often so important that the operational system becomes a part of the process.

To facilitate execution of the business process, an operational system must enable several types of database interaction, including inserts, updates, and deletes. Operational systems are often referred to as transaction systems. The focus of these interactions is almost always atomic—a specific order, a shipment, a refund. These interactions will be highly predictable in nature. For example, an order entry system must provide for the management of lists of products, customers, and salespeople; the entering of orders; the printing of order summaries, invoices, and packing lists; and the tracking of order status.

Implemented in a relational database, the optimal design for an operational schema is widely accepted to be one that is in *third normal form*. This design supports the high performance insertion, update, and deletion of atomic data in a consistent and predictable manner. This form of schema design is discussed in more detail in Chapter 8.

Because it is focused on process execution, the operational system is likely to update data as things change, and purge or archive data once its operational usefulness has ended. Once a customer has established a new address, for example, the old one is unnecessary. A year after a sales order has been fulfilled and reflected in financial reports, it is no longer necessary to maintain information about it in the order entry system.

Data Warehouse Systems

While the focus of the operational system is the *execution* of a business process, a data warehouse system supports the *evaluation* of the process. How are orders trending this month versus last? Where does this put us in comparison to our sales goals for the quarter? Is a particular marketing promotion having an impact on sales? Who are our best customers? These questions deal with the *measurement* of the overall orders process, rather than asking about individual orders.

Interaction with the data warehouse takes place exclusively through queries that retrieve data; information is not created or modified. These interactions will involve large numbers of transactions, rather than focusing on individual transactions. Specific questions asked are less predictable, and more likely to change over time. And historic data will remain important in the data warehouse system long after its operational use has passed. The differences between operational systems and data warehouse systems are highlighted in Figure 1.1.

The principles of dimensional modeling address the unique requirements of data warehouse systems. A star schema design is optimized for queries that access large volumes of data, rather than individual transactions. It supports the maintenance of historic data, even as the operational systems change or delete information. As a model of process measurements, the dimensional schema is able to address a wide variety of questions, even those that are not posed in advance of its implementation.

	Operational System	Data Warehouse
Also Known as	Transaction System On Line Transaction Processing (OLTP) System Source system	Analytic system Data mart
Purpose	Execution of a business process	Measurement of a business process
Primary Interaction Style	Insert, Update, Query, Delete	Query
Scope of Interaction	Individual transaction	Aggregated transactions
Query Patterns	Predictable and stable	Unpredictable and changing
Temporal Focus	Current	Current and historic
Design Principle	Third normal form (3NF)	Dimensional design (star schema)

Figure 1.1   Operational systems versus data warehouse systems.

Facts and Dimensions

A dimensional model divides the information associated with a business process into two major categories, called *facts* and *dimensions*. Facts are the measurements by which a process is evaluated. For example, the business process of taking customer orders is measured in at least three ways: quantities ordered, the dollar amount of orders, and the internal cost of the products ordered. These process measurements are listed as facts in Table 1.1.

On its own, a fact offers little value. If someone were to tell you, "Order dollars were $200,000," you would not have enough information to evaluate the process of booking orders. Over what time period was the $200,000 in orders taken? Who were the customers? Which products were sold? Without some context, the measurement is useless.

Dimensions give facts their context. They specify the parameters by which a measurement is stated. Consider the statement "January 2006 orders for packing materials from customers in the nortßheast totaled $200,000." This time, the order dollars fact is given context that makes it useful. The $200,000 represents orders taken in a specific *month* and *year* (January 2006) for all products in a *category* (packing materials) by customers in a *region* (the northeast). These dimensions give context to the order dollars fact. Additional dimensions for the orders process are listed in Table 1.1.

Table 1.1 Facts and Dimensions Associated with the Orders Process

FACTS	DIMENSIONS	
Quantity Sold	Date of Order	Sales Region
Order Dollars	Month of Order	Region Code
Cost Dollars	Year of Order	Region Vice President
	Product	Customer
	Product Description	Customer Headquarters State
	Product SKU	Customer's Billing Address
	Unit of Measure	Customer's Billing City
	Product Brand	Customer's Billing State
	Brand Code	Customer's Billing Zip Code
	Brand Manager	Customer Industry SIC Code
	Product Category	Customer Industry Name
	Category Code	Order Number
	Salesperson	Credit Flag
	Salesperson ID	Carryover Flag
	Sales Territory	Solicited Order Flag
	Territory Code	Reorder Flag
	Territory Manager	

TIP A dimensional model describes a process in terms of facts and dimensions. Facts are metrics that describe the process; dimensions give facts their context.

The dimensions associated with a process usually fall into groups that are readily understood within the business. The dimensions in Table 1.1 can be sorted into groups for the product (including name, SKU, category, and brand), the salesperson (including name, sales territory, and sales region), the customer (including billing information and industry classification data), and the date of the order. This leaves a group of miscellaneous dimensions, including the order number and several flags that describe various characteristics.

The Star Schema

In a dimensional model, each group of dimensions is placed in a *dimension table*; the facts are placed in a *fact table*. The result is a *star schema*, so called because it resembles a star when diagrammed with the fact table in the center. A star schema for the orders process is shown in Figure 1.2.

The dimension tables in a star schema are *wide*. They contain a large number of attributes providing rich contextual data to support a wide variety of reports and analyses. Each dimension table has a primary key, specifically assigned for the data warehouse, called a *surrogate key*. This will allow the data warehouse to track the history of changes to data elements, even if source systems do not.

Fact tables are *deep*. They contain a large number of rows, each of which is relatively compact. Foreign key columns associate each fact table row with the dimension tables. The level of detail represented by each row in a fact table must be consistent; this level of detail is referred to as *grain*.

Dimension Tables and Surrogate Keys

A dimension table contains a set of dimensional attributes and a key column. The star schema for the orders process contains dimension tables for groups of attributes describing the Product, Customer, Salesperson, Date, and Order Type. Each dimensional attribute appears as a column in one of these tables, with the exception of order_id, which is examined shortly. Each key column is a new data element, assigned during the load process and used exclusively by the warehouse.

> **TIP** In popular usage, the word *dimension* has two meanings. It is used to describe a dimension table within a star schema, as well as the individual attributes it contains. This book distinguishes between the table and its attributes by using the terms *dimension table* for the table, and *dimension* for the attribute.

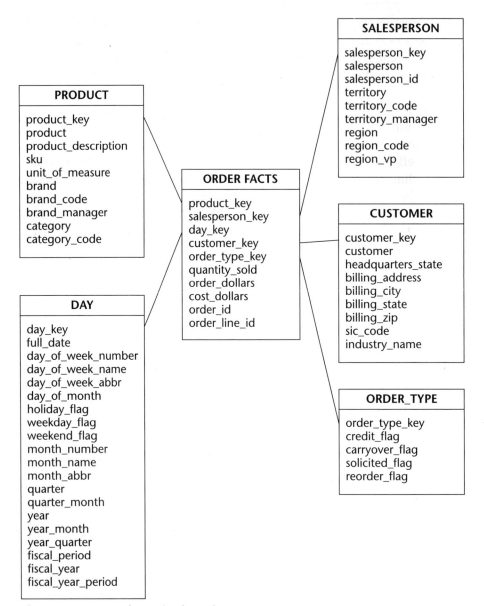

Figure 1.2   A star schema for the orders process.

Dimensions provide all context for facts. They are used to filter data for reports, drive master detail relationships, determine how facts will be aggregated, and appear with facts on reports. A rich set of descriptive dimensional attributes provides for powerful and informative reporting. Schema designers therefore focus a significant amount of time and energy identifying useful dimensional attributes. Columns whose instance values are codes, such as brand_id, may be supplemented with additional columns that decode these values into descriptive text, such as brand_name. The contents of Boolean columns or flags, such as credit_flag, are recorded in descriptive manners, such as Credit Order and Non-Credit Order. Multi-part fields or codes, such as an account code, may exist in a dimension table, along with additional columns that represent the different parts. When multiple dimensional attributes are commonly combined, such as title, first_name, and last_name, the concatenations are added to the dimension table as well.

All these efforts serve to provide a set of dimensions that will drive a rich set of reports. Dimension tables are often referred to as wide because they contain a large number of attributes, most of which are textual. Although this may consume some additional space, it makes the schema more usable. And in comparison to the fact table, the number of rows in most dimension tables is small.

TIP Dimension tables should be wide. A rich set of dimensional attributes enables useful and powerful reports.

Each dimension table has a primary key. Rather than reuse a key that exists in a transaction system, a *surrogate key* is assigned specifically for the data warehouse. Surrogate keys in this book are identifiable by the usage of the suffix *_key*, as in *product_key*, *customer_key*, and so forth. A surrogate key allows the data warehouse to track the history of changes to dimensions, even if the source systems do not. The ways in which a surrogate key supports the tracking of history will be studied in Chapter 5.

Any key that carries over from the transaction system, such as *sku* or *salesperson_id*, is referred to as a *natural key*. These columns may have analytic value, and are placed in the dimension tables as dimensional attributes. Their presence will also enable the process that loads fact tables to identify dimension records to which new fact table records will be associated. You learn more about the relationship between natural and surrogate keys, and the lookup process, in Chapter 5.

TIP A *surrogate key* is assigned to each dimension table and managed by the data warehouse load process. Key columns or unique identifiers from source systems will not participate in the primary key of the dimension table, but are included as dimensional attributes. These natural keys may have analytic value, and will also support the assignment of warehouse keys to new records being added to fact tables.

Dimension tables commonly store repeating values. For example, the Product table in Figure 1.2 contains several dimensional attributes related to a brand. Assuming there are several products within a given brand, the attribute values for these columns will be stored repeatedly, once for each product. An alternative schema design, known as the *snowflake schema*, seeks to eliminate this redundancy by further normalizing the dimensions. Figure 1.3 shows a snowflaked version of the Orders schema.

The snowflake approach saves some storage space but introduces new considerations. When the size of the dimension tables is compared to that of fact tables, the space saved by a snowflake design is negligible. In exchange for this small savings, the schema itself has become more complex. More tables must be loaded by the ETL process. Queries against the snowflake will require additional joins, potentially affecting performance. However, some data warehouse tools are optimized for a snowflake design. If such a tool is part of the data warehouse architecture, a snowflake design may be the best choice.

TIP Avoid the snowflake design unless a component of the architecture requires it. The space saved is minimal, and complexity is added to the query and reporting processes.

Fact Tables and Grain

A fact table contains the facts associated with a process, and foreign keys that provide dimensional context. The fact table for the order entry process appears in the center of Figure 1.2. It contains the three facts for the orders process: quantity_sold, order_dollars, and cost_dollars. In addition to the facts, it contains foreign keys that reference each of the relevant dimension tables: Customer, Product, Salesperson, Day, and order_type.

TIP Although a fact table is not always placed in the center of a diagram, it is easily identifiable as a dependent table, carrying a set of foreign keys.

The fact table in Figure 1.2 contains two additional attributes, order_id and order_line_id, which are neither facts nor foreign keys. These columns reference a specific order and the line number within an order respectively. They are dimensional attributes that have been placed in the fact table rather than a dimension table. Although they could have been placed in the order_type table, doing so would have dramatically increased the number of rows in the table. When a dimensional attribute is located in the fact table, it is known as a *degenerate dimension*.

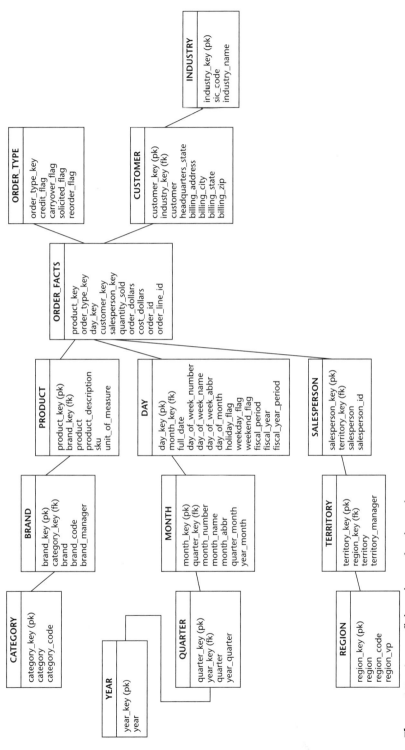

Figure 1.3 A snowflake schema for the orders process.

TIP Fact tables contain facts, foreign keys that reference dimension tables, and degenerate dimensions.

In each row of a fact table, all facts are recorded at the same level of detail. This level of detail is determined by the dimensional attributes present in the schema design. In the case of order_facts, the design requires each fact to have an associated order date, customer, salesperson, product, order_type, order_id, and order_line_id. If certain dimensional attributes do not apply to certain facts, these facts must be placed in a separate fact table. I examine designs involving multiple fact tables shortly.

The level of detail represented by a fact table row is referred to as its *grain*. Declaring the grain of a fact table is an important part of the schema design process. It ensures that there is no confusion about the meaning of a fact table row, and guarantees that all facts will be recorded at the same level of detail. A clear understanding of grain is also necessary when designing aggregate tables, as you will see in Chapter 2.

Grain may be declared in dimensional terms, or through reference to an artifact of the business process. The grain of order_facts, declared dimensionally, is "order facts by order Date, Customer, Salesperson, Product, order_id, and order_line." Because an individual line on a specific order contains all this information, the grain of order_facts can also be declared as "order facts at the order line level of detail."

The grain of a fact table row is always set at the lowest possible level of detail, based on what is available in the transaction systems where data is collected. The schema can always be used to produce less detailed summaries of the facts, as you will see in a moment. Detail not captured by the schema can never be reported on. Schema designers therefore look to capture data at an atomic level.

TIP The level of detail represented by a fact table row is referred to as its *grain*. Grain may be declared dimensionally or through reference to an artifact of the business process. The grain of a dimensional schema should capture data at the lowest possible level of detail.

The rate of growth of a fact table is greater than that of a dimension table. Although a fact table may start out small, it will quickly surpass dimensions in terms of number of rows, and become the largest table in the schema design. For example, consider the star schema for order facts. There may be several hundred products in the Product dimension table, a few hundred salespeople in the Salesperson table, one hundred thousand customers in the Customer table, sixteen possible combinations of flags in the Order_Type table, and five years worth of dates, or 1826 rows, in the Day table. Of these tables, the Product dimension table is the largest, and it may be expected to grow by about 10 percent per year. Fact table size can be estimated based on an average volume of orders. If the number of order lines per day averages 10,000, the fact table will contain 3,650,000 rows by the end of one year.

Although fact tables contain far more rows than dimension tables, each row is far more compact. Because its primary contents are facts and foreign keys, each fact table row is a very efficient consumer of storage space. Contrast this to dimension tables, which contain a large number of attributes, many of which are textual. Although the typical dimension row will require far more bytes of storage, these tables will contain far fewer rows. Over time, most fact tables become several orders of magnitude larger than the largest dimension table.

TIP Because they will accumulate a large number of rows, fact tables are often referred to as *deep*. Fact table rows are naturally compact because they contain primarily numeric data. This makes the most efficient use of physical storage.

Last, note that the fact table does not contain a row for every combination of dimension values. Rows are added only when there is a transaction. If a specific customer does not buy a specific product on a specific date, there is no fact table row for the associated set of keys. In most applications, the number of key combinations that actually appear in the fact table is actually relatively small. This property of the fact table is referred to as *sparsity*.

Using the Star Schema

The queries against a star schema follow a consistent pattern. One or more facts are typically requested, along with the dimensional attributes that provide the desired context. The facts are summarized as appropriate, based on the dimensions. Dimension attributes are also used to limit the scope of the query and serve as the basis for filters or constraints on the data to be fetched and aggregated.

A properly configured relational database is well equipped to respond to such a query, which is issued using Structured Query Language (SQL). Suppose that the vice president of sales has asked to see a report showing order_dollars by Category and Product during the month of January 2006. The Orders star schema from Figure 1.2 can provide this information. The SQL query in Figure 1.4 produces the required results, summarizing tens of thousands of fact table rows.

SQL Query

Dimension attributes that
will appear in the report {

A fact, which will be
aggregated from detail {

Dimension tables
involved in the query {

The fact table {

Constraints on
dimensional attributes {

Join tables in the
query using surrogate
key columns {

Specifies scope of
aggregation {

```
SELECT

    product.category,

    product.product,

    sum ( order_facts.order_dollars ) AS
    "Order  Dollars"

FROM

    product,

    day,

    order_facts

WHERE

    day.month_name = "January" AND

    day.year = 2006 AND

    product.product_key = order_facts.product_key AND

    day.day_key = order_facts.day_key

GROUP BY

    product.category,

    product.product
```

Query Results (Partial)

Each line of query
results summarizes
numerous fact
table rows {

```
CATEGORY          PRODUCT              ORDER DOLLARS
--------------    -------------------  ----------------
Packing Matter    5x7 bubble mailer      23,520.00
Packing Matter    8X10 bubble mailer     33,120.00
Packing Matter    9X12 bubble mailer     31,920.00
Packing Matter    Packing tape            8,544.00
Packing Matter    Box Type A             49,920.00
Packing Matter    Box Type B             29,088.00
Packing Matter    Box Type C             64,416.00
Snacks            Crackers               14,997.84
Snacks            Packaged peanuts        2,880.00
Snacks            Pretzels                3,120.00
                      .                      .
                      .                      .
                      .                      .
```

Dimension attribute values
serve as row headers

The fact is aggregated
according to
dimensional context

Figure 1.4   Querying the star schema.

The SELECT clause of the query indicates the dimensions that should appear in the query results (category and product), the fact that is requested (order dollars), and the manner in which it will be aggregated (through the SQL sum() operation). The relational database is well equipped to perform this aggregation operation. The FROM clause specifies the star schema tables that are involved in the query.

The WHERE clause constrains the query based on the values of specific dimensional attributes (month and year) and specifies the join relationships between tables in the query. Joins are among the most expensive operations the database must perform; notice that in the case of a star schema, dimension attributes are always a maximum of one join away from facts. Finally, the GROUP BY clause specifies the context to which the fact will be aggregated.

Most queries against a star schema follow the structure of this basic template. Any combination of facts and dimensions can be retrieved, subject to any filters, simply by adding and removing attributes from the various clauses of the query. More complex reports build on this same basic query structure by adding subqueries, performing set operations with the results of more than one query, or, as you will see in a moment, by merging query result sets from different fact tables.

TIP The star schema maximizes query performance by limiting the number of joins that must be performed and leveraging native RDBMS aggregation capabilities. Fact and dimension attributes can be mixed and matched as required, which enables the schema to answer a wide variety of questions— many of which were not anticipated at design time.

The example query takes advantage of the fact that order_dollars is *fully additive*. That is, individual order_dollars amounts can be added together over any of the dimensions in the schema. Order_dollar amounts can be summed over time, across products, across customers, and so forth. While most facts are fully additive, many are not. Facts that are *semi-additive* can be summed across some dimensions but not others. Other facts, such as ratios, percentages, or averages, are not additive at all. Examples of semi-additive and non-additive facts appear in Chapter 8. Also note that facts can be summarized in other ways; examples include counts, minimum values, maximum values, averages, and running totals.

Multiple Stars and Conformance

An enterprise data warehouse contains numerous star schemas. The data warehouse for a manufacturing business may include fact tables for orders, shipments, returns, inventory management, purchasing, manufacturing, sales goals, receivables, payables, and so forth. Each star schema permits detailed analysis of a specific business process.

Some business questions deal not with a single process, but with multiple processes. Answering these questions will require consulting multiple fact tables. This process is referred to as *drilling across*. Construction of drill-across reports requires each fact table be queried separately. Failure to do so can result in incorrect results.

Suppose that senior management wishes to compare the performance of salespeople to sales goals on a monthly basis. The order_facts fact table, which you have already seen, tracks the actual performance of salespeople. A separate star schema records sales goals. The grain of the fact table, sales_goal_facts, is salesperson, month, and plan version. Comparison of salesperson performance to goal requires that you consult both fact tables, which appear in the top of Figure 1.5.

You cannot access both fact tables using a single query. For a given month and salesperson, there may be a single goal value in sales_goals_facts, but there may be numerous rows in order_facts. Combining both fact tables in a single query would cause the goal value for a salesperson to be repeated once for each corresponding row in order_facts. In addition, you do not want to lose track of salespeople with goals but no orders, or those with orders but no goals. Further, the month associated with an order is in the Day table, while the month associated with a sales goal is stored in the Month table. You don't want two different month values in the report.

These problems are overcome in a multiple-step process. First, each fact table is queried separately. Each query retrieves any needed facts specific to that fact table, plus dimensions that will appear in the report. The dimensions, therefore, will appear in both result sets. Next, these interim result sets are merged together. You accomplish this by performing a full outer join, based on the common dimension values. Comparisons of facts from the different fact tables can be performed once the result sets have been merged.

This process is depicted in the bottom portion of Figure 1.5. To compare order_dollars and goal_dollars by Salesperson and Month, two queries are constructed. Each is similar in form to the one described earlier in this chapter. The first query fetches Year, Month, Salesperson, and the sum of sales_dollars from the order_facts schema. The second query fetches Year, Month, Salesperson, and the sum of goal_dollars from the sales_goal_facts schema.

Because each query aggregates a fact to the same set of dimensions, the intermediate result sets now have the same grain. Each will have a maximum of one row for each combination of year, month, and salesperson. The results can now be safely joined together, without concern for double counting. This is achieved by performing a full outer join on their common dimensional attributes, which are month, year, and salesperson. The full outer join ensures that you do not lose rows from one result set that do not have a corresponding row in the other. This might occur if there is a salesperson with a goal but no orders, or vice versa. As part of this merge process, a percent of goal figure can be calculated by computing the ratio of the two facts. The result of the drill-across operation is shown in the bottom of the figure.

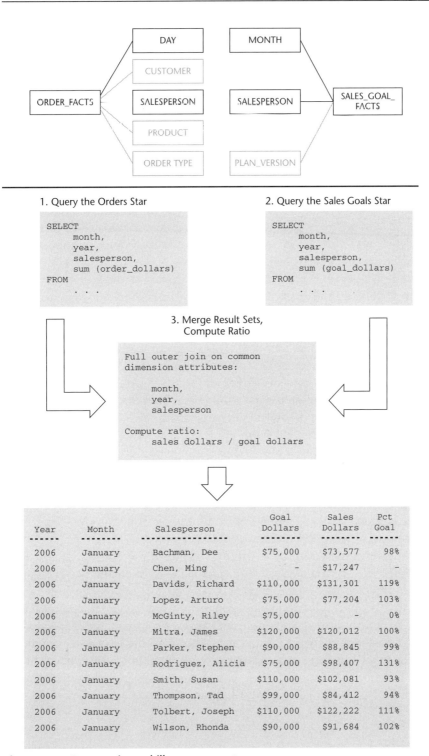

Figure 1.5 Constructing a drill-across report.

TIP Drill-across reports combine data from multiple fact tables by querying each star separately and then merging the result sets by performing a full outer join on the common dimension values.

The way the drill-across operation is carried out varies based on the tools available in the data warehouse environment and the preferences of the report developer. One option is to fetch multiple result sets from the database and then join them on a client machine or application server. Another technique stores interim result sets in temporary tables and then issues a new query that joins them. Extended SQL syntax can also be leveraged, permitting construction of a single statement that performs a full outer join on the results of multiple SELECT statements. Some query and reporting software products are star schema aware, and will automatically perform drill-across operations when required, using one or more of these techniques.

Successful drill-across reports cannot be constructed without consistent representation of dimensional attributes and values. The comparison of goal dollars to order dollars would not have been possible if each schema represented salesperson differently. To drill across the two fact tables, the salesperson dimension attributes and values must be identical. This is guaranteed if each star uses the same physical Salesperson table. This may not be possible if the two stars reside in different databases, perhaps even running RDBMS products from different vendors. But if the Salesperson table is the same in both databases, it is still possible to drill across. The warehouse team must ensure that both tables have the same columns, the attribute values are identical, and the same combinations of attribute values exist in both tables. When these conditions are met, the tables are identical in form and content, and are said to *conform*.

Dimensions are also said to conform if one is a perfect subset of the other. The Month table, for example, contains a subset of the attributes of the Day table. This is illustrated in Figure 1.6. The values of the common attributes must be recorded identically, and each table must have exactly the same set of distinct values for the common attributes. When these conditions are met, Month is referred to as a *conformed rollup* of the Day dimension.

Without dimensional conformance, it is not possible to pose business questions that involve multiple fact tables. You would not be able to compare performance to goals, orders to shipments, sales to inventory, contracts to payments, and so forth. Instead, individual stars become known as *stovepipes*. Each works on its own but cannot integrate with the others. And incompatible representations of the same business concept, such as product or customer, may foster distrust in the individual stars as well.

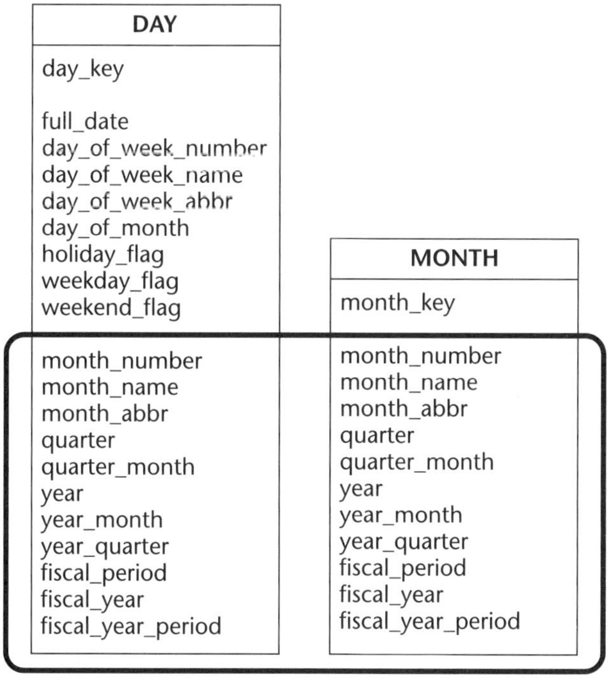

```
┌─────────────────────────────┐
│             DAY             │
├─────────────────────────────┤
│ day_key                     │
│                             │
│ full_date                   │
│ day_of_week_number          │
│ day_of_week_name            │
│ day_of_week_abbr            │
│ day_of_month          ┌──────────────────────────┐
│ holiday_flag          │           MONTH          │
│ weekday_flag          ├──────────────────────────┤
│ weekend_flag          │ month_key                │
├─────────────────────┬─┴──────────────────────────┤
│ month_number        │ month_number               │
│ month_name          │ month_name                 │
│ month_abbr          │ month_abbr                 │
│ quarter             │ quarter                    │
│ quarter_month       │ quarter_month              │
│ year                │ year                       │
│ year_month          │ year_month                 │
│ year_quarter        │ year_quarter               │
│ fiscal_period       │ fiscal_period              │
│ fiscal_year         │ fiscal_year                │
│ fiscal_year_period  │ fiscal_year_period         │
└─────────────────────┴────────────────────────────┘
```

Conformed Dimensions:

- Attributes of one table are a subset of the other's.

   The only exception is the key column.

- Attribute values are recorded identically.

   "January" does not conform with "JANUARY" or "Jan"

- Each table contains the same distinct combinations of values for the common attributes.

   There is no month/year combination present in one table but not in the other.

Figure 1.6 Month is a conformed rollup of Day.

   To maximize the value and success of a dimensional data warehouse, it is therefore critical to ensure dimensional conformance. A common set of dimensions is planned and cross-referenced with the various business processes that will be represented by fact tables. This common dimensional framework is referred to as the *data warehouse bus*. As you will see in Chapter 7, planning dimensional conformance in advance allows the data warehouse to be implemented one subject area at a time, while avoiding the potential of stovepipes. These subject areas are called *data marts*. Each data mart provides direct value when implemented, and will integrate with others as they are brought on-line.

TIP Conformed dimensions are required to compare data from multiple fact tables. The set of conformed dimensions for an enterprise data warehouse is referred to as the *warehouse bus*. Planned in advance, the warehouse bus avoids incompatibilities between subject areas.

Data Warehouse Architecture

Before exploring the use of aggregate tables to augment star schema performance, it is necessary to introduce the basic technical architecture of a data warehouse. Two major components of the data warehouse have already been discussed: the operational systems and the data warehouse. In addition to these databases, every data warehouse requires two additional components: software programs that move data from the operational systems to the data warehouse, and software that is used to develop queries and reports. These major components are illustrated in Figure 1.7.

The architecture of every data warehouse includes each of these fundamental components. Each component may comprise one or more products or physical servers. Whether custom-built or implemented using commercial off-the-shelf products, each of these components is a necessary piece of infrastructure.

- **Operational systems:** An operational system is an application that supports the execution of a business process, recording business activity and serving as the system of record. Operational systems may be packaged or custom-built applications. Their databases may reside on a variety of platforms, including relational database systems, mainframe-based systems, or proprietary data stores. For some data, such as budgeting information, the system of record may be as simple as a user spreadsheet.

- **Dimensional data warehouse:** The dimensional data warehouse is a database that supports the measurement of enterprise business processes. It stores a copy of operational data that has been organized for analytic purposes, according to the principles of dimensional modeling. Information is organized around a set of conformed dimensions, supporting enterprise-wide cross-process analysis. A subject area within the data warehouse is referred to as a *data mart*. The dimensional data warehouse is usually implemented on a relational database management system (RDBMS.)

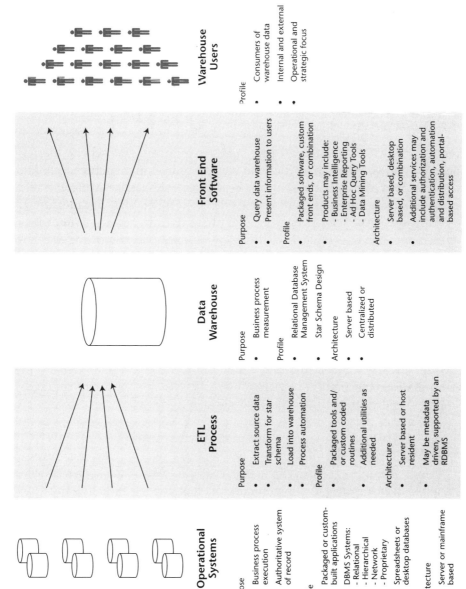

Operational Systems

Purpose
- Business process execution
- Authoritative system of record

Profile
- Packaged or custom-built applications
- DBMS Systems:
  - Relational
  - Hierarchical
  - Network
  - Proprietary
- Spreadsheets or desktop databases

Architecture
- Server or mainframe based

ETL Process

Purpose
- Extract source data
- Transform for star schema
- Load into warehouse
- Process automation

Profile
- Packaged tools and/or custom coded routines
- Additional utilities as needed

Architecture
- Server based or host resident
- May be metadata driven, supported by an RDBMS

Data Warehouse

Purpose
- Business process measurement

Profile
- Relational Database Management System
- Star Schema Design

Architecture
- Server based
- Centralized or distributed

Front End Software

Purpose
- Query data warehouse
- Present information to users

Profile
- Packaged software, custom front ends, or combination
- Products may include:
  - Business Intelligence
  - Enterprise Reporting
  - Ad Hoc Query Tools
  - Data Mining Tools

Architecture
- Server based, desktop based, or combination
- Additional services may include authorization and authentication, automation and distribution, portal-based access

Warehouse Users

Profile
- Consumers of warehouse data
- Internal and external
- Operational and strategic focus

Figure 1.7 Data warehouse architecture.

- **Extract Transform Load (ETL) software:** ETL software is used to move data into data warehouse tables. This process involves fetching data from source systems (*extract*), reorganizing it as required by the star schema design (*transform*), and inserting it into warehouse tables (*load*). ETL may be accomplished using specialized, packaged software, or by writing custom code. The ETL process may rely on a number of additional utilities and databases for staging data, cleansing it, automating the process, and so forth. A detailed overview of the ETL process is provided in Chapter 5.

- **Front-end software:** Any tool that consumes information from the data warehouse, typically by issuing a SQL query to the data warehouse and presenting results in a number of different formats. Most architectures incorporate more than one front-end product. Common front-end tools include business intelligence (BI) software, enterprise reporting software, ad hoc query tools, data mining tools, and basic SQL execution tools. These services may be provided by commercial off-the-shelf software packages or custom developed. Front-end software often provides additional services, such as user- and group-based security administration, automation of report execution and distribution, and portal-based access to available information products.

Having developed a basic understanding of the dimensional model and the data warehouse architecture, you are now ready to begin studying aggregate tables.

Invisible Aggregates

Aggregate tables improve data warehouse performance by reducing the number of rows the RDBMS must access when responding to a query. At the simplest level, this is accomplished by partially summarizing the data in a base fact table and storing the result in a new fact table. Some new terminology will be necessary to differentiate aggregate tables from those in the original schema.

If the design of an aggregate schema is carefully managed, a query can be rewritten to leverage it through simple substitution of aggregate table names for base table names. Rather than expecting users or application developers to perform this substitution, an aggregate navigator is deployed. This component of the data warehouse architecture intercepts all queries and rewrites them to leverage aggregates, allowing users and applications to issue SQL written for the original schema.

For all of this to come off smoothly, it is important that the aggregates be designed and built according to some basic principles. These principles will shape the best practices detailed throughout this book.

Improving Performance

As you have seen, the best practices of dimensional design dictate that fact table grain is set at the lowest possible level of detail. This ensures that it will be possible to present the facts in any dimensional context desired. But most queries do not call for presentation of these individual atomic measurements. Instead, some group of these measurements will be aggregated. Although the atomic measurements do not appear in the final query results, the RDBMS must access them in order to compute their aggregates.

Consider again the query from Figure 1.4, which requests order_dollars by category and product for the month of January 2006. Each row of the final result set summarizes a large number of fact table rows. That's because the grain of the order_facts table, shown in Figure 1.2, is an individual order line. With over 10,000 order lines generated per day, the sample query requires the RDBMS to access over 300,000 rows of fact table data.

Most of the time the RDBMS spends executing the query will be spent reading these 300,000 rows of data. More specifically, the time will be spent waiting for the storage hardware to provide the data, as described in Chapter 2. Of course, the RDBMS has other tasks to perform. For example, it must first identify which rows of data it needs. And after the data has been returned, it needs to perform the necessary joins and aggregation. But in comparison to the time spent reading data, these tasks will be completed relatively quickly.

Aggregate tables seek to improve query performance by reducing the amount of data that must be accessed. By pre-aggregating the data in the fact table, they reduce the amount of work the RDBMS must perform to respond to a query. Put simply, query performance is increased when the number of rows that must be accessed is decreased.

Suppose a summarization of the order facts across all customers and orders is precomputed and stored in a new table called order_facts_aggregate. Shown in Figure 1.8, this table contains the same facts as the original fact table, but at a coarser grain. Gone are the relationships to the customer and order_type tables. Also omitted are the degenerate dimensions order_id and order_line_id.

All the data necessary to answer the query is present in this summary schema—it contains order_dollars, category, product, month, and year. But in this summarized version of order_facts, there are approximately 1,000 rows per day, compared to 10,000 order lines per day in the original fact table. Using this table, the RDBMS would have to access one-tenth the number of rows. Reading data from disk is one of the most time-consuming tasks the RDBMS performs while executing a query, as described in Chapter 2. By reducing the amount of data read by a factor of ten, response time is improved dramatically.

TIP An aggregate table improves response time by reducing the number of rows that must be accessed in responding to a query.

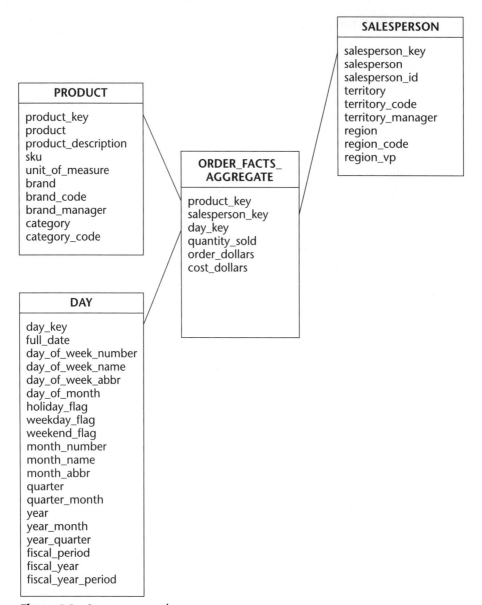

Figure 1.8 An aggregate schema.

Notice that the design of the aggregate schema in Figure 1.8 does not attempt to reuse base schema tables to store the aggregated data. Instead, a new table was created to store aggregated facts. The use of separate tables as a best practice for the storage of aggregated data is established in Chapter 3, after fully exploring the alternatives.

The Base Schema and the Aggregate Schema

The star schema in Figure 1.8 has already been referred to as an *aggregate schema*. It provides a partially aggregated summarization of data that is already stored in the data warehouse. The original schema containing the granular transactions is referred to as the *base schema*. Together, the base and aggregate stars form a *schema family*.

Similar terminology describes the individual tables in each schema. The fact table in the aggregate schema is referred to as an *aggregate fact table*. It summarizes information from the *base fact table*.

Notice that the dimension tables in the aggregate schema from Figure 1.8 are identical to those in the base schema. This aggregate schema has summarized order_facts by completely omitting the salesperson and order_type dimension tables.

For some aggregate schemas, partial summarization across a dimension may be useful. Instead of completely omitting a dimension table, it is partially summarized. For example, a monthly summary of order_facts by customer and salesperson would further reduce the number of rows in the aggregate fact table, and still be able to respond to the sample query.

In order to construct this aggregate schema, a Month dimension table is needed. The base schema includes only a Day dimension, so a new Month table must be built. This *aggregate dimension table* will be based on the Day dimension table in the base schema. As you will see in Chapter 2, its design is subject to the same rules of dimensional conformance discussed earlier in this chapter. In fact, a conformed Month table was already built for the sales goals schema, as shown in Figures 1.5 and 1.6. This same Month table can be used in an aggregate of the orders schema, as shown in Figure 1.9.

Although the aggregate schema from Figure 1.9 will go still further in improving the performance of our sample query, its overall usefulness is more limited than the daily aggregate from Figure 1.8. For example, it cannot respond to a query that requests order_dollars by day and product. Because this query requires specific days, it can be answered only by the aggregate schema in Figure 1.8, or by the base schema.

This characteristic can be generalized as follows: The more highly summarized an aggregate table is, the fewer queries it will be able to accelerate. This means that choosing aggregates involves making careful tradeoffs between the performance gain offered and the number of queries that will benefit. Chapter 2 explores how these factors are balanced when choosing aggregate tables.

With a large number of users issuing a diverse set of queries, it is to be expected that no single aggregate schema will improve the performance of every query. Notice, however, that improving the response time of a few resource-intensive queries can improve the overall throughput of the DBMS dramatically. Still, it is reasonable to expect that a *set* of aggregate tables will be deployed in support of a given star, rather than just one.

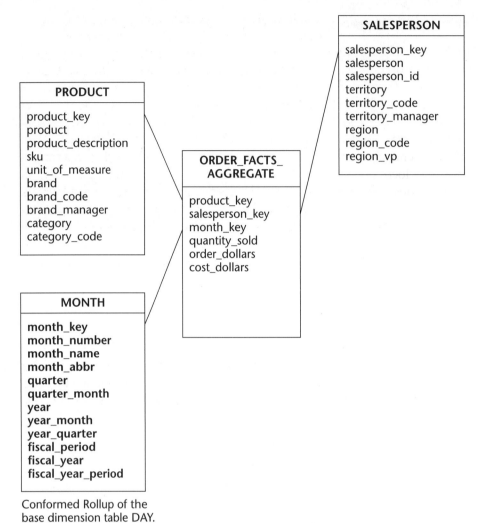

Conformed Rollup of the
base dimension table DAY.

Figure 1.9   Month as an aggregate dimension table.

The Aggregate Navigator

To receive the performance benefit offered by an aggregate schema, a query
must be written to use the aggregate. Rewriting the sample query was a simple matter of substituting the name of the aggregate fact table for that of the
base fact table. This may be easy for technical personnel, but can prove confusing for an end user. The complexity grows as additional aggregate tables
are added. Technical and business users alike may err in assessing which table
will provide the best performance. And, if more aggregate tables are added or
old ones removed, existing queries must be rewritten.

The key to avoiding these pitfalls lies in implementation of an *aggregate navigator*. A component of the data warehouse infrastructure, the aggregate navigator assumes the task of rewriting user queries to utilize aggregate tables. Users and developers need only be concerned with the base schema. At runtime, the aggregate navigator redirects the query to the most efficient aggregate schema. This process is depicted in Figure 1.10.

A number of commercial products offer aggregate navigation capabilities. Ideally, the aggregate navigator provides this service to all queries, regardless of the front-end application being used, and all back-end databases, regardless of physical location or technology. It maintains all information needed to rewrite queries, and keeps track of the status of each aggregate. This allows its services to be adjusted as aggregates are added and removed from the database, and permits aggregates to be taken off-line when being rebuilt. Detailed requirements for the aggregate navigator are presented in Chapter 4, which also describes how the aggregation strategy is altered if there is no aggregate navigator.

Principles of Aggregation

This chapter has proposed using a set of invisible aggregate tables to improve data warehouse performance. A family of aggregate star schemas will partially summarize information in a base star schema. These dimensional aggregates will be invisible to end-user applications, which will continue to issue SQL targeted at the base schema. An aggregate navigator will intercept these queries and rewrite them to leverage the aggregate tables.

For all this to come off smoothly, two key principles must be followed in the design and construction of the aggregate schemas. Subsequent chapters of this book enumerate best practices surrounding the selection, design, usage, and implementation of aggregates.

Providing the Same Results

The data warehouse must always provide accurate and consistent results. If it does not, business users will lose faith in its capability to provide accurate measurement of business processes. Use of the data warehouse will drop. Worse, those who do use it may base business decisions on inaccurate data.

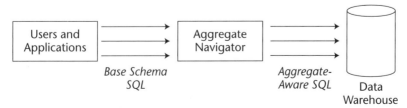

Figure 1.10 The aggregate navigator.

The importance of accuracy leads to the first guiding principle for aggregate tables. Assuming the base schema has been designed to publish operational data accurately and consistently, any aggregates must do the same. More specifically, the following can be stated:

An aggregate schema must always provide exactly the same results as the base schema.

If a rewritten query returns different results, it is returning wrong results. The data warehouse will bear the consequences. Every aggregate table must be an accurate and comprehensive summarization of its corresponding base table. This may seem obvious, but it is important to state it explicitly.

The effects of this principle are encountered throughout this book. Design options that violate this principle will be ruled out in Chapters 3 and 8. If the base schema and aggregate schema are not to be loaded simultaneously, this principle will require aggregates to be taken off-line during the load process, as discussed in Chapter 5. Design options for summaries that handle the absence of data differently than the base schema can produce results that are accurate, but different. In Chapter 9 these derived schemas are not awarded the status of invisibility and serve as base schema tables instead.

The Same Facts and Dimension Attributes as the Base Schema

The successful deployment of aggregate tables depends largely on their invisibility, particularly when more than one set of aggregates is available. The aggregate navigator will be relied upon to quickly and accurately rewrite queries through the substitution of table names and join columns in SQL queries. This suggests a second guiding principle:

The attributes of each aggregate table must be a subset of those from a base schema table. The only exception to this rule is the surrogate key for an aggregate dimension table.

The introduction of a new attribute to an aggregate table will either destroy its invisibility by requiring the aggregate be addressed by application SQL directly, or complicate the query rewrite process by requiring complex transformations of SQL syntax. Examples of potential new attributes, and their impact on schema usage, are explored in Chapter 3.

The capabilities of specific technologies may permit this principle to be relaxed slightly. For example, database features such as materialized views or materialized query tables can safely perform certain calculations on base schema attributes, or combine attributes from multiple tables into a single summary table. These possibilities are explored in Chapter 4.

Other Types of Summarization

The aggregate tables discussed thus far provide the same results as the base schema, and are leveraged by substituting the names of aggregate tables in SQL queries. Throughout this book, the term *aggregate* will be reserved for tables that exhibit these characteristics, even if an aggregate navigator is not deployed.

However, there are other ways to summarize the information in a star schema. Although not meeting the requirements for invisibility, these summary tables may provide value to the data warehouse in other ways.

Pre-Joined Aggregates

Like the dimensional aggregates you have seen so far, a pre-joined aggregate summarizes a fact across a set of dimension values. But unlike the aggregate star schemas from Figures 1.8 and 1.9, the pre-joined aggregate places the results in a single table. By doing so, the pre-joined aggregate eliminates the need for the RDBMS to perform a join operation at query time.

An example of a pre-joined aggregate appears in Figure 1.11. This table collects some dimensional attributes from Product, Day, and Salesperson, placing them in a single table with the facts from order_facts.

Like the aggregate schemas from the previous section, this pre-joined aggregate will improve the performance of our sample query by reducing the number of rows that must be consulted. While it also eliminates join processing requirements, this effect is less dramatic. All the major relational databases in use today have native support for star-join operations, optimizing the process by which fact table data is accessed and combined with dimensional data.

ORDER_PREJOINED_ AGGREGATE
product sku brand category month_name year_month salesperson territory region quantity_sold order_dollars cost_dollars

Figure 1.11 A pre-joined aggregate.

The pre-joined aggregate also has one drawback: It requires dramatically more storage space. Earlier, you saw that fact tables, although deep, consisted of very compact rows. Dimension tables contained wider rows, but were relatively small. The pre-joined aggregate is likely to be *wide and deep*. It is therefore likely to consume a very large amount of space, unless it is highly summarized. The more highly summarized an aggregate, the fewer queries it will accelerate.

> **TIP** A pre-joined aggregate table combines aggregated facts and dimension attributes in a single table. While it can improve query performance, the pre-joined aggregate tends to consume excessive amounts of storage space.

Nonetheless, pre-joined aggregates are often implemented in support of specific queries or reports. And if the second principle of aggregation is relaxed slightly, the aggregate navigator may be leveraged to rewrite base-level SQL to access pre-joined aggregates as well. The aggregate navigator will have to replace all table names with the single pre-joined aggregate, and eliminate joins from the WHERE clause.

The processes of choosing and designing pre-joined aggregates are similar to those for standard dimensional aggregates, as you learn in Chapters 2 and 3. In Chapter 4, you see that database features such as materialized views work nicely to maintain pre-joined aggregates and rewrite queries. And in Chapter 5, you see that the pre-joined aggregate is also easy to build manually because it does not require any surrogate keys.

Derived Tables

Another group of summarization techniques seeks to improve performance by altering the structure of the tables summarized or changing the scope of their content. These tables are not meant to be invisible. Instead, they are provided as base schema objects. Users or report developers must explicitly choose to use these tables; the aggregate navigator does not come into play. There are three major types of derived tables: the merged fact table, the pivoted fact table, and the sliced fact table.

The *merged fact table* combines facts from more than one fact table at a common grain. This technique is often used to construct powerful data marts that draw data from multiple business areas. The merged fact table eliminates the need to perform drill-across operations, but introduces subtle differences in the way facts are recorded. Some facts will be stored with a value of zero, where the base fact table recorded nothing.

The *pivoted fact table* transforms a set of metrics in a single row into multiple rows with a single metric, or vice versa. Pivoted fact tables greatly simplify reporting by configuring the storage of facts to match the desired presentation format. Performing a similar transformation within SQL or a reporting tool can be slow and cumbersome. Like the merged fact table, the pivoted fact table may be forced to store facts with a value of zero, even when the base fact table contains nothing.

The *sliced fact table* does nothing to transform the structure of the original schema, but does change its content. A sliced fact table contains a subset of the records of the base fact table, usually in coordination with a specific dimension attribute. This technique can be used to relocate subsets of data closer to the individuals that need it. Conversely, it can also be used to consolidate regional data stores that are identical in structure. Because the slice can be derived from the whole, or vice versa, which table is derived is a function of the business environment.

In all three cases, the derived fact tables are not expected to serve as invisible stand-ins for the base schema. The merged and pivoted fact tables significantly alter schema structure, while the sliced fact table alters its content. These tables should be considered part of the base schema, and accessed by users or report developers explicitly. Derived tables are explored in further detail in Chapter 9.

Tables with New Facts

In a paradoxical twist, the final type of summary table actually contains attributes not present in the original schema. Such summaries occur when a fact in the original schema does not exhibit the characteristic of additivity, as described previously. While these facts can be summarized, the semantics and usage of the result differ from those of the original table. Like the derived schemas, these summarizations are not expected to remain invisible to end users. Instead, they are called upon directly by application SQL.

In all the examples in this chapter, facts have been aggregated by summing their values. For some facts, this is not appropriate. Semi-additive facts may not be added together across a particular dimension; non-additive facts are never added together. In these situations, you may choose to aggregate by means other than summation.

An account balance, for example, is semi-additive. On a given day, you can add together the balances of your various bank accounts to compute a total balance. Unfortunately, you cannot add together a series of daily balances to compute a monthly total. But it may be useful to compute a monthly average of these values. The average daily balance can be used to determine the interest allied at month's end, for example. But an average daily balance means something different than the balance dollars fact of the original schema.

When you aggregate by means other than summation, you create new facts. These facts have different meanings than the original fact, and their usage is governed by different rules. Tables with new facts, therefore, are not expected to remain invisible. Like the derived tables, they will be made available as part of the base schema. Users and applications will access them explicitly. Tables with new facts will be encountered in Chapter 8, which explores the impact of advanced dimensional design techniques on aggregates.

Summary

This chapter has laid the foundation for the chapters to come, reviewing the basics of star schema design, introducing the aggregate table and aggregate navigator, defining some standard vocabulary, and establishing some guiding principles for invisible aggregates.

- While operational systems focus on process *execution*, data warehouse systems focus on process *evaluation*. These contrasting purposes lead to distinct operational profiles, which in turn suggest different principles to guide schema design.

- The principles of *dimensional modeling* govern the development of warehouse systems. Process evaluation is enabled by identifying the *facts* that measure a business process and the *dimensions* that give them context. These attributes are grouped into tables that form a star schema design.

- *Dimension tables* contain sets of dimensional attributes. They drive access to the facts, constrain queries, and serve as row headers on reports. The use of a *surrogate key* permits the dimension table to track history, regardless of how changes are handled in operational systems.

- Facts are placed in *fact tables*, along with foreign key references to the appropriate dimension tables. The *grain* of a fact table identifies the level of detail represented by each row. It is set at the lowest level possible, as determined by available data.

- Although the specific questions asked by end users are unpredictable and change over time, queries follow a *standard pattern*. Questions that cross subject areas can be answered through a process called *drilling across*, provided the warehouse had been designed around a set of conformed dimensions referred to as the warehouse bus.

- Aggregate tables improve the response time of a star schema query by reducing the number of rows the database must read. Ideally, the aggregate tables are *invisible* to end uses and applications, which issue queries to the base schema. An *aggregate navigator* is deployed, rewriting these queries to leverage aggregates as appropriate.

- To facilitate this invisibility, two basic principles guide aggregate schema design. Aggregates must always provide the same results as the base schema, and the attributes of each aggregate table must be a subset of those of a base table.

- Not all forms of summarization meet the requirements of invisible aggregates. Other forms of summarization include *pre-joined aggregates*, *derived tables*, and tables with *new facts*. Although not serviced by the aggregate navigator, these summaries can serve as useful additions to the base schema of the data warehouse, accessed explicitly through application SQL.

With these fundamentals out of the way, you are ready to turn to the first and most perplexing task: choosing which aggregates to design and build.

CHAPTER 2

Choosing Aggregates

One of the most vexing tasks in deploying dimensional aggregates is choosing which aggregates to design and deploy. Your aim is to strike the correct balance between the performance gain provided by aggregate schemas and their cost in terms of resource requirements.

Several factors make it difficult to achieve this balance. The sheer number of possible aggregates is much larger than you might expect. Of course, they can't all be included in the data warehouse. But it would be exceedingly tedious to study each permutation of attributes to identify those aggregates that might produce useful cost savings. If your system is not yet in production, you do not have existing query patterns to optimize so you might not even be able to tell if the cost savings offered by a particular aggregate would ever be realized. And if you do have usage data, it does not tell you the relative importance of different queries. Last, you may find that you need to choose between the needs of different user constituencies.

This chapter shows you how to cut through these issues and determine which aggregates make sense to deploy in your situation.

The first section briefly examines how to describe an aggregate schema.

The next section gives you a variety of techniques you can use to identify aggregates that are likely to be of value in your implementation. These techniques are used to establish a pool of aggregates for potential inclusion in your data warehouse.

The last part of this chapter shows you how to evaluate the value of potential aggregate tables from this pool and choose those that make the most sense for your application.

What Is a Potential Aggregate?

To identify potential aggregates, distinguish between them, and choose which ones to add to the data warehouse, it is necessary to have a way to describe each candidate. The easiest way to do this is to describe them in terms of their dimensional grain. If a potential aggregate schema partially summarizes a dimension table, the grain statement should indicate the base dimension table to which it conforms. Grain can be used to describe pre-joined aggregates as well.

Aggregate Fact Tables: A Question of Grain

As you saw in Chapter 1, an aggregate schema is a special type of star schema. Like a base schema, the aggregate schema comprises a fact table and several dimension tables. The fact table of the aggregate schema is an aggregate fact table. Like a base fact table, it is composed of facts and foreign keys. Each of the dimension tables of the aggregate schema is a base dimension table or a rollup dimension. Like any other dimension table, these are composed of dimensional attributes and warehouse keys.

The only real difference between a base star and an aggregate star is one of grain. Consider the orders example from Chapter 1. The grain of the base schema from Figure 1.2 is:

- Order lines by day, customer, salesperson, product, order, and order line

The grain of the aggregate schema from Figure 1.8 is:

- Orders by day, salesperson and product

A potential aggregate, then, can be identified using a grain statement. Some other potential aggregates of the schema might include:

- Orders by day, customer, and product
- Orders by month, product, and salesperson

By defining the aggregate schema in terms of fact table grain, you have identified its essential characteristics.

TIP Express potential aggregates as fact table grain statements.

Each of the preceding grain statements defined the aggregate fact table specifically in terms of its dimensionality. Most aggregate grain statements take such a form. Sometimes, however, the grain can be expressed differently.

The grain statement of a fact table can also take its definition from an artifact of the business process. For example, the grain of the schema from Figure 1.2 can also be stated as "Order facts at the order line level of detail." Instead of explicitly identifying dimensionality, this statement of grain refers to the individual order lines of a purchase order.

This approach is often used because it avoids any confusion about what a row in the fact table means. The definition is easily understood by business users. It remains a valid statement of grain because it implies dimensionality. Each order line will include a date, product, and customer.

The grain of an aggregate fact table might be described in this manner as well. If the base fact table is defined as "Order facts at the order line" then an aggregate might be defined as "Order facts by order header." This would be equivalent to the dimensional definition "Order facts by customer, salesperson, and day." As you will see later, the latter expression of grain will be more helpful when it is time to sort through the candidate aggregates and identify those that will be built.

Aggregate Dimensions Must Conform

Most of the aggregate schemas mentioned so far have summarized the base schema through omission of a dimension table. These are the simplest form of aggregates. As you will see in Chapter 7, these aggregates are also the easiest to build. The aggregate fact table can be defined through a very simple SQL SELECT statement.

Many potential aggregates partially summarize a dimension. The most intuitive example of this form of aggregation involves time. Consider again the schema from Figure 1.2. Notice that it contains sales by day, product, customer, salesperson, and order_type. Potential aggregates can be conceived by dropping various dimension tables from the schema. But you will always want to keep a time component to your data, so it would never make sense to eliminate the Day dimension table. However, you might find value in summarizing this data by month, as in Figure 1.9.

Like the others this aggregate fact table can be described by its grain:

■ Orders by Product, Salesperson, and Month (day)

The word "day" appears in parentheses after "Month" to indicate that the Month dimension conforms to the Day dimension. In Chapter 1, you learned that one dimension conforms with another if it is identical, or if it contains a subset of the attributes of the first. It is also required that the attributes have the same name, that the data values are expressed the same way, and that all data values appear in both dimensions. These rollup dimensions can also serve as aggregate dimensions.

> **TIP** When an aggregate schema partially summarizes a dimension table, note the base dimension table summarized by the aggregate dimension table. Be sure the tables follow the rules of conformance.

Just as one speaks of fact table grain, one sometimes speaks of dimension table grain. The grain of a dimension table describes the level of detail represented by one of its rows. The simplest example is time: The grain of a Day dimension is the individual day; the grain of a Month dimension is the month, and so forth.

The Month dimension table does include a column that is not part of the original date table: the month_key. This warehouse assigned key is used to associate records in the aggregate fact table with records in the aggregate dimension table. This makes aggregates that partially summarize a dimension slightly harder to build, as discussed in Chapter 6.

In a snowflake schema, you do not need to construct the aggregate dimension. It already exists as part of the normalized time dimension. Figure 2.1 shows the snowflake schema from Figure 1.3 with an aggregate based on month.

Notice that the Month dimension is not a simple list of months. A row in this Month dimension represents a month in a year. Whether the target schema is a star with conformed dimensions or a snowflake, it is important to highlight such nuances during the design process.

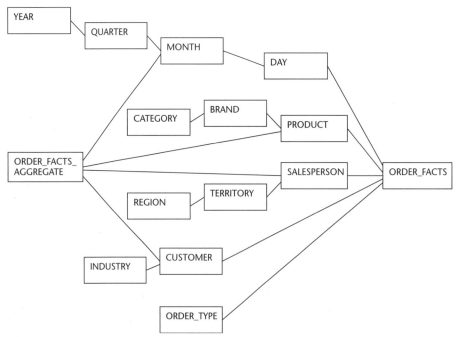

Figure 2.1   A snowflaked version of the Orders schema with an aggregate table.

Pre-Joined Aggregates Have Grain Too

The preceding examples have described aggregate star schemas. Recall from Chapter 1 that an aggregate star schema comprises an aggregate fact table, and a combination of base dimensions and/or aggregate dimensions.

The other type of invisible aggregate discussed in Chapter 1 is the pre-joined aggregate. Unlike an aggregate star schema, this type of aggregate forgoes the separation of facts and dimensions into separate tables. Instead, it combines them into a single table.

While it no longer resembles a star, the pre-joined aggregate is queried in the same manner as a star. A series of dimension attributes are selected, along with the sum of one or more measures. Because everything is now located in a single table, the RDBMS does not need to execute joins when retrieving anything from this table. But the pre-joined aggregate can still be conceptualized and described in purely dimensional terms.

TIP Requirements for a pre-joined aggregate can be described in the same way as they are described for star schema aggregates: as a grain statement that optionally includes conformed dimensions.

The grain of the pre-joined aggregate from Figure 1.11 is:

- Order facts by month (day), product, and salesperson.

Dimensionally, this statement is identical to the grain statements for an aggregate fact table. It describes exactly what is represented by a row in the pre-joined aggregate table in dimensional terms, and identifies the base dimensions to which the summarized dimensions conform.

Enumerating Potential Aggregates

By identifying the potential points of aggregation within the dimensions for a given star, it is possible to enumerate all the potential aggregates. This list turns out to be longer than you might expect.

Table 2.1 shows all the potential levels of aggregation for the dimension tables of the orders schema in Figure 1.2. Notice that each dimension includes an option to remove the entire dimension (for example, across all products, or across all customers.) An exception is made for Time, assuming that you will always want to analyze at least by annual totals.

Table 2.1   Potential Aggregation Levels for the Orders Schema

TABLE	POTENTIAL AGGREGATION LEVELS	#
Day	Date, Month, Quarter, Year, Fiscal Period, Fiscal Year	6
Product	Product, Brand, Category, All Products	4
Customer	Customer, Industry, State, All Customers	4
Salesperson	Salesperson, Division, Region, All Salespeople	4
Order Type	Order Type, All Orders	2
Order Number	Order Number, All Orders	2

Observe that this list does not impose a hierarchical viewpoint on aggregation. For example, the Customer dimension table might be aggregated by State. The list also recognizes what might be considered orthogonal hierarchies. For example, the Day dimension table can be aggregated by calendar Quarter and Year, or Fiscal Period and Fiscal Year. Last, the degenerate dimension, Order Number, is acknowledged as a source of potential aggregation; the order may or may not be included in aggregate tables, affecting their grain as any other dimension would.

The total number of combinations of these aggregation points is 1536. One of these combinations represents the base fact table; another is a single row with grand totals for the entire fact table. So the number of potential aggregate fact tables is 1534.

Careful observation can narrow this number down a bit. For example, Order Types correspond to Order Numbers, so any aggregate that includes the Order Number may as well include the Order Type. Other relationships between dimensional elements might also be observable, while some will be hard to see. Even accounting for these observations, you will still be facing a very large pool of candidates.

Before sitting down and trying to gauge the performance gain offered by each of these aggregates, it is useful to use business requirements to limit the number of potential options.

Identifying Potentially Useful Aggregates

The description of an aggregate has been reduced to familiar dimensional terms: fact table grain and dimensional conformance. You've also seen that the number of aggregates can be quite large. The next step is to link potential aggregates to actual business requirements. This process is not hard if you remember one thing: *think dimensionally*.

This section provides techniques you can use during three different stages of the lifecycle of the base schema:

- During the initial design of the base schema
- Once the schema design has been frozen
- When the base schema is in production

During design of the base schema, you will be provided with numerous clues to potentially valuable aggregates. If your base schema has already been designed, consult with the designers or examine notes and artifacts of the schema design process.

The next place to look is the base schema design itself. More specifically, you will scrutinize the dimensional conformance bus. Looking at fact tables that will be used together in "drill-across" reports will suggest aggregates that are quite likely to be among the most valuable.

Last, once your base schema is in production, you can consult a large number of new artifacts.

Wherever you look to find aggregates, remember: Think dimensionally.

Drawing on Initial Design

One of the keys to identifying potential aggregates is being able to think like an end user. If you think about the business the way an end user does, you know what types of business questions are likely to be asked of the data warehouse. Many business questions reveal potential aggregates.

During the initial design of a base schema, good data modelers become immersed in the business process. This is necessary to achieve a sound dimensional design. As pointed out in Chapter 1, dimensional modeling aims to capture how a business process is viewed and understood. It follows, then, that this is a good time to identify potential aggregates.

TIP Identify and document potential aggregates during schema design, even if initial implementation will not include aggregates. This information will be useful in the future.

If initial design is completed without special attention to aggregates, all is not lost. The process is likely to have left several artifacts, which can be scoured for clues. These can include interview notes, samples of operational reports, descriptions of user workflows, and so forth.

Design Decisions

During the design process for the base schema, much attention will be paid to the grain of the fact tables, how dimensional attributes should be divided into dimension tables, and conformance. Deliberations around each of these design issues will reveal potential aggregates.

Grain Decisions

One of the cardinal rules of star schema design is to set the grain of the fact table at the lowest level of detail possible. Doing so ensures that the schema will endure into the future. While it is easy to add or remove attributes to or from a dimensional model without invalidating existing fact table records, it is not possible to set a deeper grain. Doing so requires data that is not already present in the schema.

During the design process, the grain of a fact table may not be immediately obvious. As user interviews get underway, designers will immediately begin sketching draft models that support the business requirements they are hearing. The draft model will include one or more fact tables. Each fact table has a grain.

It is often the case that a newly discovered requirement shatters a working assumption about fact table grain. The draft design is then modified to reflect a finer grain, complete with new dimensionality.

For example, the sales schema from Figure 1.2 has a grain that corresponds to an order line. Suppose that interviews are still underway, and this is a working draft that reflects the needs of those interviewed thus far. The designers now interview one of the last people on their list: the pricing manager. During this interview, they learn that order lines are internally further decomposed by pricing algorithms. A given order line may actually contain many sub-lines, each of which includes information according to pricing policies. These sub-lines are not visible to most of the users, but are important from a pricing perspective. As a result of this new information, the schema designers add a new pricing dimension and alter the grain of the fact table.

Notice something important here. The detail has been added to the schema in the name of fixing grain at the finest level possible and satisfying the needs of the few who required it. But the interviewers have already discussed requirements with a large number of users, *none of whom needed the additional detail* to perform their analysis. The original draft design, prior to the grain change, is a strong candidate for an aggregate schema.

> **TIP** Any decision to set the grain of a fact table at a finer level reveals a potential aggregate.

The aggregate will certainly be used by a large number of users, but this doesn't mean it will be useful. It is also important to examine the actual performance improvement that can be expected from the aggregate. Performance improvement will be discussed later in this chapter.

Groups of Dimension Attributes

Good dimensional modelers work hard to find a rich set of dimensional attributes. As the model is filled out, decisions are made about distribution of those attributes across dimension tables. Generally, dimensional modelers attempt to keep attributes in the same table if users are likely to browse them together. This need is balanced with the need to manage the size of the table and the frequency with which its attributes will require updates.

Through this process, sets of attributes that clearly belong together are identified. Designers often create dimensions that contain more than one of these groups. They may be directly related, loosely correlated, or even completely unrelated. But whatever the reason, the presence of these groupings indicates a potential level of aggregation.

For example, product name and SKU clearly relate to a product, and are found in the Product dimension from Figure 1.2. This dimension also contains Brand and Category information. A full-blown Product dimension might have dozens of attributes for each of these groups (Product, Brand, and Category). Brand and Category information is observed to change independently of the individual products, and in fact may come from a different system.

In this case, the designers choose to keep these three sets of attributes in a single dimension table. This decision is based on the observation that users would want to browse these attributes together, and that their inclusion in a single table will not generate an unmanageable number of slow changes. But the process of making this decision has revealed potential aggregations for all related facts: conformed dimensions for Brand and for Category.

TIP Decisions about where to place groups of dimensional attributes reveal potential levels of aggregation.

It may strike you that the example used here is obvious, and that you don't need any special techniques to identify Category and Brand as possible aggregation points for Product. But not all instances will be as clear-cut.

The groupings in the example are easily identified because they would correspond to distinct entities in an E/R model. But sometimes groupings are more arbitrary. A set of demographic attributes, for example, may actually correspond to instances of a single entity in an E/R model. A so-called *junk dimension* may bear no relationship to an E/R entity at all. The important point is that any time you find yourself deciding what to do with a group of attributes, you should keep in mind that they represent a potential level of aggregation.

Drill Paths and Hierarchies

Thus far, the word "hierarchy" has been largely avoided. While it is tempting to describe the product dimension as a hierarchy involving Product, Brand, and Category, this line of thought can be dangerous. A hierarchical perspective on dimensions can obscure valid patterns of analysis where a hierarchy does not exist, or where multiple hierarchies can be found among the same set of attributes.

These concerns notwithstanding, hierarchies are often clearly understood by end users. Moreover, the drill-up/drill-down capabilities of most business intelligence tools are limited by a myopic dependency on predefined hierarchies. For these reasons, it is often prudent to model hierarchies during the design process. This information is not part of the star schema, but it will assist in user education or the configuration of your business intelligence tool.

NOTE Notice that if you instantiate them in your dimensional model, you have a snowflake schema rather than a star.

TIP Discussion of hierarchies or drill paths point to potential aggregates.

As you will see in Chapter 3, it is important that any documentation of hierarchies within a dimension acknowledge alternatives. For example, an organization dimension may have two hierarchies that subset the attributes in two different ways. One subsets them geographically, perhaps including location, region, and country. Another subsets them according to chain of command, perhaps including location, division, and company.

Listening to Users

The techniques for recognizing potential aggregates discussed thus far correspond to critical decision points that occur during the process of developing the base schema. But even before pen is set to paper for initial designs, you will be provided with clues to potential aggregates. Again, the key is to think dimensionally.

During the design process, you identify business requirements in several ways. Users will explicitly tell you things they look at on a regular basis and why. They will tell you what they need to do manually today and what information they get from existing reports. Managers will tell you how they evaluate a business process or how they evaluate employees who participate in that process. Developers of operational applications will share with you the complexities of fulfilling certain report requests, and what they have done to support them. Database administrators will share their travails in tuning the database to support the needs of a report that is in demand.

Most requirements that are expressed to you will suggest an aggregate. In fact, it is often (but not always) the case that very few requirements require the most granular data available. Someone reconstructing an Order from the Order schema, for example, may well be wasting their time. Such a report is surely available from the operational system used for order entry.

If you think in terms of facts and dimensions, you should be able to identify the grain of a given user request. For example, a manager of the sales process might show you a report she uses. It shows order amounts by region, and perhaps over time. This reflects her viewpoint on the business; each region is overseen by a regional vice president. This manager's needs do not require the individual sales representative. Her requirements, expressed dimensionally, might be "Orders by Product, Region (salesperson), and Day."

TIP User work products reveal potential aggregates. These may include reports from operational systems, manually compiled briefings, or spreadsheets. They will also be revealed by manual processes and requirements not currently met.

If the dimensionality of user requests does not come to you naturally, there are some things you can look out for. Recall that anything a user measures is a fact. This will live in a fact table and will have a dimensional grain. If it is tallied, summed, counted, or averaged, it is likely a fact.

The dimensions will appear as row or column headers on a report. When someone describes a report, the dimensions will often follow the word "by" or "for each," revealing the level of aggregation requested. For example, "Sales by Region and Product Category" suggests an aggregation to the Region and Category levels. It may not be until later that you determine that Region conforms to the base dimension Salesperson and that Category conforms to the based dimension Product. But you clearly have a statement that describes the level of detail that is important to this user.

Where Subject Areas Meet

One of the key components of a dimensional design is the identification of a set of fact tables or business processes and their dimensionality. This ensures that business questions spanning subject areas will be answerable by the data warehouse. This data warehouse bus, and its attendant set of conformed dimensions, can be used to identify potential aggregates that will be leveraged with great frequency.

The Conformance Bus

A dimensional data warehouse is often subdivided into subject areas and implemented incrementally. Sometimes these subject areas are referred to as *data marts*. On its own, each data mart provides valuable capability to a set of users. Together, they are exceptionally powerful.

Examples of data marts might include a Sales data mart, which deals with order management; a Shipments data mart, which addresses order fulfillment; and an Inventory data mart, which analyzes product stock. In addition, there may be data marts that deal with planning data. Perhaps there is an annual plan for sales, as set by management. There may also be a data mart that holds forecasting data as generated by the salespeople on a monthly basis.

If these data marts have been well designed, they are based on a set of conformed dimensions that allow another type of analysis—one that spans subject areas. In addition to permitting powerful analysis within each subject area, they permit analysis that crosses subject areas.

A key tool in planning for this capability is the dimensional bus. Part of any good schema design, the dimensional bus maps fact tables or business processes against a set of dimensions. Figure 2.2 is a conformance matrix for this example. The rows of the matrix represent fact tables; the columns represent dimensions.

Consider the data warehouse described by the conformance matrix in Figure 2.2. The Order Facts data mart and the Inventory Snapshot Facts data mart are each useful in their own right. Together, they can provide more powerful insights into the efficiency of the fulfillment process. Inventory and Order history can be analyzed together to determine the efficiency with which inventory is managed, and to predict shortfalls or prevent overstocks.

This synergy is one of the key benefits of the dimensional approach. By carefully considering and conforming dimensions up front, a data warehouse can be built incrementally. This avoids the dreaded *stovepipe*, which some critics have unfairly attempted to equate with the term data mart.

The principle of conformance demands that the dimensions are consistent through the warehouse, even if they are implemented redundantly. For example, Order Facts and Sales Forecast Facts must use the same Customer dimension. If these stars live in separate databases, the Customer dimensions must be identical; they must contain the same columns, same customer rows, and same warehouse keys.

Rollups can also be said to conform. In Figure 2.2, you see that annual planning is done at the Product Category level. All Category attributes must be identical to those in the Product table, and they must contain exactly the same values. This allows the annual plan to be compared with actual orders at the lowest level of common dimensionality—the Category level.

Aggregates for Drilling Across

The process of combining information from multiple fact tables is called drilling across, as discussed in Chapter 1. Each fact table is queried individually, and the results are combined through a full outer join on the common dimensions of the queries.

The lowest level of common dimensionality between two fact tables that will participate in a drill-across query is usually an aggregation of at least one of these fact tables. Such drill-across aggregates deserve consideration in your portfolio of aggregates because if they exist they are likely to be used frequently.

	Time			Product			Sales Org.		Promotion	Customer	Order Type	Shipment Method	Return Reason	Warehouse
	Date	Month	Quarter	Product	Brand	Category	Salesperson	Sales Region						
Order Facts	✓			✓			✓		✓	✓	✓			
Promotion Facts	✓			✓					✓					
Shipment Facts	✓			✓			✓		✓	✓	✓	✓		✓
Return Facts	✓			✓			✓		✓	✓	✓		✓	✓
Inventory Snapshot Facts	✓			✓										✓
Annual Plan Facts			✓			✓		✓						
Sales Forecast Facts		✓			✓			✓		✓				

Figure 2.2 The data warehouse bus: a dimensional conformance matrix.

Suppose that drill-across queries will be used to compare Orders with the Annual Plan. Consulting Figure 2.2, you see that the Orders data is available at a lower level of detail than the Annual Plan data. The lowest level at which the two fact tables can be compared is at the Quarter, Category, and Sales Region. In addition, the comparison must not include Promotion, Customer, or Order_type. This potential aggregate is depicted in Figure 2.3.

It is also possible that users will compare Order information to Inventory data. The lowest level at which these two processes can be compared suggests two aggregate fact tables. Sales must be summarized across all Salespeople, Promotions, Customers, and Order_types. Inventory must be summarized across all warehouses.

> **TIP** The words "across all" are often used as shorthand in describing the grain of an aggregate table. Instead of expressing the aggregate in terms of its explicit dimensionality, this shortcut allows you to define it in terms of what has been omitted. The dimensions that appear after "across all" are removed from the base table's grain to determine the aggregate grain.

You may be tempted to construct a drill-across fact table that combines the plan data and sales data in a single fact table. This approach seems logical but does not always make sense. It can get in the way of some aggregate navigation schemes and can also introduce unwanted zero-values into some reports. Chapter 9 explores the ramifications of merging fact tables and explains why they should not be considered invisible aggregates.

> **TIP** Consult the conformance bus to identify aggregates that will be used in drill-across reports. The lowest common dimensionality between two fact tables often suggests one or more aggregates.

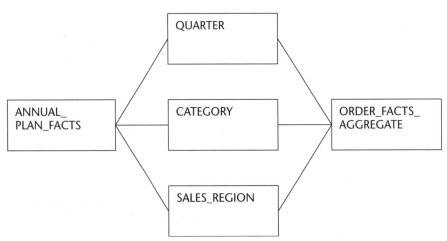

Figure 2.3 A drill-across aggregate of order data.

Query Patterns of an Existing System

If the data warehouse is in production, there are more places to look for potential aggregates. These include existing reports and their summary pages, usage logs and recommendations generated by the database or business intelligence tools, performance complaints from end users, and batched or scheduled report runs.

Analyzing Reports for Potential Aggregates

You have already seen that during the design phase, you can identify potential aggregates from work products of the operational system. It follows that, once the star schema is in production, you can identify potential aggregates from data warehouse reports as well. From the design perspective, the process is the same. Identify and express dimensionally the grain of the facts used in the reports.

A single report may suggest multiple potential aggregates. This is common for reports that drill across multiple fact tables, reports that contain one or more levels of summarization, and reports that facilitate user drilling.

TIP Reports can be used to identify candidate aggregates. Careful review of a report will reveal the grain of the report detail, summary level(s) including grand totals, separate drill-across queries, and drill-up/drill-down levels.

Note that the word *report* is used here to designate any information product of the data warehouse. In addition to the tabular and matrix reports that the word normally brings to mind, these same techniques can be used to extract requirements from charts, dashboards, or automated alerts. Any information extracted from the warehouse has an implied grain; your job is to identify it.

Drill-Across Reports

You have already seen that the lowest common dimensionality shared between two fact tables suggests potential aggregates that may be used quite often. When you look at a drill-across report, you can identify the specific dimensional requirements of the individual fact table queries.

These may turn out to be more highly summarized than the lowest level at which the fact tables conform. Make note of them as candidate aggregates. As you will see in the next section, they may prove more valuable than the lowest common dimensionality.

Summary Rows and Pages

Most reports present some form of detail data along with summaries. The simplest case is a grand total. Typically, tabular data will often be divided into subtotals as well.

The report in Figure 2.4 shows some product sales data. The report detail shows sales by Product. The sales data are also summarized by Category, and the Grand Total shows sales for all Products.

If you think dimensionally, this report suggests three levels of aggregation. The detail rows require order facts by product and month. The summary rows require order facts by category and month. The grand total requires order facts by month. Each of these is a potential aggregation of the base schema.

The fact that these levels of aggregation appear on a report indicates that there is business value in looking at the data at particular levels of summarization. This may help users who look only at the summaries—they may have similar reports that omit the details. And if the reporting tool re-queries the database for summary rows, the report itself may be aided by the summaries.

	Orders by Product For: January 2006 (cont'd.)				
Category	Product	SKU	Quantity Sold	Avg. Unit Price	Order Dollars
Packing Matter	5x7 bubble mailer	011-4822	2,000	.49	$ 980.00
	8x10 bubble mailer	011-4899	3,450	.40	$ 1,380.00
	9x12 bubble mailer	011-5744	3,800	.35	$ 1,330.00
	Packing tape	011-1729	400	.89	$ 356.00
	Box Type A	021-0011	2,000	1.04	$ 2,080.00
	Box Type B	021-0012	1,200	1.01	$ 1,212.00
	Box Type C	021-0017	2,200	1.22	$ 2,684.00
	All Packing Matter				*$ 10,022.00*
Snacks	Packaged peanuts	017-1999	500	.24	$ 120.00
	Crackers	017-2444	299	2.09	$ 634.91
	Pretzels	017-3001	500	.26	$ 130.00
	All Snacks				*$ 874.91*
Grand Total					*$ 214,896.91*
Page 10 of 10					

Figure 2.4   Excerpt from a report with subtotals.

In this simple report, some of these aggregates may prove of little value. For example, most categories seem to contain a small number of products. The Category level aggregate does not summarize very many rows of data compared to the Product aggregate. The next section discusses the evaluation of these potential aggregates.

Reports may contain summarized data in other ways as well. Reports are often divided into sections based on a dimensional attribute (or a combination of attributes). For example, the report in Figure 2.5 shows the performance of the sales team. Its primary audience is senior executives and vice presidents of the major sales regions. Each region has a summary page containing high-level information about that region. The summary page is followed by detail pages on the individual salespeople. Like subtotals, the summary pages suggest aggregates.

Often, a summary page will include some related detail that includes dimensions or facts that are not part of the body rows being summarized. Reporting tools often call this a *subreport*. For example, the regional report from Figure 2.5 might be expanded to include overall performance by customer industry on the summary page for each region. The reporting tool may handle this through the same query because the data is available in the same star. Or, it may generate a set of additional industry queries, one for each region. In either case, you have identified a part of the report that shows potential aggregation: order facts by region and industry.

Drilling

Many business intelligence tools provide an OLAP-style interaction with SQL-based reports. They may do this by re-querying the database when the user drills, adding additional dimensions to the original query. Alternatively, some tools provide the same functionality by querying more dimensional detail than the initial report displays, summarizing the facts appropriately. When the user drills, additional dimensions are added, and the facts are recalculated.

In either case, the fact that the user wants to drill up and down within the data reveals potential aggregates. Figure 2.6 shows a user drilling down from Brand to Product. The before and after states of the report reveal two different levels of aggregation.

Notice that there is no requirement to remain within a given dimension when drilling down. Starting with the same category report for January 2006, the user might have added Salesperson instead of Product. The effect is the same; an extra dimension has been added to the report, and it now displays facts at a different level of aggregation (or grain).

As discussed earlier, it is tempting to think about aggregation points within the product dimension as hierarchical. Indeed, some business intelligence products require hierarchies to be defined in advance of drill operations. If a hierarchical understanding of the dimension makes sense in your environment, document it. However, be aware that drilling is not necessarily hierarchical and that some dimensions can have multiple hierarchies.

Regional Performance Report				
Month-to-date				
January 2006				
(cont'd.)				

Eastern Region Summary

Region Code:	407
Regional Sales VP:	Domingo, Birch
Number of Territories:	23
Number of Sales Reps:	102
Number of Orders:	2113
Total Sales:	$ 2,421,443.01
Number of Sales Reps:	$ 2,400,000.00
Percent of Forecast	101%
Number of Sales Reps:	12

Page 17 of 33

Regional Performance Report				
Month-to-date				
January 2006				
(cont'd.)				

Regional Detail: Eastern Region

Territory	Sales Rep	Rep ID	Orders	Sales Dollars
Little Falls County	Chen, Ming	3011-1001	20	$ 17,247.01
	Davids, Richard	3494-2999	19	$ 131,301.00
	Lopez, Arturo	4832-1111	33	$ 77,204.00
	Rodriquez, Alicia	5934-0200	42	$ 98,407.00
	Smith, Susan	9999-9999	22	$ 102,080.55
	Thompson, Tad	2010-3993	47	$ 84,412.09
	Wilson, Rhonda	4788-2999	12	$ 91,683.77
	Little Falls			*$ 486,681.41*
River City	Mitra, James	3939-2999	17	$ 120,012.12
	Parker, Stephen	4887-2192	22	$ 88,844.91
	Tolbert, Joseph	5539-3999	44	$ 122,222.08
	River City			*$ 331,079.11*

Page 18 of 33

Figure 2.5 A report with summary pages.

Sales Drillable Report For: January 2006		
Brand	**Manager**	**Sales Dollars**
Grip Set	Dawson, Peter	$ 43,229.22
Redi-Bubble	Jones, Sheila	$ 55,011.21
Snack Packs	Nguyen, Peter	$ 15,932.54
Well-Packed	Jamison, Avery	$ 34,977.06
Grand Total		*$ 149,150.03*

User Drills Down
by Adding "Product"

Sales Drillable Report For: January 2006			
Brand	Manager	Product	Sales Dollars
Grip Set	Dawson, Peter	Packing Tape	$ 22,117.00
Grip Set	Dawson, Peter	Dura Tape	$ 21,112.22
Redi-Bubble	Jones, Sheila	5x7 bubble mailer	$ 17,380.20
Redi-Bubble	Jones, Sheila	8x10 bubble mailer	$ 19,370.44
Redi-Bubble	Jones, Sheila	9x12 bubble mailer	$ 18,260.57
Snack Packs	Nguyen, Peter	Peanuts	$ 2,406.11
Snack Packs	Nguyen, Peter	Crackers	$ 6,319.42
Snack Packs	Nguyen, Peter	Pretzels	$ 7,207.01
Well-Packed	Jamison, Avery	Box Type A	$ 10,080.00
Well-Packed	Jamison, Avery	Box Type B	$ 12,212.07
Well-Packed	Jamison, Avery	Box Type C	$ 12,684.99
Grand Total:			*$ 149,150.03*

Figure 2.6   Drill paths suggest aggregates.

Choosing Which Reports to Analyze

The number of available reports to examine can quickly exceed the number of potential dimensional aggregates. In this situation, you may choose to limit your investigation into the reports that are used most often.

> **TIP** Don't study every report for candidate aggregates. Instead, look at the popular ones, batch subscriptions, poorly performing reports, and those that are required by key users.

Popularity

The resources available to you for identification of popular reports are determined primarily by the products that your data warehouse application comprises. Most RDBMS products can log user queries; you can consult with the DBA to profile the queries being issued. The logs may also provide information about query execution time; this information will help in determining whether a particular aggregate would offer value.

Many of the business intelligence tools and reporting tools provide a log of report access. Such logs enable you to study the frequency of report access; you can then refer to the most accessed reports to look for potential aggregates. Once again, response time may be maintained as part of these logs.

You may also find that pieces of your data warehouse architecture are capable of providing suggestions on aggregates or summaries. These utilities balance the popularity of a report with the potential time savings of an aggregate.

Scheduling and Subscriptions

Many reporting tools also enable users to subscribe to reports that have been scheduled to run on a regular basis. These are often the core reports for the subject area, pre-built and parameterized as part of the data warehouse implementation. Designed to provide thorough analysis of the business process, these reports are frequently among the most used.

These reports may be referred to as *scheduled, batched, bursted,* or *broadcasted*. Some tools deliver key information only when certain conditions are met. This is often called *pushing*. Both the conditions being evaluated and the resultant report will offer potential aggregates.

Poor Performers

Even if your aim is to be proactive, there will always be reports that users complain about. When a good data warehouse is available, this is inevitable. Reports that perform poorly should not be taken as a sign that the designers have failed to identify the proper portfolio of aggregates. Instead, they can be taken to represent the growing analytic sophistication of the users—a sign of a successful data warehouse implementation.

Of course, if these reports are frequently requested or popular, they deserve special attention when it comes to the aggregate portfolio. Sometimes, a report with a relatively small audience deserves this special attention as well; its use of system resources affects those running other reports.

The Needs of Key Users

Last, you may choose to identify potential aggregates by looking at the analytic needs of key users, or *power users*. These may be the same individuals who were chosen for interviews during the design of the data warehouse. They use the data warehouse often, and have a vested interest in its success.

Often, a data mart is sponsored by a department or group. If these folks are paying the bills, then they deserve first attention when it comes to optimization. In any event, it is likely that they have the deepest relationship with the data being used and will provide the best insights into the logical patterns of analysis.

Assessing the Value of Potential Aggregates

After identifying a pool of potential aggregates, the next step is to sort through them and determine which ones to build. Three major factors will come into play. First, the resources available in your data warehouse environment will dictate how many aggregates can be built. Second, the aggregates must be compared to the base table (and each other) to determine what real performance benefit is provided. Last, each aggregate must be gauged by how many users it serves, and potentially the relative importance of different users.

Number of Aggregates

The production data warehouse environment works to limit the number of aggregates that is practical to deploy in two ways. First, the technology available to perform aggregate navigation may limit the number of aggregates that it makes sense to build. Second, a portfolio of aggregates gets very large, very fast. The available computing resources will place a maximum cap on the amount of space you are willing to reserve for aggregates.

Presence of an Aggregate Navigator

The number of aggregates that can reasonably be managed is largely determined by the presence or absence of an aggregate navigator, and by the capability of the navigator. Recall from Chapter 1 that the aggregate navigator's function is to transform base-level SQL into aggregate-aware SQL.

If there is no aggregate navigator, end users are forced to make choices about which aggregate to use. Most end users will find this technical decision confusing. As you see in Chapter 4, the best way to help users cope with this confusion is to limit the number of aggregates. For each fact table, a limit of one to two aggregates makes the most sense.

If the data warehouse includes some sort of aggregate navigation functionality, the number of potential aggregates can be larger. Users and developers are freed of making decisions regarding which tables to access. Only the base schema is visible to them; the aggregate navigator rewrites queries as appropriate.

This capability does not necessarily remove the cap on the practical number of aggregates. Some aggregate navigators require painstaking manual configuration before their query rewrite capability will properly exploit an aggregate. A complex configuration task that enumerates aggregate options on an attribute-by-attribute basis is a task that cannot be revisited lightly.

If the process of registering aggregates is too onerous, there is a disincentive to adding or removing an aggregate. Careful reconfiguration and testing will be required. In such a case, the number of aggregates may be limited in order to minimize the impact of a change to the aggregate portfolio. This will allow the warehouse team to change the aggregate portfolio as the needs of the business change.

Space Consumed by Aggregate Tables

While aggregate tables are smaller than the base schema, they are not necessarily insignificant. Even a small number of aggregate tables can easily eclipse the original base schema in terms of occupied space. And like the base schema, the aggregate schema may require indexing.

Fortunately, aggregate fact tables that approach the original fact table in size are less likely to provide a significant performance gain. As long as close attention is paid to the relative performance boost of each aggregate, it is reasonable to expect that several can be built, which together consume the same amount of space as the base schema.

Pre-joined aggregates are a different story. Because the dimensions have been collapsed together with the fact table to produce a pre-joined aggregate, dimension values are stored redundantly. A pre-joined aggregate that contains one-twentieth the rows of a base fact table may well consume more space. That's because the costly dimension values are now being stored with each fact, instead of a compact set of keys. As I mentioned previously, aggregate fact and dimension tables are preferred for this reason.

When first adding aggregates, a good rule of thumb is to allocate the same amount of space to aggregate stars as the base star consumes.

This may be a large amount of space, but it will often pale in comparison to the amount of space reserved for indexes. Even with half the space required to store the base tables, a good portfolio of aggregate stars can be implemented. Over time, as the warehouse team becomes comfortable with the integration of aggregates into the overall architecture, more space may be allocated to aggregates.

For extremely large databases, the pressure may be on to reduce the amount of disk space required for aggregate storage. But these same large databases are often the ones that need aggregates the most. There is simply no way to avoid making the tradeoff decisions between resources and performance.

If available storage resources are flexible, you may choose to plan based on the number of aggregates to build. In this case, your objective might be to build two or three strong aggregates. Implement these aggregates and track the improvements they deliver. Measure the storage resources required, as well as the IT resources used to implement and maintain the aggregates. This information can feed resource estimates for future plans to expand the aggregate portfolio. Remember, your portfolio of aggregates can and should be changed over time.

It is important to avoid a situation in which the aggregates and their resource requirements are not planned. Pre-joined aggregates, in particular, are often abused in this way. Deployed on an ad hoc basis to improve individual reports, a collection of *one-off* pre-joined aggregates can quickly grow unmanageable and consume a large amount of space with great inefficiency. Chapter 7 offers advice on how to plan and manage aggregates to avoid this kind of situation.

In the end, the number of aggregates built, and the space they consume, is determined by the overall resources available and the importance of improving performance. Many star schemas perform nicely with two to three aggregate tables. Others develop a larger portfolio of aggregates, and one that changes frequently over time.

How Many Rows Are Summarized

The real test of the value of an aggregate is what kind of performance benefit it supplies. In general, this performance benefit relates directly to the number of base rows that an aggregate fact table row summarizes.

It is easy to fall into the trap of assuming the answer is related to the relative cardinality of the various dimensions, but variations in sparsity can be difficult to predict. The skew of data values can also render an aggregate useful for some queries but not others.

WHY THE NUMBER OF ROWS SUMMARIZED ONLY APPROXIMATES AGGREGATE SAVINGS

The goal of dimensional aggregates is to provide a performance gain by reducing the amount of work the RDBMS must do for a given query. When an RDBMS receives a query, the work it does is broken down into several tasks. In very general terms, these tasks can be described as follows:

1. The RDBMS parses the query, verifying its syntax and the existence of the data objects referenced.

2. It identifies an execution plan for the query, which determines how the results will be fetched and assembled.

3. It executes the plan, reading data from disk and performing any necessary computations.

4. It returns the results to the end users.

The single largest bottleneck in this process occurs during Step 3, when the RDBMS must read the necessary data. Disk I/O is the culprit. The database must request, and wait for, blocks of data to be read from the disk.

The RDBMS may have any number of features that are designed to improve performance of this step. These may include clustering, various types of indexing, and star-join optimization. All these features help the database determine which blocks of data must be read from disk; some of them also help the RDBMS store rows together that are likely to be read together.

Performance is improved when the RDBMS has to read fewer blocks, or when blocks to be read are stored contiguously. The question to ask about a given aggregate, then, is this: Does it reduce the I/O necessary to respond to a query?

It is often assumed that if the database needs to read one-twentieth the number of rows to query the aggregate, it may respond up to 20 times faster than it would if accessing the base schema.

As mentioned, the database actually reads data from blocks, and a block may contain more than one row. If two needed rows are in the same block, the read operation is more efficient. And the RDBMS can read two blocks that are contiguous much more quickly than if it must perform a seek operation to locate the second block.

So other factors contribute to the relative performance of the aggregate. For these reasons, you may not receive the expected 20x performance gain in this example.

In the worst possible case, the aggregate would require the same number of seeks and block reads as the fact table, providing no performance gain. In the best possible case, the needed rows are better concentrated within blocks, and the contiguity of required blocks is better, so that the performance gain is greater than 20x.

These factors are mitigated somewhat because the aggregate fact table is managed by the RDBMS and the DBA in the same way as the base fact table. The same database features used to optimize performance of the base schema will be used to optimize the aggregate. The disk *footprint* of the rows needed for a given query is likely to be smaller in the case of the aggregate fact table, the distribution of rows across blocks is likely to be as good or better, and distribution of the relevant blocks is likely to fall in a similar pattern to the base schema.

What all this technical talk means is that, as a general rule of thumb, the performance value of an aggregate fact table can be estimated if you look at how many base rows are summarized by each aggregate row. A 20:1 ratio suggests there will be significant performance gains; a 1.25:1 ratio does not.

It will, however, be important to test the performance gains offered by the aggregate. This is discussed in Chapter 7.

Examining the Number of Rows Summarized

The relative power of an aggregate is based on the average number of base rows that an aggregate row summarizes. This is only approximate, as explained in the sidebar, but will allow comparison of the relative merits of various options. After the average savings is calculated, you must also ensure that these savings are relatively consistent across the data set, and that similar savings are not already achieved elsewhere.

Figuring Out Average Savings

Your primary measure of aggregate value will be the average number of fact table rows summarized by an aggregate fact table row. This can be estimated by issuing some database queries.

Refer again to the orders schema from Figure 1.2, which contains orders by Day, Customer, Product, Salesperson, and Order Type. You have identified some reports that do not require product detail, and are considering an aggregate of order facts by Day, Customer, Category (Product), and Salesperson. This aggregate eliminates the order type information and summarizes by product category.

One way to get a peek at the potential advantage of the aggregate is to focus on a particular day and count the number of base rows that each aggregate would summarize. For example, you might issue the following query:

```
Select  product.category,               /* aggregating by category */
        order_facts.customer_key,
        order_facts salesperson_key,
        count(order_facts.product_key)   /* number of rows summarized */
from    order_facts, product, day
where   order_facts.product_key = product.product_key
  and   order_facts.day_key = day.day_key
  and   day.date = to_date('1/31/2006')      /* one day sample*/
group by
        product.category, customer_key, salesperson_key
```

The results of this query are a set of keys and a product category with a count. The count specifies exactly how many rows were summarized by the aggregate. You counted `product_key` but could have counted any mandatory column in the fact table. Here is an excerpt of some sample query results:

category	customer_key	salesperson_key	count(product_key)
Office Supplies	477	101	17
Office Supplies	479	152	19
Office Supplies	501	156	22
Office Supplies	522	152	17
Office Supplies	553	101	19
Packing Matter	477	101	17
Packing Matter	480	152	21
Packing Matter	501	156	21
Packing Matter	520	157	17
Packing Matter	553	141	22
Snacks Foods	478	191	15
Snacks Foods	522	152	22
Snacks Foods	533	156	24
Snacks Foods	550	157	14
Snacks Foods	609	141	20

The counts for each row are shown in the rightmost column and indicate exactly how many base fact table rows are summarized by the category aggregate. In this case, the average is around 19 rows, a strong candidate for consideration. A few additional queries should be run to ensure that the savings does not vary by date.

TIP A good starting rule of thumb is to identify aggregate fact tables where each row summarizes an average of 20 rows.

Of course, even limiting your analysis to one day, the number of rows returned by a query like this may be too large to scrutinize in this form. Instead, look at the total number of rows returned when selecting the distinct combination of dimensional keys and summary attributes.

The Impact of Skew

Sometimes, the distribution of individual values within a group is not even, a concept referred to as *skew*. Suppose that the previous test query had returned these results instead:

category	customer_key	salesperson_key	count(product_key)
Office Supplies	477	101	2
Office Supplies	479	152	1
Office Supplies	501	156	3
Office Supplies	522	152	2
Office Supplies	553	101	1
Packing Matter	477	101	33
Packing Matter	480	152	61
Packing Matter	501	156	44
Packing Matter	520	157	59
Packing Matter	553	141	70
Snacks Foods	478	191	1
Snacks Foods	522	152	1
Snacks Foods	533	156	2
Snacks Foods	550	157	1
Snacks Foods	609	141	1

In this case, the average number of rows summarized is still around 19. But the distribution of the savings is skewed heavily toward Packing Matter. There may be several explanations for this behavior. Perhaps the business focuses primarily on packing material, and most other categories contain only one or two products. But the explanation may be more complicated, involving a confluence of categories, products, salespeople, customers, and the date. Running this query for a larger date range may reveal different patterns.

TIP The savings afforded by aggregates can be lopsided, favoring a particular attribute value.

Evaluating the aggregate now requires understanding two things: the distribution of the savings across category values, and the focus on user queries across category values. This extends the required analysis to include actual attribute values, which easily takes you far beyond the number of possible situations to consider.

The aggregate in this case is likely to provide very large performance gains for queries that involve mainly Packing Matter. If this represents the bulk of the data, the aggregate remains a very strong candidate. Queries that involve all products will still benefit from reading around one-twentieth the rows. If, on the other hand, most sales fall outside the category of Packing Matter, the value of the aggregate is greatly diminished.

Skew in the data can be difficult to identify and quantify. There are a large number of combinations of dimensional attributes to consider over a wide spread of attribute values. A few simple queries should help you gauge if you have relatively good distribution of the average savings; testing will be important in verifying your assumptions (see Chapter 7).

Compared to What?

So far, you've looked at the number of base fact table rows that are summarized by an aggregate. If more than one aggregate is to be deployed, you also need to compare aggregates to one another.

Remember that the aggregate table functions in exactly the same way as the base schema. It can be used to answer queries that match its grain, but it can also be aggregated in exactly the same way a base schema can. This holds true for star schema aggregates and pre-joined aggregates.

For example, assume you plan to include an aggregate of order facts by Day, Category (Product), Customer, and Salesperson. Call this the "Category" aggregate. You are also considering an aggregate of order facts by Day, Customer, and Salesperson. This second aggregate completely summarizes the product dimension.

To judge the value of this aggregate, you must compare it not only to the base fact table, but also to the category aggregate. You may discover that it provides significant savings over the base fact table, but not when compared to the category aggregate. Perhaps there are not many categories, or the categories tend to participate in low cardinality relationships with Salespeople and Customers. In these cases, the proposed aggregate offers very little value over the category aggregate.

> **TIP** Remember that, like a base fact table, a dimensional aggregate can be aggregated during a query. Aggregates may be competing with other aggregates to offer performance gains.

The Cardinality Trap and Sparsity

The number of distinct values taken on by a given attribute is referred to as *cardinality*. Often, you think of the aggregation levels in terms of cardinality. For example, you might observe some cardinality characteristics of your order schema:

- Day: 1826 Days, 60 Months, 20 Quarters, 5 Years
- Product: 2,000 Products, 200 Brands, 20 Product Categories
- Customer: 1000 Customers, 15 Industries
- Salesperson: 200 Salespeople, 50 Territories, 4 Regions

These cardinalities can be very helpful as you think through potential aggregates. But they often fuel incorrect assumptions about the distribution of values in relation to one another.

If you think about the aggregates in terms of the cardinality of the dimensions, you must also take care not to make any assumptions about sparsity. In Chapter 1, you saw that fact tables are generally sparse. That is, not all combinations of keys are present.

Using the orders example, consider sales on a given day. There are 2,000 products, 1,000 customers, and 200 salespeople. (For simplicity's sake, leave order type out of the picture.) There are 400,000,000 possible combinations of these values on any given day (2,000 × 1,000 × 200).

Most days, only 20 percent of the products on the price sheet are sold to 5 percent of the customers through 10 percent of the sales force. This generates a maximum of 4,000,000 million rows in the fact table—about 1 percent of the possible combinations. The value may be even lower if there are other correlations between data values. Perhaps salespeople focus on particular customers, for example.

The trap comes if you assume a similar sparsity will be found within the aggregate. For example, consider an aggregate fact table that summarizes order facts by Month, Brand, Industry, and Salesperson. Using the preceding cardinalities, you see 600,000 possible combinations of Brand, Industry, and Salesperson for a given month (200 × 15 × 200). Assuming 1 percent sparsity, this would be a 6,000 row aggregate table, a fantastically powerful aggregate, each row summarizing about 667 base fact rows.

But the sparsity does not remain constant. As you climb to higher levels of summarization, the fact table grows more dense. Stepping back from the mathematics for a moment, this makes perfect sense. You may not sell all products to all customers on a given day. But over the course of a month, you may well sell all categories to all customers.

TIP Don't assume aggregate fact tables will exhibit the same sparsity as the tables they summarize. The higher the degree of summarization, the more dense the aggregate fact table will be.

The best way to get an idea of the relative size of the aggregate is to count the number of rows. As before, count the distinct combination of keys and/or summarized dimension attributes.

This conversation has focused on aggregate fact tables. Once again, note that everything said here applies to pre-joined aggregates as well. The savings of a pre-joined aggregate roughly correlates with the number of base fact table rows it summarizes; this savings may be skewed in favor of particular dimensional values or relatively even; you cannot assume the pre-joined aggregate will exhibit the same sparsity as the fact table it summarizes.

Who Will Benefit from the Aggregate

Who benefits from an aggregate is as important as how much benefit it provides. It goes without saying that the aggregate is of no benefit if user queries are never able to leverage it.

Earlier in this chapter, it was suggested that candidate aggregates be drawn from a pool of actual user requirements. Requirements may be drawn from user interviews, operational reports, design notes, or existing query patterns. This ensures that there is a useful business context for each aggregate considered.

Some aggregates will prove useful in more situations than others. Aggregates that are more highly summarized will offer more value in a smaller number of situations, and consume a smaller amount of system resources. Conversely, aggregates that offer benefits to a wider number of queries will tend to be less summarized, offering a lesser degree of improvements, and consuming more resources.

The first aggregates you add to your implementation are those that offer benefits across the widest number of user requirements. Aggregates that fall in the 20:1 range of savings are compared with one another to identify those that support the most common user requirements.

Next, you can eliminate aggregates that offer little incremental value over those already chosen. In the orders example, you saw that summarizing across all products did not offer much incremental value over a category aggregate. You can scratch this one off the list, along with some others.

As the pool of aggregates is narrowed down, you will arrive at a set of aggregates with very clear value and broad appeal. You will also find some aggregates that have very clear value, but which apply in far fewer situations. For example, you may have identified three aggregates that serve a very large number of existing reports quite well. You have two more that offer additional gain in some very narrow situations. Resource constraints mean you will be able to implement only one of them. Which to include?

The last step is to consider the relative importance of the business requirement the aggregate satisfies. Important queries may be those that are run by senior management and their administrative staff—for example, questions to which the CEO may demand a quick answer. Important queries may also be those issued by the department sponsoring the data warehouse or data mart. For example, if the marketing department sponsored the orders data mart, their needs carry special weight.

TIP Start by selecting aggregates that provide solid performance boosts for a wide number of common queries. To this, add more powerful (but more narrowly used) aggregates as space permits. Use the relative importance of one aggregate over another in a tiebreaker situation.

Summary

A potential aggregate is expressed in terms of grain and dimensional confor-mance. This works equally well for aggregate fact tables as for pre-joined aggregates.

In this chapter, you have seen that the number of potential aggregates can be large enough to preclude their evaluation on a case-by-case basis. Business requirements can be gathered and linked to potential aggregates, narrowing the pool that must be evaluated.

These requirements can be identified during the schema design process by looking at the dimensional conformance matrix for drill-across aggregates and by looking at actual user reports.

The number of aggregates and space they consume will be dictated by your operating environment and resource considerations. Given these limits, you will look at aggregates that seem to have wide applicability and evaluate the average number of rows each aggregate row summarizes.

This savings is compared to the base table and to other aggregates. Factors such as skew and changes in sparsity require careful testing of the proposed pool of aggregates. The relative importance of various business requirements is used as a tiebreaker in choosing between aggregates to include.

Now that the aggregates have been chosen, you need to formally document their design. This chapter has already touched on some design principles for aggregate schemas, and others have been implied. The next chapter provides a formal set of design principles that should be followed in designing and doc-umenting your chosen aggregates.

CHAPTER 3

Designing Aggregates

Once you have chosen dimensional aggregates, they must be designed and documented. This is the point of greatest risk for aggregate implementation. If not designed properly, dimensional aggregates can violate the guiding principles laid out in Chapter 1, rendering the schema very difficult to use. Worse, design errors can render aggregates capable of producing incorrect results. This chapter lays out guiding principles for avoiding these pitfalls.

Before diving into the design of the aggregate schema, this chapter examines some key elements of the base schema design. Part of *any* good schema design, these elements must be in place prior to the development of a successful group of aggregates.

Next, the chapter provides a set of principles for aggregate design. Following these principles ensures that dimensional aggregates are easy to use, and that they will always return correct results. We will also look at the problems introduced when these principles are not followed.

Unlike the base schema, dimensional aggregates are likely to change over time. As usage patterns change, aggregates will be added and removed as appropriate. This makes documentation of aggregate implementation extremely important. The last section of this chapter enumerates elements of the aggregate design that must be included in schema documentation.

The Base Schema

Often, the initial implementation of a data mart does not include aggregates. This omission can help an inexperienced project team get their feet wet by reducing project scope. Aggregates will be introduced later, and will probably be incorporated into the initial implementation of subsequent data marts. These project approaches are examined in Chapter 7.

Whether or not aggregates will be included, documentation of the base schema should include information that will aid in the future development of aggregate tables. These include grain statements, the dimensional conformance bus, and the documentation of aggregation points or hierarchies within dimensions.

When building aggregates, the base schema serves as the *source system* for the aggregate schema. Knowing this, you can include some housekeeping columns in your fact and dimension tables, which will aid the ETL process for building the aggregates.

Identification of Grain

Explicit identification of fact table grain is an essential part of any dimensional design. It is usually one of the first steps in the schema design process. Failure to properly fix the grain leads to problems. It will be difficult to get valid reports out of the schema. Confusion over what a row in the fact table represents will make the task of identifying aggregates impossible.

When Grain Is Forgotten

Inattention to grain leads to failures in design that compromise the value of the schema. *Fuzzy grain* manifests itself in several ways. Available detail is omitted from the data warehouse; inappropriate dimensional attributes are included; appropriate attributes are excluded; facts of different dimensionality are placed together in a single fact table. The result can only be characterized as a failure.

If available detail has not been included, the schema will be unable to answer key business questions. Consider a schema built to analyze the orders process, as described in Chapter 1. Failure to set the grain at the order line would have prevented this schema from answering product-related questions. This error seems unlikely because product details come up frequently in user interviews. But what about order type detail? These less popular attributes provide valuable analysis to a small group of users.

Failure to set the lowest possible grain also damages the schema's ability to be adapted to change. When grain is properly set, new dimensional attributes or facts can be added to the schema, without having to throw out data that has already been loaded and without damaging existing reports. For example, a new product attribute is easily included. Existing rows in the product dimension can be updated to include an unknown value for this attribute. An ambitious warehouse team might even go back through the transaction data from the source systems to populate this column for previously loaded facts. The fact that order number has been included in the schema design becomes critical.

There are more immediate problems with fuzzy grain declaration. Placing facts that have different grains in a single fact table leads to queries that produce incorrect results. In fact, trying to get any results can prove challenging.

In the orders example, suppose that every order includes shipping charges. These charges are not allocated to the order line. A shipping_charge fact applies only at the order level, not at the order line. If this fact is included in the fact table, several problems created by fuzzy grain appear.

First, the shipping charges may be repeated in the fact table—once for each individual product that is ordered. This means that the shipping_charge fact will not aggregate properly. Orders with multiple order lines will show incorrect results. To cope with this problem, it becomes necessary to query the shipping charge separately from the order detail. The design may be further complicated by the inclusion of a *level field*, which is discussed in detail shortly. This introduces new issues, including what values to include in a dimension row for attributes that do not apply.

Grain and Aggregates

When a schema with fuzzy grain is implemented, the data warehouse team will have their share of problems. They may not have any time left over to even consider aggregates. And if they do, they will quickly discover that identification of aggregates becomes a futile exercise.

You've seen that the aggregate schema is nothing more than a star schema itself, differing from the base schema only in terms of its dimensional grain. If there is no discipline when it comes to setting the grain of fact tables, how do you define an aggregate? The problems of the schema are likely to be compounded if any attempt to build aggregates is made. What exactly should be summarized in the aggregate schema? It is likely to exhibit fuzzy grain itself. When do you choose the aggregate schema over the base schema?

The lesson here is simple: Grain must be fully understood and documented for each and every fact table. Aggregates cannot be meaningfully expressed if the grain of the base schema is in question.

TIP Declaration of grain is an essential part of schema design. Proper definition of grain not only enables the future identification of aggregates, it is crucial to the success of the base schema itself.

Conformance Bus

Any good dimensional design should include documentation of dimensional conformance. This information will prove useful to aggregate designers in two ways. First, designers can inspect the conformance to identify candidate aggregates that will assist in drill-across queries. Second, the conformance of base dimensions and their rollup dimensions is identical to the conformance of aggregate dimensions and the base dimensions they summarize. You saw examples of these benefits in Chapter 2.

The conformance bus is often documented at different levels. Prior to the implementation of the first data mart, some organizations choose to perform a high-level analysis across all business processes. This analysis identifies dimensions that are of interest across subject areas. Conformance of these dimensions is required. These requirements are documented in a process-level conformance bus.

An example of a process-level conformance bus is shown in Figure 3.1. It shows several business processes: Planning, Sales, Fulfillment, and Inventory Management. Common warehouse dimensions in the diagram are Customer, Product, Salesperson, Time, Warehouse, and Shipper. These dimensions form a bus structure into which the subject areas connect as appropriate. For example, the Inventory Management business process involves Product, Time, and Warehouse.

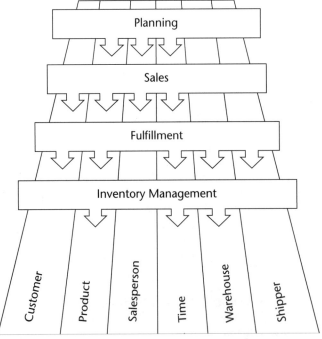

Figure 3.1   Conformance bus for business processes.

A diagram like this is more easily depicted as a simple matrix, as shown in Figure 3.2. Rows of the matrix represent business processes, and columns represent conformed dimensions. The checkmarks in a given row represent the dimensions in which that business process participates.

Any of the processes depicted in Figures 3.1 and 3.2 may involve more than one fact table. For example, inventory management may include separate fact tables for inventory snapshots and transactions. The inventory snapshot fact table captures inventory levels at a particular point in time, whereas the inventory transaction fact table captures the increases and decreases in inventory as product comes and goes. Similarly, the sales process may include separate fact tables for order lines, orders, and returns.

A process-level conformance diagram is useful but is often omitted from the model documentation. The project may be focused on a specific business process, without the prior consideration of dimensional conformance over a series of processes. Or, the diagram may be viewed as redundant if detailed schema designs are also included.

Every schema design should always include a table-level conformance diagram. Where the process-level diagram included processes, this diagram includes fact tables. You saw an example of a table-level conformance matrix in Figure 2.2. Notice that this schema also documented conformance across partially aggregated dimensions. Month, for example, is a conformed rollup of Day; Category is a conformed rollup of Product.

TIP A table-level conformance matrix is an important component of the design documentation. It illustrates conformance requirements, and will be useful in selecting aggregates as well.

	Customer	Product	Salesperson	Time	Warehouse	Shipper
Planning		✓	✓	✓		
Sales	✓	✓	✓	✓		
Fulfillment	✓	✓		✓	✓	✓
Inventory Management		✓		✓	✓	

Figure 3.2   Matrix representation of conformance bus for business processes.

Some schema designers like to include additional information about each fact table in this type of diagram, including the type of fact table and its grain. An example of this appears in Figure 3.3. Like the table-level conformance diagram found in Figure 2.2, this diagram captures the relationship between fact tables and conformed dimensions in the data warehouse.

Digging slightly deeper into the dimensional conformance matrix reveals another important design issue. Dimensions do not need to be identical in order to conform. For example, a properly designed Month table can conform with a Day table. It should be no surprise, then, that these rollups are carefully planned as well. As it turns out, the different ways a dimension can be rolled up become useful in planning aggregate schemas.

Rollup Dimensions

Fact tables can work together when they share conformed dimensions. Conformed dimensions are not necessarily identical; two dimensions conform if all of the following rules are followed:

- The attributes of one dimension are a strict subset of another (with the exception of its key).

- Value instances of the common attributes are recorded in an identical manner in both dimensions.

- Of the subset of common attributes: All combinations of values represented in the more detailed dimension are present in the second, and no others.

When these rules are met, two dimensions are said to conform. The smaller dimension is often referred to as a *rollup dimension*. The conformance matrix from Figure 2.2 includes several rollup dimensions. For the Day dimension, there are rollups for Month, Quarter, and Year. For Product, there are rollups for Brand and Category. The rollup dimensions are followed by the base dimension's name in parentheses.

When the schema design includes rollup dimensions, it is important to properly identify aggregation points, natural keys, and data sources. This information will be valuable when it comes to defining aggregates, and should be included as part of the base schema design. A conformed rollup is no different from an aggregate dimension, so these rules will also come in handy shortly, when looking at design rules for aggregate schemas.

Fact table	Type	Grain	customer	product	salesperson	time	warehouse	shipper	order_line	transaction_type
order_facts	transaction	Orders by order_line, customer, product, salesperson, and day	✔	✔	✔	✔			✔	
shipment_facts	transaction	Shipments by customer, product, time, warehouse, and shipper	✔	✔		✔	✔	✔	✔	
shipment_status_facts	snapshot	Fulfillment levels by customer, product, and time	✔	✔		✔			✔	
inventory_status_facts	snapshot	Inventory levels by product, warehouse, and date		✔		✔	✔			
inventory_transaction_facts	transaction	Changes to inventory level by product, warehouse, and date		✔		✔	✔			✔

Figure 3.3 Table-level conformance matrix with additional information.

Aggregation Points

The summarization of dimensions that conform but are not identical is described in terms of *aggregation points*. An aggregation point describes a potential summarization of a dimension. For example, Category and Brand were defined as potential aggregation points within the Product dimension. This is illustrated in Figure 3.4.

A simple list of aggregation points will be a helpful component of the design documentation. This can be provided in a tabular format, as in Table 2.1. Some teams choose to supplement this list with basic documentation of dimensional hierarchies, as you will see in a moment.

Notice that all relevant attributes are included in the rollup dimensions. The Month dimension, for example, includes all attributes relevant for a given year and month, including the fiscal period and fiscal year in which the month falls. If quarters and fiscal periods do not fall on similar boundaries, the fiscal period and fiscal year information may be absent in the Quarter dimension.

For a snowflake schema, there is no need to define the rollup dimension. The dimension is already normalized, and fact tables can connect to the dimensional structure at the appropriate point. In Figure 2.1, order_facts_aggregate connected into the Time dimension at the Month table. The foreign key for Quarter in this table can be followed to reach Quarter, and similarly from Quarter you can reach Year.

Natural Keys

Just as a base dimension includes a natural key, so too does the rollup. For example, the natural key of the Product dimension is SKU. This column uniquely identifies a product in the source system. Similarly, the category_code uniquely identifies a category on the source side. This column is the natural key of the Category rollup dimension. The natural keys of conformed dimensions are identified by the letters nk, as in Figure 3.4.

Sometimes the natural key of a rollup dimension does not exist as a primary key in the source dimension. Perhaps it is a loosely related collection of attributes, like the order_type dimension from Chapter 1. Or the natural key may not exist as individual attributes in the source system, like the Month dimension in Figure 3.4. Each row of this dimension is uniquely identified by the combination of a year and a month, although such attributes do not exist as a key on the source side.

TIP When the base schema design includes rollup dimensions, identify the aggregation point of the rollup and its natural key. The natural key may be a combination of attributes.

PRODUCT
product_key (pk) product product_description sku (nk) unit_of_measure brand brand_code brand_manager category category_code

BRAND
brand_key (pk) brand brand_code (nk) brand_manager category category_code

Aggregation Point:
Brand

CATEGORY
category_key (pk) category category_code (nk)

Aggregation Point:
Category

DAY
day_key (pk) full_date (nk) day_of_week_number day_of_week_name day_of_week_abbr day_of_month holiday_flag weekday_flag weekend_flag month_number month_name month_abbr quarter quarter_month year year_month year_quarter fiscal_period fiscal_year fiscal_year_period

MONTH
month_key (pk) month_number (nk) month_name month_abbr quarter quarter_month year (nk) year_month year_quarter fiscal_period fiscal_year fiscal_year_period

Aggregation Point:
Month in a Year

QUARTER
quarter_key (pk) quarter (nk) year (nk) year_quarter

Aggregation Point:
Quarter in a Year

YEAR
year_key (pk) year (nk)

Aggregation Point:
Year

Figure 3.4   Conforming rollup dimensions and their natural keys.

Source Mapping

As part of the design of the base schema, each column is mapped to source system attributes, with transformation rules or logic as appropriate. The design of the rollup dimension should source it from the base dimension. This greatly simplifies ETL processing, and ensures that values are expressed identically and that all combinations of attributes present in the base dimension are also present in the rollup dimension. This is discussed in more detail when the ETL process is examined in Chapters 5 and 6.

Slow Change Processing

The source system attribute values from which dimension values are drawn will change over time. The schema design must determine how the warehouse responds (or does not respond) to these changes. If an attribute value, such as the name of a product, changes on the source side, the same change may be implemented in the warehouse. This is known as a *type 1 change*. Alternatively, a new dimension row may be created with the new value. This is known as *a type 2 change*.

These rules for slowly changing dimensions are identified during the schema design process. Typically, each attribute that is not a key is assigned a slowly changing dimension property of type 1 or type 2. Sophisticated implementations may be able to handle a single attribute as either type, depending on the circumstance of the change.

By definition, these exact rules must apply to attributes that survive in a rollup dimension. If brand_manager is a type 1 attribute in the Product dimension, it must also be treated as a type 1 attribute in the Brand dimension. Otherwise, the Brand dimension could end up containing a set of brand brand_manager combinations that is different from those present in the Product dimension.

TIP Rollup dimensions should be sourced from the base dimensions, and their attributes must follow the same rules for slow change processing.

Hierarchies

It is tempting to think about dimensional data in hierarchical terms. Days fall into months, months fall into quarters, quarters fall into years . . . products group into brands, brands into categories. Moving down a hierarchy from general to specific (for example, year to quarter) is a form of drilling down. Moving up the hierarchy is drilling up.

You've already seen that these are really just special cases of drilling up and drilling down. Drilling into data is a simple matter of adding dimensional detail. Starting with a report that shows sales by product category, for example, you might add the dimensional attribute Salesperson. You have expanded the dimensional detail of the report in a meaningful way. Product Category to Salesperson represents a meaningful drill path that is not part of a hierarchy.

A hierarchy within a dimension, then, is one of many potential drill paths. However, the drill-down capability offered by many business intelligence tools requires a dimensional hierarchy. When you use such tools, drilling must take place along a predefined hierarchy within a dimension. If such a tool is part of the target implementation, identification of hierarchies within a dimension is a useful exercise, and the results will aid developers of drill-down reports.

An understanding of hierarchies will also be critical when using certain database technologies to build aggregates, such as materialized views or materialized query tables. The importance of hierarchies for these tools is explored in Chapter 4.

Hierarchies can be identified by outlining successive levels of conformance within a dimension. Each hierarchy level is defined by an aggregation point and placed on a continuum from most general to most detailed. Figure 3.5 depicts a product hierarchy.

The numbers next to each level of the hierarchy represent the approximate number of values (or members) at that level. The highest level of summarization, All Products, ignores product altogether. There are approximately 35 categories, 700 brands, and 15,000 products. This information can be used to assess the average number of rows summarized at each level. For example, each brand summarizes approximately 21 products, and each category summarizes approximately 20 brands.

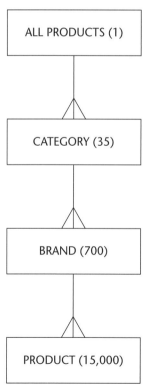

Figure 3.5   A hierarchy in the Product dimension.

TIP Documenting dimensional hierarchies may be important for business intelligence software and database features such as materialized views and materialized query tables. The hierarchies identify potential aggregation points and can aid in estimating degree of summarization.

Don't let these numbers lead you to make assumptions about the number of fact table rows that will be summarized at each level. The interaction of data values at these levels will interact with other dimensions to determine how many fact table rows there will be. As shown in Chapter 2, skew can make the average summarization meaningless. For example, 14,000 of the products may fall under a single brand. The actual summarization must be carefully evaluated.

Dimensions are not limited to a single hierarchy. It is common to find several hierarchies within a dimension. For example, a Day dimension may contain two hierarchies, one for the calendar year and one for the fiscal year. Two ways of representing these hierarchies are shown in Figure 3.6. The top half of the diagram depicts each hierarchy separately; the lower diagram shows each level only once.

In either half of the figure, working up from the lowermost level of detail, observe that both hierarchies include day and month. After that, they diverge into separate paths.

Housekeeping Columns

The design of the base schema serves as the analytic foundation for the data warehouse. Every query and report will be defined based on the facts and dimensions it contains. When it comes to aggregate tables, the base schema has a new role: It serves as the data source. This simplifies the ETL process in a number of ways. The extraction from OLTP systems occurs only once for the base schema, rather than once for each aggregate. All attribute transformation is performed only once, during the load of the base schema. Loads of aggregate schemas will not need to transform any dimensional attributes, or calculate any facts other than aggregation. These benefits are fully explored in Chapter 5.

Recognizing that the base schema will serve as the source for aggregates, you can add design features that will help with the construction of the aggregates. During an incremental load, processing time is greatly reduced if you are able to process only rows that are new or changed. For example, building a brand rollup from scratch during each load would require processing 15,000 products. If you are able to process only products that have changed, you may need to consider only a few hundred products or fewer. This will be discussed in further detail in Chapter 5.

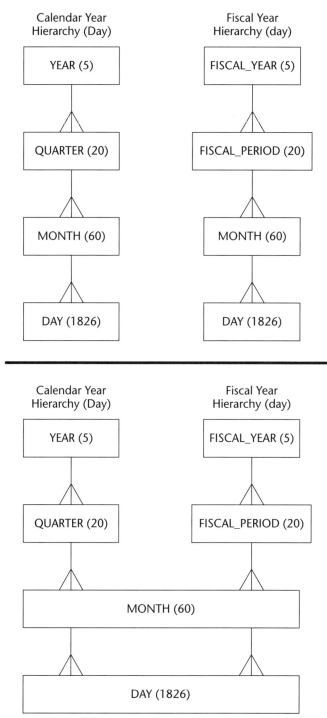

Figure 3.6 Two methods for diagramming multiple hierarchies within a dimension.

To accomplish this reduction in processing, you need a method of changed data identification. Because you are building the source of the dimensional aggregate, you can easily engineer this capability. By adding a date_inserted and a date_updated column to the base dimension, you provide a mechanism by which the ETL process can access only those records that have been added or changed since the last time the dimension was processed.

In the same manner, you can stamp fact table records with a load date. This is often accomplished by using an *audit dimension*, which includes a load date and other information pertinent to the process that loaded the record. Figure 3.7 shows a schema design that incorporates these features.

These attributes are referred to as *housekeeping columns* because, like keys, they are present for a purely technical reason. In this case, the reason is to aid the load process. Also like keys, the housekeeping columns will not be of interest to the users. Reporting and ad hoc query tools should be configured so that the end user does not see these columns.

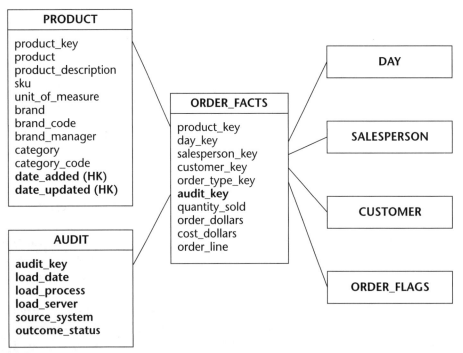

Figure 3.7 Housekeeping columns and an audit dimension.

Design Principles for the Aggregate Schema

After defining the base schema and choosing aggregates, the next major step is to design and document the aggregate schemas. Given that the aggregate schema bears a very close resemblance to the base schema, the aggregate design process will seem relatively simple. A few basic rules will ensure that aggregates adhere to the principles laid out in Chapter 1.

A Separate Star for Each Aggregation

Chapter 1 asserted that aggregates should be stored in separate schemas, either as a star schema or as a pre-joined aggregate. The best way to understand the reasons for this approach is to study the alternative.

Single Schema and the Level Field

The alternative to storing aggregate facts in separate tables is to store them in the same fact tables that hold the base data. The fact table serves multiple purposes, offering base data as well as summary data.

Consider the base Sales schema as shown in Figure 3.8. The grain of this schema is sales facts by Day, Product, Salesperson, and Customer. It is similar to the Orders schema from Chapter 1, but does not include a degenerate dimension or the order_type dimension.

Suppose that you decide to build an aggregate that contains order facts by Day, Brand, Salesperson, and Customer, and you want to store it in the same fact table The proposed aggregate summarizes sales facts by Brand, but the sales_facts table contains a product_key. This key cannot be optional; this would destroy the primary key of the fact table. And it will be necessary to find a place for the Brand attributes.

To cope with the need to include Brand summarization, the Product dimension is altered. A new column called product_level is added to the table, as shown in Figure 3.9. This field will be used to distinguish between product detail and brand-level summary facts.

The Product dimension will now serve double duty, capturing Product detail associated with the detail facts and capturing Brand detail for summary facts. Sample data is shown in Table 3.1. The Level field indicates the type of data contained in each dimension row. Dimension attributes that do not apply at the summary level contain the value N/A.

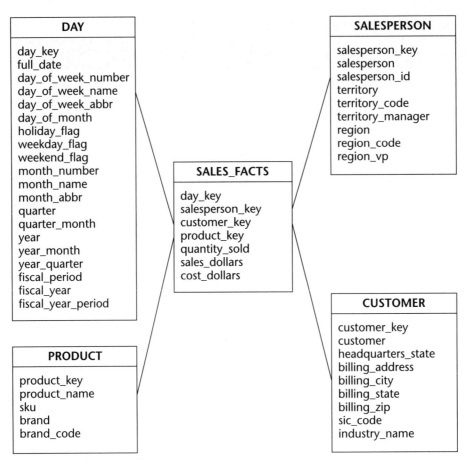

Figure 3.8 The Sales schema.

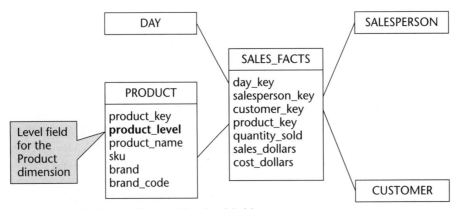

Figure 3.9 The Sales schema with a level field.

Table 3.1 Contents of the Product Dimension

PRODUCT_ KEY	PRODUCT_ LEVEL	PRODUCT_ NAME	SKU	BRAND_ CODE	BRAND_ NAME
100	Product	Packing Tape	102-293	GS01	Grip Set
101	Product	Dura Tape	281-440	GS01	Grip Set
102	Product	5x7 Bubble Mailer	339-293	RB22	Redi-Bubble
103	Product	8x10 Bubble Mailer	339-296	RB22	Redi-Bubble
104	Product	9x12 Bubble Mailer	339-297	RB22	Redi-Bubble
105	Product	Type A Box	087-993	WP1	Well-Packed
106	Product	Type B Box	087-995	WP1	Well-Packed
107	Product	Type C Box	087-996	WP1	Well-Packed
108	Brand	N/A	N/A	GS01	Grip Set
109	Brand	N/A	N/A	RB22	Redi-Bubble
110	Brand	N/A	N/A	WP1	Well-Packed

Brand aggregates can now be stored in the fact table by assigning the appropriate keys from the Product dimension. When you want to query the brand aggregates facts, you join to the Product dimension table and include this qualification in your query:

```
where product.product_level = "Brand"
```

When you want to query the base level facts, you must join to the product dimension and include this qualification in your query:

```
Where product.product_level = "Product"
```

This approach can be extended to allow for additional levels of aggregation. For example, you might also include a row in the Product dimension for summarizing across all products. The product_level for this row could contain the text All Products, and all attributes would contain the value N/A.

If an aggregate is to summarize a different dimension, this technique is repeated. For a monthly summary of facts, day_level is added to the Day dimension. This will distinguish between detail rows and rows that represent months. Because some of the attributes in the Day dimension are numeric, special values must be used for the attribute when it does not. For example, a day_number of 0 is used for rows in the table that describe months.

If an aggregate is to summarize within more than one dimension, the appropriate key values are used for the summary facts. For example, aggregate facts by brand and month would include key values that reference the appropriate summary rows in the Product and Day dimensions. The aggregate rows can now be retrieved by qualifying the query as follows:

```
where product.product_level = "Brand"
and day.day_level = "Month"
```

Now there are multiple aggregates that involve brand. The original brand level aggregate (sales by Day, Brand, Salesperson, and Customer) can no longer be selected through simple constraint on product_level. This constraint would capture both the daily summaries by Brand and the monthly summaries by Brand. The necessary qualification is now:

```
where product.product_level = "Brand"
and day.day_level = "Day"
```

In fact, for *every* query, it is necessary to fully qualify *every* dimension for which aggregation levels are available.

Drawbacks to the Single Schema Approach

There are several problems with the single schema approach, the first of which should be immediately obvious: *The schema is now capable of producing incorrect results*. Every dimension for which aggregations are available must be qualified in every query. If not, facts will be double counted, triple counted, or worse.

For example, a query that does not include any product attributes would still require a constraint on the product_level column in the Product dimension. Otherwise, the query would return fact table rows that include product-level detail and brand-level detail. In other words, the facts would be double counted.

The risk of incorrect results is a serious drawback to this approach and is reason enough to avoid it. A simple omission by a report developer or end user will produce inaccurate information. Once discovered, this error will destroy confidence in the data warehouse. Distrust will prevail, even after the error is corrected.

> **TIP** Do not store different levels of aggregation in the same schema. The schema will be capable of providing wrong results.

That should be enough reason to avoid the single-table approach, but there are other drawbacks as well. As already discussed, the contents of the dimensions will now become messy. Users browsing the dimensions will need to qualify on the level filed, or deal with the inclusion of seemingly extraneous N/A values. And as you have seen, numeric columns and date columns cannot contain the value N/A because they do not contain character data. They must contain arbitrarily selected values in place of N/A. The same holds true for columns of character data types that contain fewer than three characters.

Last, note that the data type of the facts must now be expanded in precision to accommodate the summarization. The largest sales_dollars value for the detail data (Day, Product, Salesperson, and Customer) might be safely assumed never to exceed 10,000,000. But the column must also store aggregate sales_dollar amounts, some of which could reach into the billions. The precision of the fact column has to be increased, which affects all records in the fact table.

The single-table approach is often chosen under the mistaken idea that it saves space or reduces work. But notice that this is not true. The aggregate data will take up the same amount of space, whether in the same table or a different table. In fact, the demands of increased precision may cause the base schema data to consume more storage. And regardless of where the aggregate data is stored, the ETL process is still required to compute and manage it.

Advantages of Separate Tables

All the disadvantages of the single-table approach are avoided by storing dimensional aggregates in their own fact tables. The aggregate containing sales by Day, Brand, Salesperson, and Customer from Figure 3.9 is replaced by the one shown in Figure 3.10. Instead of adding a level field to the Product dimension table, a Brand table is added. The aggregated facts are stored in a separate fact table, which references the Brand table through brand_key.

As long as each star (base or aggregate) is queried separately, there is no risk of wrong results. Using separate queries for each fact table is already a requirement for dimensional models, so this method of aggregation does not introduce new complications.

The dimensions are now clean. There is no need to populate them with level indicators, N/A values, or arbitrarily chosen values. They are understandable to the user, and they can be browsed without the need for constraints on level indicators.

TIP Dimensional aggregates should be stored in separate tables for each aggregation.

Last, the facts can be stored at a precision that is appropriate for each aggregate. Because aggregates do not reside in the same fact table, there is no need to size the fact attributes to account for the largest possible aggregation. This saves considerable space, as the base fact table columns to not have to be increased in size.

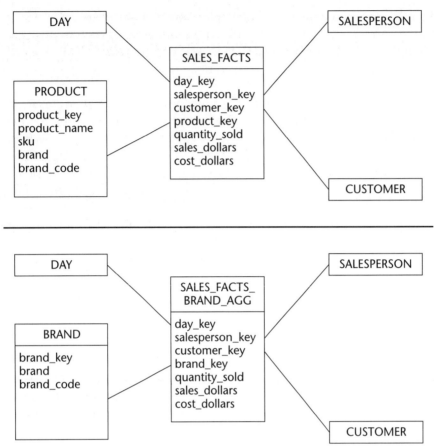

Figure 3.10   Aggregate data stored in a separate fact table.

Pre-Joined Aggregates

Pre-joined aggregates are governed by the same rule: separate tables for each aggregate. Recall from Chapter 1 that a pre-joined aggregate summarizes a fact table and dimension tables by incorporating the facts and dimensions into a single table. This wide table contains no keys, accelerating the query process.

By definition, these aggregates cannot be stored in the same table as the base data. They contain dimension columns that are not present in the base fact table, and exclude keys that are present. However, it is possible to use the same pre-joined aggregate for multiple summaries. Table 3.2 shows a pre-joined aggregate that summarizes by Product and Brand.

Table 3.2 A Pre-Joined Aggregate with Multiple Levels of Summarization

DATE	PRODUCT_ LEVEL	PRODUCT	BRAND_ NAME	SALES_ DOLLARS
1/17/2006	Product	Packing Tape	Grip Set	356.00
1/17/2006	Product	Dura Tape	Grip Set	480.00
1/17/2006	Product	5x7 Bubble Mailer	Redi-Bubble	980.00
1/17/2006	Product	8x10 Bubble Mailer	Redi-Bubble	1,380.00
1/17/2006	Product	9x12 Bubble Mailer	Redi-Bubble	1,330.00
1/17/2006	Product	Type A Box	Well-Packed	2,080.00
1/17/2006	Product	Type B Box	Well-Packed	1,212.00
1/17/2006	Product	Type C Box	Well-Packed	2,684.00
1/17/2006	Brand	N/A	Grip Set	836.00
1/17/2006	Brand	N/A	Redi-Bubble	3,690.00
1/17/2006	Brand	N/A	Well-Packed	5,976.00

Use of this pre-joined aggregate involves some of the same drawbacks seen already. Most important, it is capable of producing wrong results if not properly constrained by product_level. If aggregation takes place in multiple dimensions, then each level_field must be constrained. And the order_dollars column must be declared with a precision that permits the largest possible aggregation.

TIP Aggregate facts should be stored in separate tables for each level of aggregation. These may be separate aggregate fact tables or separate pre-joined aggregate tables.

Naming Conventions

Having established that aggregates will reside in separate fact tables or pre-joined tables, you must now begin naming the components of the aggregate tables. The examples have already implied some conventions; here they are called out explicitly.

Naming the Attributes

You may have noticed that throughout the examples, aggregate facts and dimension attributes have the same name as the corresponding attributes in the base schema. For example, in Figure 3.10, the Product table and the Brand table both contain an attribute named brand. The base fact table and aggregate fact table both contain a fact named order_dollars. This approach is practical because it is easily understandable.

This convention also helps your schema adhere to the guiding principles from Chapter 1. By naming the attributes identically, queries can be rewritten through simple substitution of table names. The values themselves must also be the same in order to guarantee correct results.

These requirements, as driven by the guiding principles of Chapter 1, should sound familiar. *They are identical to the rules of conformance.*

Introduced in Chapter 1, the rules of conformance guarantee equivalency of facts and dimensions that appear in different tables. An aggregate schema conforms with the base schema by definition. If the brand or sales dollars in the aggregate schema were different from the brand or sales dollars in the base schema, it would not be a true summarization.

> **TIP** Facts and dimensional attributes should receive the same name in an aggregate schema as they do in the base schema.

The fact that the aggregate schema is a special case of conformance also explains why the treatment of aggregate dimensions has been identical to the treatment of rollup dimensions. They are the same thing. Both allow a fact table to capture facts at a grain that partially summarizes the base dimension. In the case of a rollup dimension, the fact table relates to a separate business process; in the case of the aggregate dimension, the fact table is an aggregate.

The only columns in aggregate schemas that will require new names are the warehouse keys in aggregate dimensions. For example, the aggregate dimension Brand in Figure 3.10 contains a brand_key. This column was not present in the base schema. It is named according to the same conventions as other warehouse keys. In this case, that means it takes its name from the dimension table and contains the suffix _key.

Naming Aggregate Tables

Aggregate dimension tables should be named according to the same conventions used for base dimension tables. In this book, names have been chosen for dimension tables that indicate what a row represents. Each row in the Product table represents a product; each row in the Day table represents a day. In the same way, the aggregate dimensions have been named to describe what a row represents. Each row in a Brand table represents a brand; each row in a Month table represents a month.

This level of specificity is useful in the presence of a set of aggregates. The contents of each table are readily identified by the names of the tables, and for the most part their conformance will be obvious.

TIP The name of an aggregate dimension table should describe the contents of its rows.

Aggregate fact tables are more difficult to name. The natural tendency is to give them names that describe either their grain or what has been summarized. In either case, the names quickly become too long.

Consider the fact tables in Figure 3.10. There is a base fact table, sales_facts, and an aggregate. The aggregate contains sales by day, brand, salesperson, and customer. It has been named sales_facts_brand_agg. This name indicates that it summarizes the table sales_facts by including that name. The suffix _agg indicates that it is an aggregate fact table. The word "brand" is included in the name to indicate the level to which product data has been summarized.

This convention seems useful but unfortunately becomes unwieldy. When the aggregate summarizes more than one dimension, the name becomes more of a mouthful. For example, the base schema in Figure 3.10 may also have aggregates with names like sales_facts_brand_month_category_region_agg. Fact tables with more dimensions, such as the one in Figure 1.1, would require even wordier aggregate names.

These difficulties can be mitigated by developing short names that will correspond to fact tables and dimension tables. Sales_facts might have the corresponding short name SLS, brand's short name is BRD, and so forth. The aggregate table can be named using the fact table short name, the _agg suffix, and then short names describing the aggregation level in each dimension. For example, sls_agg_brd_mth_rg describes sales facts aggregated by Brand, Month, and Region. This is no better from the standpoint of comprehensibility, but at least it is shorter.

TIP The names of aggregate fact tables are always problematic. The best you can do is establish a convention and stick to it.

The good news is that users and report developers should never have to see the names of aggregate tables. If an aggregate navigation function is in place, all interactions will be with the base fact table; only the aggregate navigator will need to worry about the names of the aggregate fact tables. Knowing this, some designers choose to label their aggregate tables in a non-descriptive manner, as in sales_facts_agg_01. But this becomes a headache for those charged with loading and maintaining the aggregate; the use of short names is a better approach.

If there is to be no aggregate navigator, only a small number of aggregates should be built. This will allow for descriptive names. Implications of the presence or absence of an aggregate navigator are discussed in more detail in Chapter 4.

The same advice applies to the naming of pre-joined aggregates. Define a convention and stick to it. Like the convention just described, one method combines standard short names for the base fact table and the levels of dimensional aggregation. Instead of adding agg, use something like pja (for pre-joined aggregate) or my personal favorite, BWT (big wide table). This would result in tables with names such as sls_bwt_brn_mth_reg. Once again, this is a mouthful. An aggregate navigator will shield developers and end users from it.

If there is no aggregate navigator, there will be fewer aggregates and hence more freedom to name the pre-joined aggregate table descriptively. Because many pre-joined aggregates are designed for a specific report, some designers choose to name them after the report.

Aggregate Dimension Design

By now, the design principles for aggregate dimension tables should be clear. They are conformed dimensions and therefore subject to the principles of dimensional conformance.

Stated explicitly:

- The aggregate dimension must be a perfect subset of attributes from a base dimension. The only exception is its key.

- The values taken on by attributes of the aggregate dimension must be identical to those present in the base dimension.

- There must be exactly one row in the aggregate dimension that corresponds to each combination of its attribute values in the base dimension, and no others.

The first rule dictates the schema definition of the aggregate dimension table. It leaves no leeway for design tweaks; the only attribute that is up to the discretion of the designer is the name of the primary key.

The second two rules deal with the information that appears in the aggregate rows. They ensure that the aggregate summarizes the base dimension completely and that the data values match exactly.

These rules govern the design of the load process for the aggregate dimension table.

Because aggregate dimensions are likely to be shared by multiple fact tables, some additional considerations may affect load processing.

Attributes of Aggregate Dimensions

Because an aggregate dimension must conform to the base dimension, its attribute names and data types will be identical to those in the base dimension. All attributes will have the same name, business definition, and data values.

Key columns and housekeeping columns are exempt from this rule. None of these columns have business significance, and they should not be visible to the end user.

As I have already suggested, use the same naming convention for the aggregate dimension key column as you do for all warehouse keys. Typically, the name of this column identifies the fact that it is a key, and identifies the table for which it serves as primary key.

Housekeeping columns aid in the maintenance of the dimension during ETL processing. Figure 3.7 showed an example of housekeeping columns in the base schema. Typical housekeeping columns include creation date, date of last update, and sometimes an indication of the process that created the row. These columns should be present in the aggregate dimension tables as well, but are not subject to conformance requirements. Row values will differ if the base and aggregate dimension tables are loaded at different times or by different processes.

The equivalency required between the base dimension table and aggregate dimension table also applies to the slow change processing requirements of each attribute. If the change to an attribute is handled as a type 2 change in the base schema, it must be handled as a type 2 change in the aggregate schema.

Notice that while the attributes of the aggregate dimension must be identical to their counterparts in the base dimension, they may serve a slightly different role in the aggregate dimension. For example, the attribute brand_code may be a type 2 attribute in the base dimension and serve as the natural key in the aggregate dimension. All these characteristics will be incorporated into the documentation requirements described later in this chapter.

TIP Attributes of the aggregate dimension must be identical to those in the base dimension in name and data type. Slow change processing rules must be identical. The natural key of an aggregate dimension will be different from the base dimension.

One final note: There is no room for additional attributes in the aggregate dimension. Their inclusion would violate the rules of conformance, and also provide a confusing situation for end users. The additional attribute would render the aggregate capable of answering a business question the base schema cannot answer. In this situation, it is no longer a simple summary. To get at this information, it would not be possible to require that the aggregate remain invisible. Worse, the aggregate dimension seems to contain more detail than the base dimension it summarizes.

Sourcing Aggregate Dimensions

The design of every table in the data warehouse schema must include a load specification. This holds equally true for base dimension tables and aggregate dimension tables.

The last two rules of conformance suggest that data in the aggregate table must be processed in a manner that is identical to the way it is processed for inclusion in the base dimension table. They also suggest that special care must be taken to make sure that each set of attributes represented in the base table is properly represented in the aggregate table.

The easiest way to satisfy these requirements is to do one of two things: load the base and aggregate dimensions simultaneously, or source the aggregate from the base dimension. Either way, transformation of the data will be done once, ensuring that data values are identical. At the same time, redundant transformation processes are eliminated.

> **TIP** Source aggregate dimensions from the base dimension, rather than the original source system. This eliminates redundant processing, and ensures uniform presentation of data values.

Either approach is acceptable, although in Chapter 5 you will see that sourcing the aggregate from the base dimension can improve the manageability of the ETL process. In either case, the load specification must include source columns and transformation logic for each aggregate dimension column, source query or extract logic for the dimension load process, and a changed data identification strategy.

Some aggregate navigation schemes, such as materialized views, may require that aggregates be built separately from the base dimension. In such cases, the aggregates should be sourced from the base dimension. Chapter 4 examines the unique requirements of materialized views.

Shared Dimensions

It is not uncommon for a single table to serve in two roles. A single rollup dimension may serve as a dimension in a base star, visible to users and applications, and as an aggregate dimension in one or more aggregate stars, invisible to users and applications. This double-duty comes about as a byproduct of the fact that aggregate dimensions are nothing more than a special case of conformed dimension.

For example, consider the sales forecast schema encountered in Chapter 2. Sales_forecast_facts is one of several fact tables included in the table-level conformance matrix in Figure 2.2. The sales forecast process is done on a monthly basis, and the forecast itself is at the level of Brand, Region, and Customer. Referring to the table, you see that Month, Brand, and Region are conformed dimensions that summarize Day, Product, and Salesperson, respectively.

Now, the schema designers decide to build an aggregate schema that summarizes order_facts by Day, Brand, and Order Type. The aggregate will be called ord_agg_brnd. This aggregate schema will require an aggregate dimension table Brand (product). This dimension is already part of the data warehouse.

The same holds true for the use of an aggregate dimension in multiple aggregate schemas. The Brand table may be utilized in other aggregates as well. In both examples, it is useful to describe the Brand table as a *shared dimension table*.

It is not necessary to build the shared dimension table multiple times. If the fact tables that share it reside in the same database, they can make use of the same dimension table.

TIP Aggregate dimension tables are often shared by multiple aggregates, and sometimes used by base fact tables. These shared dimension tables do not need to be built redundantly; the various fact tables can use the same dimension table. If the shared table is to be instantiated more than once, build it a single time and then replicate it.

When the same dimension table is used in multiple stars, there may be special considerations for the load process. For example, the forecast schema may be loaded monthly, while the sales aggregate is loaded daily. Both schemas share the Brand dimension. The load specification for Brand must reflect the requirement for daily updates.

Shared rollup dimensions may complicate fact table loads. As you will see in Chapter 6, the application of a type 1 change to an aggregate dimension can have a peculiar effect on associated facts. If the attribute is not dependent on another attribute of the aggregate dimension, the change may necessitate the merging of two dimension rows and the recomputation of aggregate facts. As a result of this phenomenon, an aggregate fact table may require load processing outside of its normal load window.

TIP The documentation for a shared dimension must enumerate all dependent fact tables, whether part of the base schema or aggregates. In some cases, frequent updates to a dimension may require updates to fact tables outside their normal load windows.

Documentation examples provided later in this chapter will help you ensure that these important aspects of aggregate dimension tables are considered. Like the aggregate dimension tables, aggregate fact table design will require some unique considerations as well.

Aggregate Fact Table Design

Any fact table design begins with a statement of grain, and you have already seen that this holds true for aggregates. After grain has been determined, the attributes of the aggregate fact table can be documented. Most of the rules you have reviewed for aggregate dimensions apply here as well; the only real difference pertains to data types.

Aggregate Facts: Names and Data Types

The main attributes present in a fact table are the facts and foreign keys to the dimensions. The presence of dimension keys is dictated by the grain of the fact table. This leaves only the design of facts to consider.

Each aggregate fact summarizes a fact from the base fact table. By definition, then, aggregate facts are measuring the exact same thing as base level facts—albeit at a different level of detail. The aggregate fact is a special type of conforming fact. The aggregate fact should have the same business definition and column name as the base fact.

Unlike dimensional attributes, the aggregate fact may have a different data type than its counterpart in the base schema. This results from its status as an aggregate. Put simply, the numbers may be much larger. For example, order_dollars from individual order_lines may never exceed $99,999,999.99. But aggregates of order_dollars may far exceed this amount. In a base schema, then, order_amount may receive the data type number(10,2). Aggregates by category and day may require number(12,2) and aggregates by year may require number(15,2).

No New Facts, Including Counts

One of the guiding principles for aggregates is that they must always return exactly the same answer as the base schema does. Unfortunately, there is one situation where this cannot be guaranteed, even if the aggregate fully conforms to the base schema: counts.

Many business questions are answered by counting rows in the fact table or in the dimensions. A planner studying fulfillment, for example, might want to look at the total number of product shipment lines processed by warehouse. This is accomplished by counting rows in the shipments fact table. For example:

```
select warehouse,
       count(shipment_facts.product_key)
  from shipment_facts,
       warehouse,
       day
 where shipment_facts.warhouse_key = warehouse.warehouse_key
   and shipment_facts.day_key = day.day_key
   and day.month = 'January'
   and day.year = 2006
group by warehouse
```

This query counts rows in the fact tables and groups them by warehouse. Product_key is chosen arbitrarily—any attribute will serve the purpose for counting rows.

An aggregate table that summarizes shipment facts by warehouse and month will not provide the same answer, even though it contains all the columns in this query. Rows in the aggregate table no longer represent the shipment lines in which the manager is interested.

TIP Counts cannot be accurately performed against aggregate schemas, even if all attributes are the same. All counts must be performed against the base schema.

Your impulse to solve this problem may be to add the count to the aggregate schema. A new fact, perhaps called number_of_shipment_lines is added. It shows exactly how many base rows each aggregate row summarizes. Notice that the SQL will have to change. Instead of *counting*, you must *sum*:

```
select  warehouse,
        sum(number_of_shipment_lines)
  from  shipment_facts_month_agg,
        warehouse,
        month
 where  shipment_facts_month_agg.warhouse_key = warehouse.warehouse_key
   and  shipment_facts_month_agg.month_key = month.month_key
   and  month.month = 'January'
   and  month.year = 2006
group by warehouse
```

Adding this fact, however, renders the aggregate capable of responding to a query that the base table cannot. There is no number_of_shipment_lines column in the base schema. A solution to this dilemma is to add the number_of_shipment_lines to the base schema. Here, the fact will always be populated with a value of 1. Aggregates will simply sum this value. The symmetry between base and aggregate schema is restored; counts can always be performed using sum().

Be warned, however, that the aggregate will not necessarily improve the performance of the count. This may seem odd, particularly if each aggregate row summarizes several hundred transactions. But in the case of the original query, *the database may never need to read the fact table.* All the information needed to compute the count may be found in the compound index on the fact table's primary key! By contrast, the query against the aggregate uses the sum function. The aggregate fact table must be read in order to obtain the number_of_shipment_lines values.

Additionally, consider that you may decide to add additional counts to your aggregate. For example, you might want to include a number of products if aggregating to the Brand level, a number of regions if aggregating to the Territory level, and so on. This quickly becomes an overwhelming number of new facts for inclusion in the base and aggregate schemas.

> **TIP** As a general rule of thumb, the only count to be added to an aggregate should show the number of base rows summarized. If this fact is added to the aggregate, it should also appear in the base fact table with a constant value of 1. Counts of any other attribute should be directed to the base schema only.

In addition to accommodating the facts, it is also necessary that the aggregate fact table design account for another data element sometimes found in fact tables: the degenerate dimension.

Degenerate Dimensions

Fact tables often include degenerate dimensions. These are dimension attributes that have not been isolated within a dimension table. This may be done because the attribute takes on a very large number of values, or because there are not any additional attributes that would reside with it in a dimension table.

When degenerate dimensions conform across fact tables, promoting them to dimension table status makes drill-across queries more understandable. This does add a join to each fact table query, which the DBA may wish to avoid.

Whatever the reason for its presence, the degenerate dimension is still a dimension. It may or may not participate in the aggregate schema; this is determined by the grain of the aggregate fact table. If it survives in an aggregate, it is subject to all the same rules that have been outlined for dimensional attributes: its name and value must be expressed identically.

Audit Dimension

Previously, you saw that an audit dimension can be used to aid in the loading and management of a fact table. In Figure 3.7, an Audit dimension was added to the fact table design to capture information about the process that loaded or updated the fact table row. The Audit dimension will be very helpful in the load of aggregate facts because it provides a built-in mechanism for changed data identification.

If an audit dimension is part of a base fact table design, it makes sense to include one in the aggregate dimension as well. While the aggregate fact table may not be the source for other fact tables, the presence of this audit information will provide consistency and aid in the maintenance of the warehouse.

Like the housekeeping columns of an aggregate dimension table, the audit_key is an exception to the conformance rules of the aggregate fact table. The audit record associated with a row in the aggregate fact table does not summarize the audit data associated with the base fact table. It describes the process by which the aggregate row was inserted or updated.

Sourcing Aggregate Fact Tables

The load specification for the aggregate fact table should use the base fact table as its source. This makes sense for the same reasons that aggregate dimensions are best sourced from the base dimension: It reduces redundant processing and guarantees identical attribute values.

Facts will be sourced from the base fact table and aggregated by the load process as appropriate. Dimension keys that do not participate in aggregation can also be drawn from the base fact table.

For foreign keys that reference aggregate dimension tables, the load specification must identify natural keys in the base schema that will be used to locate the corresponding record in the aggregate dimension. For example, the aggregate schema in Figure 3.10 summarizes product detail by brand. Rows will be selected from the base schema and aggregated for insertion into the aggregate schema. But there is no brand_key to select. Instead, the natural key for a brand is selected: brand_code. This code will be used to locate the correct brand_key through a lookup process. This process will be explored more fully in Chapter 6.

All these source attributes can be included in a single query against the source star. For the aggregate in Figure 3.10, this query would be:

```
select  day_key,
        salesperson_key,
        customer_key,
        brand_code,          /* will be used to look up brand_key */
        sum(quantity_sold),  /* aggregate fact */
        sum(sales_dollars),  /* aggregate fact */
        sum(cost_dollars)    /* aggregate fact */
from    sales_facts,
        day,
        salesperson,
        customer,
        product
where   sales_facts.day_key = day.day_key
   and  sales_facts.salesperson_key = salesperson.salesperson_key
   and  sales_facts.customer_key = customer.customer_key
   and  sales_facts.product_key = product.product_key
group by day_key, salesperson_key, customer_key, brand_code
```

Additional qualification on the audit dimension would be included so that only new rows are selected.

Pre-Joined Aggregate Design

The design of the pre-joined aggregate follows the same rules that have been enumerated for aggregate stars:

- Facts and dimensions should have the same names as they do in the base schema.

- Facts may require a larger data type declaration, but in all other respects should remain the same.

- Housekeeping columns, if included, describe the creation of the aggregate rather than summarize the creation of the source tables.

- The pre-joined aggregate schema should be sourced from the base schema.

- Careful attention must be paid to dependencies if any source dimensions are shared with other fact or aggregate tables.

- The pre-joined aggregate should easily be defined using a single query against the source schema.

Having applied a set of principles to the process of aggregate table design, you are now ready to document the aggregate schema. The suggestions in the next section will help you ensure that important design considerations have not been overlooked and that critical information about the aggregate schema is communicated to any developers who need to know it, such as those who will design the load process.

Documenting the Aggregate Schema

Documentation of the data warehouse schema is an important product of the schema design process. Disciplined documentation of schema design prevents the team from omitting important steps in the design process, such as the setting of fact table grain. Schema documentation will drive the development of the schema itself and the ETL processes that load it. Once in production, the documentation will also become a valuable reference for maintenance of the data warehouse.

The aggregate schema is no different in these respects. Good documentation will enforce critical design steps, drive aggregate development, and serve as a reference for warehouse maintenance. This last point is important, because the aggregate portfolio is more likely to change over time than the base schema.

This section defines a set of documentation requirements for the aggregate schema that reflect the principles that have been discussed. Examples are provided to illustrate the requirements. You may choose to document your aggregates differently, but be sure each of these requirements is addressed.

Identify Schema Families

Organize your aggregate documentation around the base fact tables. A base fact table and its aggregates form a *schema family*. Each schema family is a set of stars that convey the same information at various levels of summarization. A pre-joined aggregate is also part of the base fact table's schema family.

This organizational approach will come naturally if you are including aggregate documentation with the base schema documentation. Information on aggregates logically follows the base fact tables from which they are derived. You may prefer to document aggregates separately, especially considering that they are more likely to change over time. Even so, you can still organize the aggregate documentation by base fact table.

For each base fact table, begin by enumerating the aggregate tables derived from it. These may be aggregate star schemas or pre-joined aggregates. Each aggregate is described in terms of its grain, expressed dimensionally. One way to do this is to enumerate the aggregate fact tables immediately after enumerating the aggregation points in the base schema. An example appears in Fig-ure 3.11.

This example shows a base fact table and two aggregate fact tables. Each aggregate schema is defined dimensionally, so grain is clearly defined. Dimensionality is expressed in relation to the base fact table; the entry for each aggregate has the same number of lines as that of the base fact table.

For a given aggregate fact table, this information can be scanned to identify dimensions that are summarized by the aggregate. For example, sls_agg_day_brd_cst partially summarizes day and product, and completely summarizes salesperson.

Many schema designers also include a diagram of the aggregate schema. The diagram might look like the lower star in Figure 3.10. It should include all the dimensions that are related to the aggregate fact table, whether they are base dimensions or aggregate dimensions.

Once you have identified the schema families, you can divide the remaining documentation into sections for dimensional conformance, dimension tables, and fact tables.

Identify Dimensional Conformance

The aggregate portfolio may include aggregate dimension tables. It is important to document their conformance to the base dimension table explicitly. This information may be included with documentation of the base dimension tables, or as a section in separate aggregate documentation. Either way, organize the information by base dimension table.

For example, the Sales schema might require a set of dimensional aggregates for each of the Day, Product, and Salesperson dimensions. These can be described quite simply in tabular format. An example documenting these aggregates appears in Figure 3.12.

Fact Table: sales_facts

Dimension	Potential Aggregation Points
Day	day, month, quarter, year, fiscal_period, fiscal_year
Product	product, brand, category, all products
Customer	customer, industry, state, all customers
Salesperson	Salesperson, territory, region, all salespeople

Aggregate Fact Table: SLS_AGG_DAY_BRD_CST

Dimension	Potential Aggregation Points
Day	base dimension
Brand	conforms to Product dimension
Customer	base dimension
(all salespeople)	

Aggregate Fact Table: SLS_AGG_FP_PRD_REG

Dimension	Note
Fiscal_period	conforms to Day dimension
(all products)	
Customer	base dimension
Region	conforms to Salesperson dimension

Figure 3.11   A schema family.

Conformance of Aggregate Dimensions

Dimension	Conformed Aggregates
Day	Month, Quarter, Year, Fiscal_Period, Fiscal_Year
Product	Brand, Category
Customer	Industry, State
Salesperson	Division, Region

The design and load specification for these aggregate dimension tables is included in the same section of their document as the base dimension tables. All dimension tables appear in alphabetical order.

Figure 3.12   Conformed aggregate dimensions by base dimension.

The conformance of aggregate dimensions may be intuitive or even obvious. But the attributes of the aggregate dimension table should be documented anyway. Subsets of a demographic dimension, for example, might require explanation; overlapping hierarchies may lead to confusion. Conformed rollups can be documented using a matrix of attributes to dimension tables, by documenting the same information graphically as in Figure 3.4, or by adding attributes to hierarchy diagrams like the one in Figure 3.6.

Next, the documentation must fully describe the aggregate dimension tables and aggregate fact tables. You'll look at the dimensions first.

Documenting Aggregate Dimension Tables

Documenting aggregate dimension tables is no different than documenting the base dimension tables. It requires basic information on column names and data types. Additional information must include slow change disposition, load specifications, and sizing estimates. The format of this documentation should match that of the documentation for your base dimension tables.

For each attribute of the aggregate dimension table, the documentation will capture table-level information and attribute-level information. At the table level, the information in Table 3.3 should be included.

Table 3.3   Documentation Requirements for an Aggregate Dimension Table

	DESCRIPTION	NOTES
Table Name	Name of the aggregate dimension table	*Follow naming standard (for example, name after level of detail represented).*
Location(s)	Database or schema that will hold the aggregate dimension table	*List multiple locations if replicas of the conformed dimension will appear in multiple physical schemas.*
Initial Rows	An estimate of the initial number of rows in the aggregate dimension table	*Arrive at estimate through data exploration.*
Initial Size	An estimate of the initial size of the dimension table	*Multiply Initial rows by row size.*
Growth Rate	Number of new rows	*Can be expressed as number of new rows per load, per month, per year, and so on.*
Dependent Fact Tables	List of aggregate fact tables that reference this aggregate dimension table	*May also include base fact tables for which this table serves as a rollup dimension.*
Load Frequency	Frequency of incremental loads	*Must reflect dependencies across fact tables.*
Change Data Identification	Query against base dimension table that fetches necessary rows	*Compares housekeeping columns of base table to date/time of last aggregate load.*

At the attribute level, the additional information outlined in Table 3.4 is gathered.

Table 3.4   Documentation Requirements for the Columns of an Aggregate Dimension Table

	DESCRIPTION	NOTES
Column Name	Name of the column in the aggregate dimension table	*Must be identical to name of corresponding column in base dimension table. (Exceptions: keys and housekeeping columns.)*

Table 3.4   *(continued)*

	DESCRIPTION	NOTES
Data Type	Data type of the column	*Must be identical to corresponding column in base dimension.* *(Exceptions: keys and housekeeping columns.)*
Attribute Type	Indicates whether column is a synthetic key, natural key, type 1 slowly changing attribute, type 2 slowly changing attribute, or housekeeping column	*Slow change rules must be identical to those in the base dimension table.*
Source Column	Maps the column back to its source table	*The source for the aggregate dimension is the base dimension.*

All this information combines to define the aggregate dimension table and serves as a specification for the ETL process that will load it. Figure 3.13 puts all this information together to document a Territory dimension table, which conforms with the base dimension table Salesperson.

Figure 3.13 is meant only as an example. The documentation for any given project may vary. That's okay, as long as the core information described in Tables 3.3 and 3.4 has been included. It may be supplemented with additional information, such as data dictionary information, user help text, and so forth. In addition, it will be necessary to document storage characteristics specific to the database, and indexes that will be built.

Documenting Aggregate Fact Tables

The documentation format for aggregate fact tables should mirror that of the base fact tables. There is information to be documented regarding each aggregate table, as well as information to be documented for each attribute of an aggregate table.

The table-level documentation is much the same as that gathered for the aggregate dimension table. At a minimum, it should include the items listed in Table 3.5.

Table Name: **TERRITORY**
Location: SALES_DATA_MART

Column Name	Data Type	Attribute Type	Source Columns/Fields	Note
TERRITORY_KEY	Int	PK	(warehouse generated)	Surrogate key generated for data warehouse.
TERRITORY	varchar (20)	NK	warehouse schema: SALESPERSON. TERRITORY	
TERRITORY_ CODE	char (4)	Type 1	warehouse schema: SALESPERSON. TERRITORY_CODE	
TERRITORY_ MANAGER	varchar (80)	Type 1	warehouse schema: SALESPERSON. TERRITORY_MANAGER	
REGION	varchar (20)	Type 2	warehouse schema: SALESPERSON.REGION	
REGION_CODE	char (4)	Type 2	warehouse schema: SALESPERSON.REGION_CODE	
REGION_VP	varchar (80)	Type 2	warehouse schema: SALESPERSON.REGION_VP	
DATE_CREATED	Date	HK	(warehouse generated)	Date record was created
DATE_UPDATED	Date	HK	(warehouse generated)	Date record was updated
UPDATED_BY	varchar (10)	HK	(warehouse generated)	Name of process that updated record

Initial Rows: 300

Initial Size: 71 KB

Growth Rate: 30% per year

Dependent Fact Tables: Sls_agg_day_trt_cst
Sls_agg_mon_trt_cst_prd
Sls_agg_mon_trt_bnd

Load Frequency: Daily

Change Data Identification: Where SALESPERSON.DATE_UPDATED > {date of last aggregation}

Figure 3.13 Documenting an aggregate dimension table.

Table 3.5 Documentation Requirements for Aggregate Fact Tables

	DESCRIPTION	NOTES
Table Name	Name of the aggregate fact table	*Follow naming standard (for example, short name concatenation).*
Location(s)	Database or schema that will hold the aggregate fact table	
Initial Rows	An estimate of the initial number of rows in the aggregate fact table	*Arrive at estimate through data exploration.*
Initial Size	An estimate of the initial size of the aggregate fact table	*Multiply Initial rows by row size.*
Growth Rate	Number of new rows	*Can be expressed as number of new rows per load, per month, per year, and so on.*
Load Frequency	Frequency of incremental loads	*Must reflect dependencies on dimension tables.*
Change Data Identification	Query against base dimension fact that fetches necessary rows	*Compares housekeeping columns of base table to date/time of last aggregate load.*

At the attribute level, the additional information outlined in Table 3.6 must be documented.

Table 3.6 Documentation Requirements for the Columns of an Aggregate Fact Table

	DESCRIPTION	NOTES
Column Name	Name of the column in the aggregate fact table	*Must be identical to name of corresponding column in base fact table. (Exceptions: keys and housekeeping columns.)*
Data Type	Data type of the column	*Aggregate facts may have greater precision than the corresponding fact in the base fact table.*
Key	Indicates if the column participates in the primary key of the aggregate fact table	*The primary key is typically a concatenation of the foreign keys, plus any degenerate dimensions.*

(continued)

Table 3.6   *(continued)*

	DESCRIPTION	NOTES
Attribute Type	Indicates whether column is a foreign key, fact, or degenerate dimension	*For facts, indicate additivity rules.*
Source Column	Maps the column back to its source table	*The source for foreign key columns is defined as the natural key found in the base schema, which will be used to look up the warehouse key in the aggregate dimension.*

There are two main differences between this list of documentation requirements and the one for dimension table attributes in Table 3.4. First, the data type for aggregate facts may differ from that of the corresponding base facts. You have already seen that this is necessary because the aggregations can grow significantly larger.

Second, the source column information is a bit more complex. Foreign key references to aggregate dimensions are not present in the base schema, so the corresponding natural keys are identified, along with information on which dimension table to use to look up the synthetic key. Facts are identified as the sum of a base fact.

All this information serves to define the aggregate fact table, and serves as the specification for the ETL process that will load it. Figure 3.14 puts all this information together for an aggregate fact table based on the Sales schema.

Again, the format and specifics will vary by project. This information may also be supplemented by standard data dictionary definitions, database storage parameters, and indexing schemes.

Pre-Joined Aggregates

Pre-joined aggregates can be documented in the same way as aggregate fact tables. You can use a documentation page like the one in Figure 3.14. For dimension attributes in the pre-joined aggregate, the Attribute Type column would include the value dimension.

Unlike aggregate star schemas, the pre-joined aggregates will not require locating the warehouse key for aggregate dimensions. The source query for a pre-joined aggregate will include all information needed to populate the aggregate table, with the possible exception of housekeeping columns.

Table Name: **SLS_AGG_MO_TRT_PRD**
Location: SALES_DATA_MART

Column Name	Data Type	Attribute Type	Source Columns/Fields	Note
MONTH_KEY	Int	PK/FK	DAY.MONTH DAY.YEAR	Lookup to MONTH dimension table
TERRITORY_KEY	int	PK/FK	SALESPERSON.TERRITORY_CODE	Lookup to TERRITORY table
PRODUCT_KEY	int	PK/FK	PRODUCT.SKU	Lookup to PRODUCT table
QUANTITY_SOLD	decimal (12,2)	Additive Fact	sum(SALES_FACTS.QUANTITY_SOLD)	
SALES_DOLLARS	decimal (12,2)	Additive Fact	sum(SALES_FACTS.SALES_DOLLARS)	
COST_DOLLARS	decimal (12,2)	Additive Fact	sum(SALES_FACTS.COST_DOLLARS)	

Initial Rows: 200,000

Initial Size: 8 MB

Growth Rate: 10% per month

Load Frequency: Daily (because of slow changes in Salesperson)

Source Query: select
                                 DAY.MONTH,
                                 DAY.YEAR,
                                 SALESPERSON.TERRITORY_CODE,
                                 SALES_FACTS.PRODUCT_KEY,
                                 SUM(SALES_FACTS.QUANTITY_SOLD),
                                 SUM(SALES_FACTS.SALES_DOLLARS),
                                 SUM(SALES_FACTS.COST_DOLLARS
                             from
                                 SALES_FACTS, DAY, SALESPERSON
                             where
                                 SALES_FACTS.DAY_KEY
                                 = DAY.DAY_KEY AND
                                 SALES_FACTS.SALESPERSON_KEY
                                 = SALESPERSON.SALESPERSON_KEY
                             group by
                                 MONTH, YEAR, TERRITORY_CODE, PRODUCT_KEY

Change Data Identification: SALES_FACTS.DATE_UPDATED > {date of last aggregation}

Figure 3.14 Documenting an aggregate fact table.

Materialized Views and Materialized Query Tables

Specific technologies that will be used in the data warehouse architecture may introduce additional documentation requirements.

Relational database products offer features such as materialized views or materialized query tables that can be used in the construction and aggregation of aggregates. These products will be examined in the Chapter 4. But a brief mention is necessary here because their use may affect the design and documentation of the base and aggregate schemas.

As you will see in the next chapter, defining a materialized view requires specification of a query. The documentation for each materialized view should include a source query, similar to the one at the bottom of Figure 3.14. This query should include each attribute of the aggregate fact or dimension table. If the documentation follows the format of the examples in Figures 3.13 and 3.14, the source columns can be omitted—everything will appear in a source query.

In addition, the use of materialized views or materialized query tables may require explicit identification of hierarchies. This is described in Chapter 4. Hierarchies should therefore be documented in a manner similar to Figure 3.5, with some small additions. For each level of the hierarchy, the documentation should identify the natural keys that define that level of the hierarchy and the dependent data elements that are included at that level. For example, the Brand level in Figure 3.5 is defined by the brand_code. Its dependent attributes include a brand_name and brand_manager.

Summary

Aggregates can offer tremendous performance advantages, but they must be designed properly. An improper approach to aggregate design can destroy the usability and accuracy of aggregates, and even of the base schema itself.

Good aggregate design begins with the base schema. Grain should be defined explicitly for each and every fact table; the conformance bus must be documented; and rollup dimensions must be treated carefully. Once the base schema design is in order, aggregate design begins.

The process of designing the aggregates is much like the process of designing the base schema. It requires definition of grain, facts, and dimensions. The difference is that these aggregate tables will be based on the base schema. This means the design is governed by the same rules of conformance that govern rollup dimensions in a base schema. This chapter looked at the specific principles that apply to the design of the dimensional aggregates, and then enumerated design elements that should be explicitly documented.

The next chapter studies how these aggregates will be used. Here, the power of the aggregates is showcased in the context of various technologies that can leverage them.

Using Aggregates

For the well-designed portfolio of aggregates to deliver on its promise of substantial performance gains, it must be used. While this may go without saying, the proper use of aggregates introduces a new set of requirements for the data warehouse architecture. Mechanisms must be in place to ensure that the most appropriate table is used to respond to every warehouse query. Errors can result in inefficiencies or inaccurate results.

The best practices explored in this chapter ensure that the power of aggregates is fully leveraged. The chapter begins by looking at the query environment of a dimensional data warehouse that includes aggregates, and studies how it differs from one that does not. Next, these differences will be translated into a set of requirements for the data for an aggregate navigation function.

A wide variety of commercial products offer aggregate navigation capabilities. Each implementation is different; each has its own pros and cons; all are constantly changing. Implementations are classified into three styles, and each style is evaluated against the requirements.

This process will equip you to evaluate the aggregate navigation capabilities of specific commercial products, even as the capabilities of these products evolve. In addition, you will study two of the most commonly implemented technologies: Oracle's materialized views and DB2's materialized query tables. Last, this chapter looks at the implications of working without an aggregate navigator.

Which Tables to Use?

Without aggregates, all queries are directed to the base schema. *With* aggregates, there are potentially several database tables capable of answering a query. Each fact table may have several aggregates derived from it. Some will be capable of providing an answer to a given query; some will not. Of those that can provide an answer, some will be faster than others.

A fundamental question must now be answered for every query issued: Which tables will be used? This new requirement is driven by the presence of aggregates.

Consider the Orders schema at the top of Figure 4.1, for which a set of dimensional aggregates has been designed. You are interested in looking at order dollars by month for the year 2006. Without the aggregates, this and any question about orders would be directed to the order_facts star. Now, there are several options. Some will be faster than others. There are also some tables that cannot respond to the query.

Deciding which table will best answer the query requires considering a number of factors: the schema design itself, the relative size of each option, the availability of each option, and its location. As you will see later, these choices are best left to an aggregate navigator. But even if this task is to be automated, it is important to understand what it needs to do.

The Schema Design

The identification of tables *capable* of providing query results should be simple, even if the process is performed manually. The dimensionality of a given question is compared to the dimensionality of the tables in the schema. Those with sufficient dimensional detail are able to answer the question.

Several principles from previous chapters aid this identification. The base schema and dimensional aggregates were defined in families. For each base and aggregate, dimensional grain was explicitly defined. Rules of conformance were applied, ensuring that equivalencies between dimension tables and aggregate dimension tables are understood, and that conformed facts and dimensions have the same name each place they appear. Hierarchies may have been defined to aid in this understanding.

TIP Dimensionally designed aggregates can answer a question if all facts and dimensions required by the question are present in the aggregate.

The example "Order dollars by month for 2006" is relatively simple. Dimensionally, it requires only the Day dimension, aggregated to the Month level. This means that any schema that includes the Month or Day dimensions will be able to answer the question. In Figure 4.2, these are easily identified by scanning the appropriate columns for check marks.

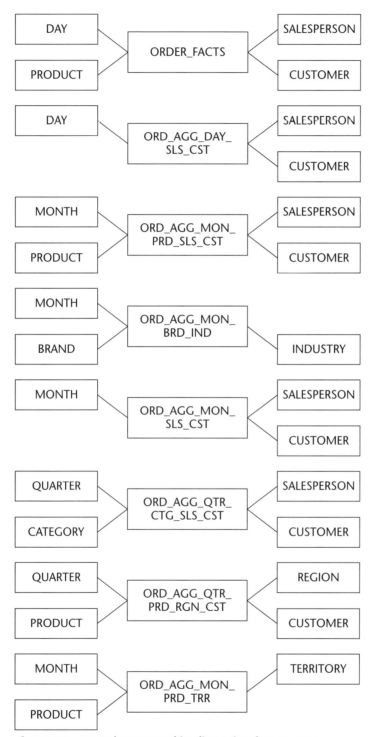

Figure 4.1 An Orders star and its dimensional aggregates.

	time			product			salesperson			customer	
	day	month	quarter	product	brand	category	salesperson	region	territory	customer	industry
order_facts	✓			✓			✓			✓	
ord_agg_day_sls_cst	✓						✓			✓	
ord_agg_mon_prd_sls_cst		✓		✓			✓			✓	
ord_agg_mon_brd_ind		✓			✓						✓
ord_agg_mon_sls_cst		✓					✓			✓	
ord_agg_qtr_ctg_sls_cst			✓			✓	✓			✓	
ord_agg_qtr_prd_rgn_cst			✓	✓				✓		✓	
ord_agg_mon_prd_trr		✓		✓					✓		

Figure 4.2 Dimensionality of the Orders star and its aggregates.

In the example, every aggregate is capable of answering the question except the two that include quarter: ord_agg_qtr_ctg_sls_cst and ord_agg_qtr_prd_rgn_cst. These aggregates do not contain Month and so cannot provide the monthly totals that are needed. For other questions, the number of tables capable of responding may vary; for some, only the base schema will suffice.

Relative Size

If multiple aggregates are capable of responding to a given query, the most appropriate aggregate must be chosen. The most appropriate table is the one that will respond the fastest. This can be approximated by comparing the number of rows in tables that are capable of responding and choosing the table with the fewest rows.

> **TIP** Use the relative number of rows in each aggregate fact table or pre-joined aggregate to estimate the performance ranking of each option.

Unlike the schema design, the number of rows in the tables will change on a regular basis. This choice, then, must be informed by up-to-date information on the contents of the tables. Using row counts that are outdated may lead to a failure to select the most appropriate table. The more current this information, the better informed the decision.

In the example query "Order dollars by month for 2006," the tables capable of responding and their row sizes appear in Table 4.1. Based on this information, any of the aggregates are likely to provide improved response time. The table ord_agg_mon_sls_cst is likely to be the most efficient at answering the question; ord_agg_mon_brd_ind would also be able to respond quite efficiently as well.

Table 4.1   Aggregates Capable of Responding to the Example Query

AGGREGATE	NUMBER OF ROWS
order_facts (base table)	600,000,000
ord_agg_day_sls_cst	100,000,000
ord_agg_mon_prd_sls_cst	200,000,000
ord_agg_mon_brd_ind	75,000,000
ord_agg_mon_sls_cst	20,000,000
ord_agg_mon_prd_trr	100,000,000

Notice that this is an approximation. The actual performance will be affected by factors that include the way in which rows are organized into contiguous blocks by the database (as explored in Chapter 3), along with the availability of indexes, the implementation of partitioning and parallelization schemes, and a variety of other factors. Because all these factors are managed by the RDBMS, you can make a strong case for database-level aggregate navigation, as you will see later in this chapter.

Aggregate Portfolio and Availability

Ideally, the tables used to answer a query should not be chosen until the query is issued. This permits the use of up-to-date information about aggregate table sizes, as described in the previous section. It also allows the current availability of the aggregates to be considered. This is important if base fact tables and aggregate tables are not updated simultaneously, and also allows for the aggregate portfolio to be changed over time.

Like the base schema, the information in dimensional aggregate tables must be loaded. The loading process for a dimensional aggregate may be similar to a standard ETL process or may be refreshed automatically by a specialized technology. In most cases, aggregates are populated directly from the base tables. Because of this dependency, the aggregates are often updated *after* the base tables have been updated. This simplifies the loading process by breaking it down into discrete subtasks. It also allows the base table to be available to end users before the work involved to populate the aggregates has taken place. These processes will be studied in Chapters 5 and 6.

TIP   Aggregates should be chosen each time a query is run. This allows consideration of availability status and accommodates a changing portfolio of aggregates.

For example, Figure 4.3 shows the tasks involved in loading a sample fact table and its aggregates. In this example, the warehouse tables are loaded while the database is unavailable to end users. At T0, the warehouse is taken off-line, and ETL processes that load the base schema begin. At T1, base schema processing is completed, and it is placed on-line. At this point, only the base schema is available to respond to queries.

After the base schema has been loaded, the processing for three sets of aggregate tables begins. Each aggregate becomes available once its load process has completed (T2, T3, and T4). At T2, for example, only the base schema and Aggregate 3 are available; at T4, all tables are available.

When selecting a table to respond to a query in this example, availability must be considered. Suppose that for a particular query, all three aggregates are capable of responding. The relative size and availability of each option is shown in Table 4.2.

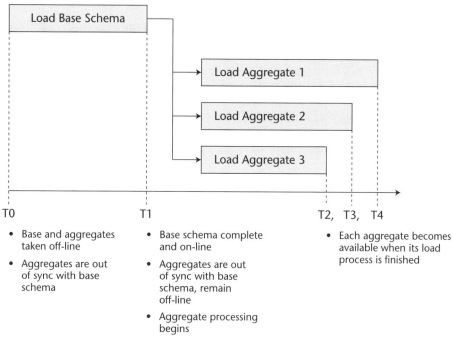

Figure 4.3 Loading a base schema and three aggregates.

Table 4.2 Aggregates and Their Availability at T3

AGGREGATE	NUMBER OF ROWS	AVAILABILITY
Base Schema	600,000,000	On-Line
Aggregate 1	7,000,000	Off-Line
Aggregate 2	95,000,000	On-Line
Aggregate 3	220,000,000	On-Line

While Aggregate 1 will be the fastest responder, it is currently off-line. Aggregate 2 is the best choice to resolve the query—it is the fastest responder of all available options. At another point in time, the choice may be different.

Not all warehouses are taken off-line during the load process, and sometimes base tables and aggregates are refreshed simultaneously. These issues will be explored more fully in Chapter 5. However, the selection of aggregates should still take place each time a query is executed. This allows the consideration of aggregates that have been recently added or removed from the warehouse in response to changes in query patterns.

Requirements for the Aggregate Navigator

Evaluating schema design, table size, and availability can be confusing for an end user. And since these evaluations should be made each time a query is run, how is a query to be saved in a report? The aggregate navigator solves these problems.

The aggregate navigator is an important part of the data warehouse architecture. It maintains its own inventory of aggregates, their size, and availability, and rewrites queries as appropriate. In doing so, it shields users from the table selection process and allows all queries and reports to be expressed in terms of the base schema.

Commercial products handle aggregate navigation in a variety of ways. Before you study the different styles of aggregate navigation, it is useful to establish a set of requirements for the aggregate navigation function.

Why an Aggregate Navigator?

Without an aggregate navigator, aggregates damage the understandability of the schema, threaten its acceptance by end users, weaken its efficiency, and introduce maintenance issues. If aggregates are queried at a time when they are not in synch with the base tables, they may also provide wrong results.

As you have seen, the appropriate table to respond to a given query is a function of (1) the dimensionality of the query, (2) the dimensionality of the aggregate schema design, (3) the relative size of the potential responders, and (4) their availability status. Weighing these factors can be a tedious and counterintuitive process for end users. This violates one of the guiding principles of star schema design: *understandability*. The user can no longer think in terms of facts and dimensions. Now, she is asked to make technical judgments.

User acceptance of the data warehouse can be damaged by this breakdown of understandability. Some will be able to make these technical judgments when designing queries or reports, but others will not. Faced with a confusing array of choices, many will default to using the base schema and never reap the advantages of aggregates. Others will begin working with an aggregate, only to become frustrated when adding a new dimension to their report requires shifting to a different aggregate. In many cases, queries will not use the most efficient tables.

This entire process becomes inefficient, or even impossible, if the user is also asked to consider aggregate availability status. You have seen that if aggregates are taken off-line during the load process, the same query must be directed to different tables at different times. Embedding this logic in a report may be impossible using some reporting tools, and very difficult with others.

A major maintenance issue develops as aggregates are added to or removed from the warehouse over time. The addition of a new aggregate to the data warehouse will require that existing reports be rewritten. Without this rewrite, they will not benefit from the aggregate. If an aggregate is removed from the warehouse, reports that use it will no longer work.

The aggregate navigator solves these problems. While aggregates can be used without the presence of an aggregate navigator, their deployment must be severely limited to avoid these issues. Later, this chapter provides techniques for coping without an aggregate navigator.

Two Views and Query Rewrite

The aggregate navigator maintains two logical views of the data warehouse schema. One, known to end users and applications, consists only of the base schema. A second view of the data warehouse, known only to the aggregate navigator, includes the aggregates, table sizes, and availability status. The aggregate navigator uses this information to rewrite user queries at runtime.

TIP The aggregate navigator should permit users and applications to deal with the base schema only.

An aggregate navigator should support aggregate star schemas. If pre-joined aggregates are to be used in the data warehouse, the aggregate navigator should support them as well. Some products will support one or the other, or require the use of a snowflake schema design technique. This may or may not be a significant limitation based on the operating environment in which it will be deployed.

TIP The aggregate navigator should support aggregate star schemas (including aggregate dimensions) and pre-joined aggregates (if desired). It should not require changes to the base schema design.

The information needed by the aggregate navigator should be easy to configure. If dimensional aggregates have been designed following the principles of the previous chapter, aggregates can be detected automatically. Families of base and aggregate schemas and their conformance are readily identified because care has been taken to name facts and dimensions identically. Likewise, table sizes are easily ascertained from the RDBMS. Complex mapping or hierarchy modeling should not be required, although some products do require this.

TIP The aggregate navigator should be able to identify all necessary information automatically, through examination of the database catalog. This includes aggregate families, conformance, and relative table size.

The aggregate navigator tracks all this information so that applications that query the database do not need to. Applications are concerned only with the base schema. All SQL is written or generated to access base fact tables. The aggregate navigator takes this SQL and rewrites it to take advantage of the most efficient aggregate. It forwards the rewritten, or *aggregate-aware*, query to the database.

TIP The aggregate navigator translates base-schema SQL into aggregate-aware SQL at runtime. This process is transparent to the applications that issue SQL queries.

Imagine a simple data mart that consists of one fact table. It has been augmented with six aggregate star schemas and two pre-joined aggregates. The major dimensions are summarized at various aggregation points that conform, and are understood in terms of hierarchies. Each fact table has a known size, and two are currently off-line. Figure 4.4 summarizes this environment.

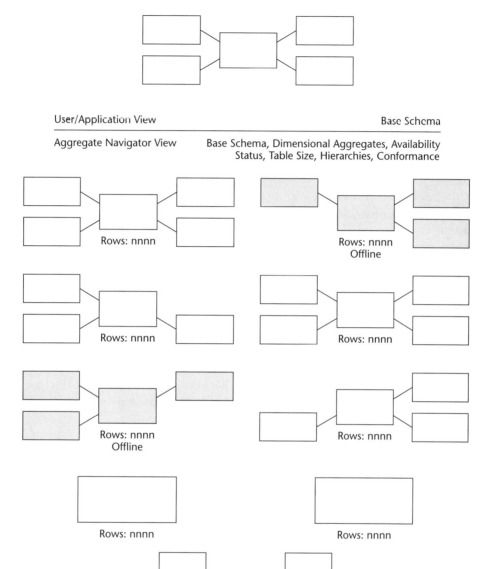

User/Application View   Base Schema

Aggregate Navigator View   Base Schema, Dimensional Aggregates, Availability
                                Status, Table Size, Hierarchies, Conformance

Figure 4.4   Two views of the data warehouse.

The top portion of Figure 4.4 shows the information with which end users or applications are concerned: the base star schema. The aggregates, their sizes and status, and dimensional conformance are known only to the aggregate navigator. This additional information does not clutter or complicate the user view of the data warehouse.

Users issue queries written against the base schema. The aggregate navigator intercepts these queries and rewrites them based on the detailed information on aggregates. This process is depicted in Figure 4.5.

By isolating the user application from the aggregates, the aggregate navigator restores schema understandability. The user application on the left side of the diagram deals with the base schema exclusively and is not required to make any decisions about which tables to use. The aggregate navigator is aware of the presence of aggregates, and automatically makes these decisions each time a query is run.

Dynamic Availability

The aggregate navigator should accommodate the dynamic nature of the aggregate pool. This means that the availability status of aggregate tables should be considered, and that the overall portfolio of aggregates should be easily changed.

You have seen that aggregate tables may become out of synch with the base tables when not loaded simultaneously. At times like this, the aggregate table must not be used to respond to a query—otherwise, it will provide different results than the base table. That is a clear violation of one of the guiding principles: *correct results.*

An aggregate navigator can avoid this situation by capturing the status of aggregate tables. It may do this automatically, or provide an interface that allows an external process to update the status of each aggregate table. This information is used to avoid the use of out-of-synch tables during the query rewrite process. The aggregate navigator is able to respond to the same query in different ways at different times, depending on the status of the aggregate tables.

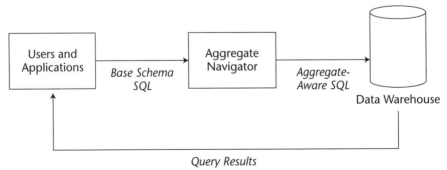

Figure 4.5   The aggregate navigator translates between two views by rewriting queries.

TIP The aggregate navigator should respond to the dynamic availability of aggregates.

In the same vein, the aggregate navigator should support changes to the aggregate pool. New aggregates may be implemented, and should be automatically exploited without rewriting queries. Existing aggregates may be removed without causing existing queries to fail.

TIP The aggregate navigator should facilitate easy addition and removal of aggregates from the data warehouse.

While this seems an obvious requirement, there are some aggregate navigators that require extensive reprogramming when the mix of tables is changed. While this may minimize impact on a large library of queries and reports, a complex process unnecessarily impedes progress. As you will see, most aggregates should be easily identifiable without human intervention.

Multiple Front Ends

A front-end tool is a software product that takes information from the data warehouse and presents it to the end user. They are most commonly referred to as *query and reporting tools*, or *business intelligence software*. A data warehouse may have several types of front-end tools, including:

- Desktop or enterprise reporting software
- Business intelligence software
- Ad hoc query and analysis software
- Data mining tools
- Statistical analysis tools
- Dashboard products
- Desktop spreadsheet plug-ins
- Analytic applications that embed one or more of the above capabilities
- SQL queries written manually by expert analysts or developers

A single environment may include front-end tools in several of these categories. And often, multiple products within a single category will be deployed. Heterogeneous front ends may have been adopted by choice, resulted from a decentralized product selection process, arrived via the acquisition of a packaged application, or arrived via mergers and acquisitions. While the reasons vary, diversity is commonplace.

Most enterprises will not have this many different applications accessing the data warehouse. But it is commonplace to find more than one front end. For example, there may be an ad hoc reporting tool, enterprise reporting software, and analysts who issue their own SQL statements. As shown in the top portion of Figure 4.6, each of these applications issues SQL statements to the data warehouse.

Ideally, a single aggregate navigation solution should service each of these front ends. This ensures that all applications benefit from the dimensional aggregates, and avoids the need to configure separate aggregate navigation solutions for each application.

TIP   A single aggregate navigator should service all front-end applications.

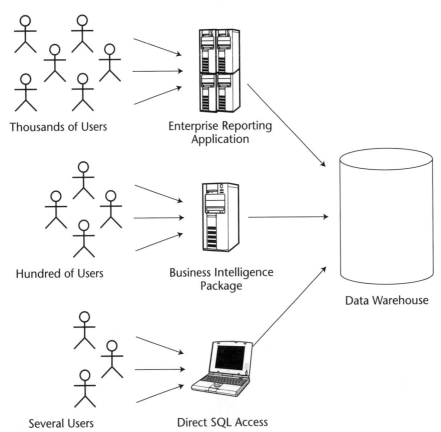

Figure 4.6   A data warehouse with multiple front-end applications.

Figure 4.7 shows an aggregate navigator that works with multiple front-end applications. Its services are available to any application that issues SQL to the database. It permits all aggregate navigation to be administered from a single point, which means you avoid the need to redundantly configure multiple applications.

Multiple Back Ends

The data warehouse is not always a single database. Often, a dimensional data warehouse is spread across multiple physical databases. By carefully planning a set of conformed dimensions, the data warehouse architect can structure an enterprise data warehouse that is divided into subject areas, each residing on a different physical database. For example, one database hosts sales and fulfillment subject areas, another hosts inventory data, and a third hosts financial data. These back ends do not necessarily reside on similar RDBMS platforms.

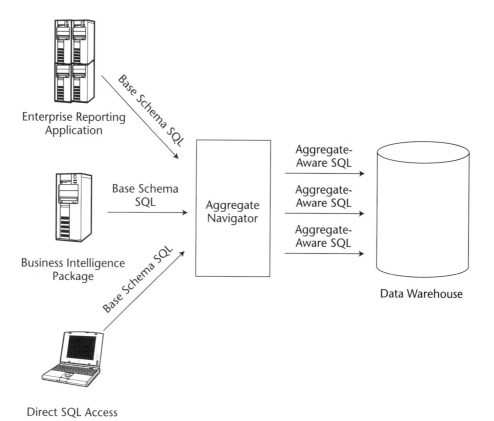

Figure 4.7   An aggregate navigator servicing multiple front ends.

Like the base schema, the aggregate tables, too, may be spread across multiple platforms. They may be on the same database server as the base tables, or on a separate database server. When on separate servers, the aggregates may be hosted by a different RDBMS platform, or by the same RDBMS platform. These various distributions are illustrated in Figure 4.8.

Ideally, a single technology would provide aggregate navigation services in all these situations. This reduces the set of necessary skills to develop and maintain the data warehouse, and makes most efficient use of available resources. A separate aggregate navigation system for each back end increases the demand on I.T. resources.

TIP A single aggregate navigation system should service all back-end databases.

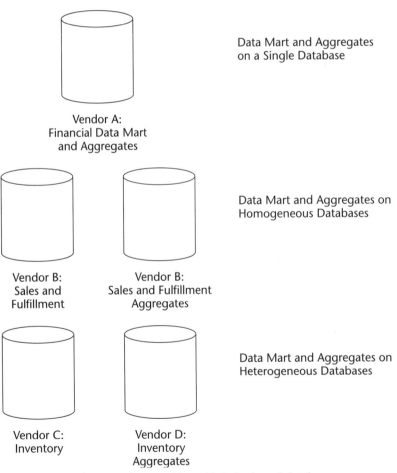

Vendor A:
Financial Data Mart
and Aggregates

Data Mart and Aggregates
on a Single Database

Vendor B:
Sales and
Fulfillment

Vendor B:
Sales and Fulfillment
Aggregates

Data Mart and Aggregates on
Homogeneous Databases

Vendor C:
Inventory

Vendor D:
Inventory
Aggregates

Data Mart and Aggregates on
Heterogeneous Databases

Figure 4.8   A data warehouse with multiple back-end databases.

The aggregate navigator in Figure 4.9 services multiple back-end databases. The same architectural component provides query rewrite services for all RDBMS platforms, regardless of vendor. It is also capable of taking a query written for a base schema on one platform and rewriting it to leverage aggregates on another platform.

The geographic distribution of data may factor into the warehouse design as well. For example, aggregates may be placed on an RDBMS server that is physically closer to a particular group of users likely to use them. The requirements of the aggregate navigator could conceivably be extended to acknowledge physical proximity between users and aggregate tables.

The list of requirements for the aggregate navigator is relatively short. Many enterprises may even be willing to forgo some of the proposed capabilities. The need to support multiple back-end databases, for example, may not be important in some enterprises. Manual configuration of aggregates may prove acceptable. Some organizations may even be willing to accept limitations on the base schema design required in order to support a particular implementation.

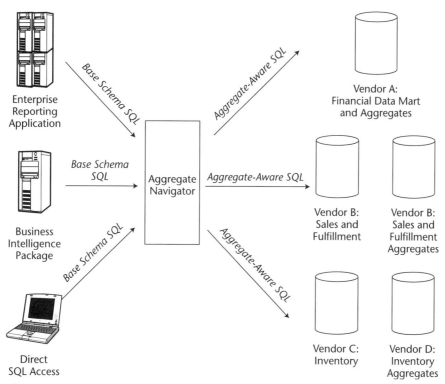

Figure 4.9 An aggregate navigator servicing multiple back-end databases.

SUMMARY OF REQUIREMENTS FOR THE AGGREGATE NAVIGATOR

1. The aggregate navigator should permit users and applications to deal with the base schema only.

2. The aggregate navigator should support aggregate star schemas (including aggregate dimensions) and pre-joined aggregates. It should not require changes to the base schema design.

3. The aggregate navigator should be able to identify all necessary information automatically, through examination of the database catalog. This includes aggregate families, conformance, and relative table size.

4. The aggregate navigator translates base-schema SQL into aggregate-aware SQL at runtime. This process is transparent to the applications that issue SQL queries.

5. The aggregate navigator should respond to the dynamic availability of aggregates.

6. The aggregate navigator should facilitate easy addition and removal of aggregates from the data warehouse.

7. A single aggregate navigator should service all front-end applications.

8. A single aggregate navigation system should service all back-end databases.

The next section looks at the three approaches to aggregate navigation that characterize most commercial products. These styles will be evaluated according to the requirements that have been outlined. This approach can be used to evaluate a commercial product, shedding light on how its implementation will impact the data warehouse.

Evaluating Aggregate Navigators

Most enterprises that have not implemented dimensional aggregates are already in possession of products that offer aggregate support. The capability is found in business intelligence tools, reporting tools, and RDBMS products, for example.

But the reality is that trade-offs will be required. Commercial products usually support dimensional aggregates through a feature of a larger product. As a result, the aggregate navigation capability is either tailored to the capabilities of the product, or is a specific application of a more generalized capability.

This section examines the three most common approaches to aggregate navigation. For each style, the overall approach is compared to the requirements developed in the previous section. Advantages and potential shortcomings will be identified, along with questions to ask that will bring to light any operational impacts of the solution.

By looking at aggregate navigators in this way, you should be able to evaluate specific products and understand their implications on the data warehouse architecture. Later, this chapter examines some specific technologies that are commonly used.

Front-End Aggregate Navigators

A decade ago, aggregate navigation features were found mostly in commercial front-end products. While there are more options today, many front-end tools still offer some form of support. Because front-end tools manage the process of submitting SQL to the database, their developers can easily extend them to support a query rewrite capability.

Front-end aggregate navigators can allow users to work with a single logical schema design (the base schema), automatically rewriting queries to take advantage of available aggregates. While they may be able to meet many of the requirements for an aggregate navigator, they will typically fall short in at least one respect: They fail to provide their services for other front-end applications.

Approach

Commercially available front-end products can incorporate aggregate navigation capability because they control the process of generating and executing queries. Navigation of aggregates is a logical extension of this process.

Typically, front-end tools maintain some form of metadata describing a database schema. This metadata is used as a foundation for the construction of queries or reports, which are managed by the tool. The specifics of the report design process vary by product. But in most cases, when users execute the query or report, all database interaction is handled by the tool. It generates SQL, sends it to the database, retrieves the results, and displays them according to the report specification.

Because they maintain control of these aspects of database interaction, these products can be extended by their developers to perform query rewrite services. In most cases, they are already generating the SQL queries required by the report. Aggregate navigation is simply an extension to this query generation process.

To provide aggregate navigation services, the product must incorporate a means for the collection of metadata on the aggregate schema and a query rewrite mechanism. It can continue to generate SQL as always, even letting end users write it freehand. At query execution time, it takes the SQL statement and compares it to metadata describing aggregates. The query is rewritten as appropriate and, still under control of the tool, submitted to the database.

Pros and Cons

This approach to aggregate navigation is appealing because it does not rely on any specialized back-end technology. The same approach to aggregate navigation can be used, even if the enterprise has heterogeneous RDBMS implementations. This reduces the I.T. skill set required to manage aggregates in a multi-database enterprise.

The obvious downside to this approach is that aggregate navigation capabilities are limited to the front-end tool that provides it. Additional front-end tools will not benefit. The business intelligence product in Figure 4.10 has built-in aggregate navigation capabilities. Its queries are aggregate-aware, but the queries issued by other front-end products are not.

This situation may be acceptable if the majority of database interaction takes place through the business intelligence tool. Perhaps the enterprise reporting tool is used primarily for the automation and caching of reports during overnight processes, when query execution time is less important. The users writing their own SQL for direct access to the database are developers, who can be expected to understand how to leverage aggregates manually.

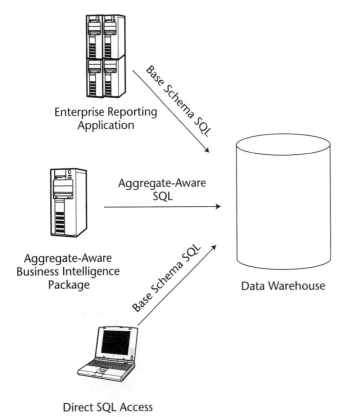

Figure 4.10 An aggregate-aware front-end tool.

It is reasonable to expect the front-end aggregate navigator to meet most of the other requirements we have established. One question that should be looked at carefully is the manner in which the solution identifies aggregates and maintains the appropriate metadata. Because these tools establish a metadata layer as a foundation for building queries, they may require manual definition of aggregates as part of this layer. If so, the process of adding and removing aggregates will be hindered by the need to reconfigure this layer. This is a workable situation, although not ideal.

As with any aggregate navigator, be sure to fully understand how the mechanism works and whether there are any implications for the schema design. Are aggregate fact and dimension tables supported? How? What about prejoined aggregates? Does the implementation require adjusting the schema design approach, or use of a snowflake model? Again, restrictions such as these may be workable. It is important to understand them in advance of the implementation.

Back-End Aggregate Navigation

Ten years ago, aggregate navigation capability was mostly found in front-end products, or in specialized *middle-tier* applications that sat between the front-end and the database. Since then, RDBMS products have matured considerably. They have grown to include a wealth of features in support of data warehousing, including query optimization for star schemas, specialized indexes for low-cardinality attributes, partitioning and parallelization for very large tables, and ETL capabilities. Among these new capabilities, most RDBMS products now provide features that can be used to perform aggregate navigation.

Specific implementation varies by vendor, but the overall approach is similar. In most cases, the RDBMS can not only perform aggregate navigation services, but also build and manage the aggregates for you. However, the mechanisms by which these features work tend to introduce complications for aggregate design. This is partly because these mechanisms have a wider applicability than dimensional aggregates. If you understand their limitations, they can be put to use intelligently.

Approach

Commercial RDBMS products can provide aggregate navigation capability because they already maintain most of the necessary metadata, and because they are already designed around an architecture that parses and rewrites queries to optimize performance. Most of the factors relating to the performance of a query are directly managed by the RDBMS, a strong argument in favor of it providing aggregate navigation services.

RDBMS products also provide a mix of other capabilities that in some way relate to aggregate management. For example, many provide mechanisms for replicating data from one table to another. Many also provide the capability to define views that are cached in permanent storage, or *materialized*. Aggregate navigation in the RDBMS is achieved by combining several of these features.

RDBMS-based solutions provide more than aggregate navigation; they are also used to build and maintain the aggregates. This can have tremendous advantages, eliminating the need to develop ETL processing for the maintenance of dimensional aggregates. There are also some disadvantages, which are explored shortly.

The use of a back-end aggregate navigation capability begins by declaring the aggregate table to the RDBMS. This is done through vendor-specific SQL to define the aggregate, which is a special type of database object. Examples include Oracle's materialized views and DB2's materialized query tables. These specific examples are examined in the section "Living with Specific Solutions" later in this chapter.

The declaration process is similar to the process of creating a view. The aggregate is based on a SQL SELECT statement, or query. The SQL query may include aggregations of facts, dimensions, and joins. In fact, it will look like a typical star schema query. Unlike a standard view, however, the results of the query are stored in the database. This allows the database to use these pre-cached results when appropriate. Figure 4.11 depicts the process of building an aggregate based on order_facts that summarizes order_dollars for all products.

The definition of the aggregate fact table includes a defining query that summarizes data from the base fact table. In this case, it includes three of the four dimensions referenced by the base fact table. The foreign keys for these dimensions are included in the SELECT clause of the query, along with the sum of order_dollars. The same set of keys is used to define the level of aggregation, specified in the GROUP BY clause.

The defining query serves two purposes. First, it is used to build the aggregate fact table, populate it with data, and keep it up-to-date. Additional parameters identify how this initial population and refresh process will work.

Second, the RDBMS uses the defining query to determine if the aggregate can be substituted in a given query. In this manner, user queries are rewritten to leverage the most efficient aggregate. This process is referred to as *query rewrite*, and is not used exclusively with aggregates.

Pros and Cons

There are two major advantages to RDBMS-based aggregate navigation solutions. First, a commercial RDBMS is designed to evaluate various options for query execution and choose the one that is likely to be most efficient. Aggregate selection fits naturally into this process. The RDBMS knows the relative size of the various options and their indexing schemes, and can determine the relative execution costs for each choice. In this respect, it is potentially able to go beyond the imperfect approximation offered by row counts.

Second, the fact that the RDBMS can build and maintain the aggregate offers significant advantages. Because the RDBMS will manage the creation and refresh of the aggregate table, there is no need to develop an ETL process to do so. This transforms the maintenance of aggregates from an ETL task, which requires specialized expertise for development and maintenance, into a DBA task, which involves mastery of a set of additional database commands and procedures.

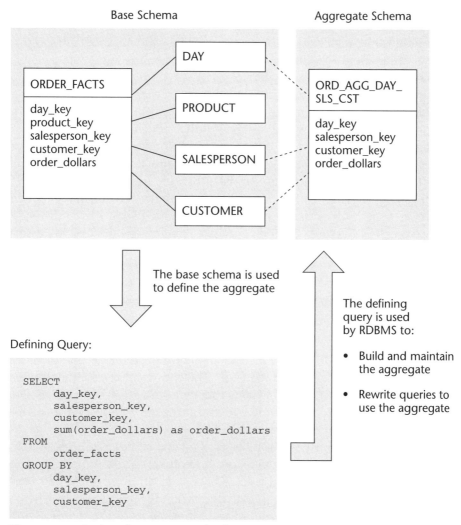

Figure 4.11 Back-end aggregate navigation.

There are two primary drawbacks to the RDBMS-based aggregate navigator. The first is that it typically performs aggregate navigation services only for a single back-end. Proprietary extensions can often be used to incorporate additional database servers, sometimes even from a different vendor. But to benefit from these aggregate navigation services, the original query must always be directed to the particular database on which the aggregates are being managed. If aggregate navigation is to be provided on heterogeneous databases, multiple solutions will be necessary.

Second, RDBMS-based solutions often have difficulty in handling an aggregate schema that includes an aggregate dimension table. The declaration of the aggregate tables is complicated by the fact that the base schema does not include the warehouse key for the aggregate dimension. While this may be compensated for by inclusion of the key in the base schema, the RDBMS optimizer will fail to identify a direct relationship between the aggregate fact and aggregate dimension table.

This problem is depicted in Figure 4.12. A new aggregate schema is planned for the Orders star. The aggregate star includes Day and Brand. Brand is an aggregate dimension that summarizes the Product dimension. The declaration of each aggregate table includes a defining query. Notice that to facilitate these declarations, a brand_key has been introduced into the base schema. The RDBMS learns that each aggregate can be substituted for the corresponding base table as appropriate. But it may fail to identify the relationship between the aggregates themselves, as represented by the dotted join.

The end result is that the back-end aggregate navigators work best in the following situations:

- Pre-joined aggregates
- Star schema aggregates that do not involve an aggregate dimension

As you will see in the next section, Oracle and IBM now offer capabilities that enable the use of aggregate dimensions on a logical level. The aggregate dimensions are not built, but are instead defined by declaring one or more hierarchies that exist in the base dimension. The end result is a solution that is functionally equivalent to aggregate stars that include a rollup dimension. For these implementations, you may say that aggregate dimensions are supported, although they are not actually built.

The solution may be further complicated if a table serves as a base table in one schema, and an aggregate dimension in another. For example, planning data may be provided at the Brand level. A base star with financial targets uses Brand, which also serves as an aggregate dimension for the aggregate schema discussed. The Brand table must be built and refreshed prior to any processing that builds or refreshes the planning facts. In addition, its definition must enable the optimizer to rewrite order queries, while not confusing planning queries.

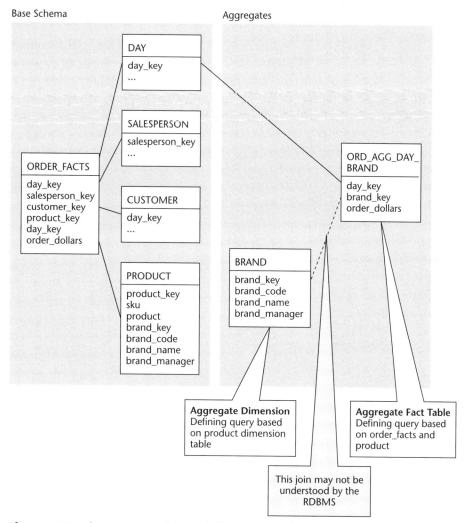

Figure 4.12 The aggregate fact and dimension tables are declared individually; their relationship to one another is not understood by the RDBMS.

In the case of an RDBMS-based solution, be sure to understand exactly how aggregates are defined, and match this against the different types of aggregates. Can each type of aggregate be implemented? If so, how? The answers to these questions will determine what you need to do to work with the aggregate navigator, or how it may limit your implementation.

Performance Add-On Technologies and OLAP

The last major category of aggregate navigator is a catch-all for solutions that go beyond the relational model to provide performance. It is a bit out of place here because it does not really operate on dimensional aggregates. However, as more and more variations on this theme become prevalent, it is prudent to consider the option.

The solutions under this umbrella cache aggregated information outside the relational database or in a non-relational format. These solutions provide accelerated access to aggregated data, enabling accelerated performance for many queries. But often, they require the use of a separate front-end tool, using an access language other than SQL.

Approach

Performance add-on technologies augment the capabilities of the RDBMS by providing a non-relational cache of data. In some cases, the relational database itself may perform this service, but the cache is not a relational data store. Microsoft's Analysis Services are an example. For the sake of clarity, the examples here will place this cache outside of the RDBMS.

Facts and dimensions are extracted from the base star and stored externally. The dimensionality of the extraction determines the level of aggregation provided by the external data store. A second level of aggregation or partial aggregation may be supported, based on a proprietary architecture that allows the facts to be fully or partially pre-computed across dimensions in the extract. Optimized for highly interactive analytical queries, this external repository generally has its own interface, which is not SQL. Alternative front-end tools leverage this non-SQL interface to access aggregated data. They can be configured to reach back to the original star when the user requests data that is not in the external repository.

A logical picture of this architecture is provided in Figure 4.13. The RDBMS on the upper left is home to a series of star schemas, based on a set of conformed dimensions. It is accessed in the usual manner by Application A, an enterprise reporting product. In the upper right, a performance technology has been implemented. Its proprietary data structures are populated using queries against the base stars. Front-end Application B accesses this data store through a non-SQL interface. When users wish to drill into detail not present, it issues a SQL query to the base star, or passes control to a SQL-enabled application.

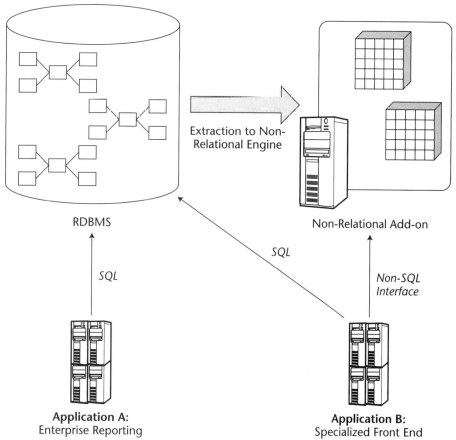

Figure 4.13 Performance add-on technologies.

The most common form of non-relational cache is an OLAP server. The high performance extract is stored in a format known as a *cube* and accessed through a non-SQL interface. This may be a proprietary interface or an open standard such as MDX. If the cube has been explicitly sourced from the relational star schema, cube users can be dynamically passed to the relational data source as required.

Pros and Cons

Strictly speaking, this technology is not aggregate navigation as defined in this book. Access to the aggregates is not provided via a transparent mechanism that hides it from the end user. The aggregate structures must be accessed explicitly and through a different interface than the base fact table.

However, this approach is included here because it fits with the dimensional approach. The extracted aggregates have grain and can be defined in terms of facts and dimensions. Hierarchies may aid in their definition, especially where OLAP technologies are concerned.

The advantages of this approach may be many. Certainly, if the packaging of relational data into external structures such as cubes is automated, there is no need to build ETL processes that construct the aggregates. This may be replaced by some necessary customization of the process that generates the non-relational storage structures but is often a simpler process.

The external structures themselves may be very fast compared to relational tables. For the queries that they accelerate, they are likely to be much faster than an aggregate fact table of similar grain. Each fact is partially pre-computed across all major dimensions in each aggregate.

The primary disadvantage here is the limitation on the technology used to access the aggregate. By working with a separate front-end product when accessing an aggregate, the invisibility rule is violated; users must select a different tool when they wish to access summarized data. However, this workflow may be logical in some situations. Sales managers may look at aggregate data when analyzing sales representative performance over time across customers, then access a traditional SQL-based report to see the customer detail for a particular sales representative.

Over time, you are likely to see this style of solution evolve. While the differences between SQL and OLAP syntax are many, some products are beginning to blur the distinctions. There will likely be a time when an RDBMS will also contain OLAP data, and allow SQL access to it. Similarly, the RDBMS solutions of the previous section are likely to evolve to contain proprietary technologies similar to those in this category.

Specific Solutions

Commercial products that offer aggregate navigation features are numerous. To explore the pros and cons of each would fill the pages of a book this size. And because they are constantly evolving, the book would be out of date almost as soon as it was published. Instead, this chapter has provided the critical skills needed to evaluate a particular solution.

However, there are specific solutions worth a more detailed treatment because they are within reach of most implementations. These approaches are: Oracle's Materialized Views, the Materialized Query Tables of IBM's DB2, and the implementation of aggregates without an aggregate navigator.

Keep in mind that this overview should not be considered the final word regarding specific products. The products will continue to evolve. Instead, consider this overview to be a starting point. As suggested in Chapter 7, implementation of any product, whether discussed here or not, should be informed by a careful evaluation of its capabilities against the requirements that have been developed in this chapter and the priorities of the enterprise.

Living with Materialized Views

The Oracle RDBMS provides aggregate navigation capability through a combination of features, centering on materialized views. The RDBMS's query rewrite capability is aware of the presence of aggregates built using this feature, and uses them as appropriate to rewrite user queries. The RDBMS can also manage the synchronization of materialized views with the base schema, eliminating the need for an ETL process.

Using Materialized Views

Materialized views are a back-end aggregate navigation solution, as discussed in the previous section. Similar to a standard relational view, a materialized view is defined based on a SQL SELECT statement. Unlike a standard view, the results of this query are saved, or materialized, in a table.

When a user submits a query that involves the tables, columns, and joins included in this defining query, the RDBMS optimizer is able to rewrite the query to access the view. This allows the RDBMS to bypass work that was done to produce the view, including the evaluation of joins or the aggregation of facts.

This approach is consistent to the one depicted in Figure 4.12. In this case, the materialized view is the aggregate table. Its defining query is used by the RDMBS to populate it with data, and is leveraged by the query rewrite mechanism to provide aggregate navigation services.

Materialized Views as Pre-Joined Aggregates

The simplest application of the materialized view is a pre-joined aggregate. The defining query for the materialized view simply selects the appropriate dimensions and fact aggregations, joining to the necessary dimension tables.

Consider once again an Orders schema that includes dimensions for Product, Day, Salesperson, and Customer. A pre-joined aggregate is desired that aggregates order dollars by Day and Brand. Figure 4.14 shows the base schema and the pre-joined aggregate.

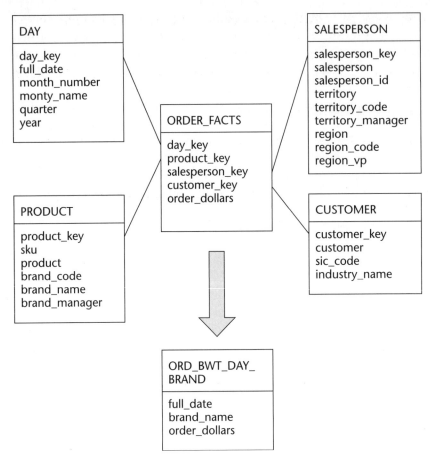

Figure 4.14 An Orders schema with a pre-joined aggregate.

This aggregate is easy to create using a materialized view. The defining query for the pre-joined aggregate simply selects the desired attributes from the base star:

```
CREATE MATERIALIZED VIEW ord_bwt_date_brand
    ...          /* options and parameters go here */
AS SELECT     /* the defining query begins here */
  day.full_date,
  product.brand_name,
  sum( order_facts.order_dollars )as order_dollars
FROM
  order_facts, day, product
WHERE
  order_facts.day_key = day.day_key and
  order_facts.product_key = product.product_key
GROUP BY
  day.full_date,
  product.brand_name
```

The CREATE MATERIALIZED VIEW statement would also include several parameters and options that control the behavior of the materialized view. The RDBMS uses this query to build the aggregate.

Once this materialized view is in place, populated with data, and enabled for query rewrite, it will automatically be leveraged as appropriate. The query optimizer compares user queries to the defining query in order to identify potential query rewrites. If the materialized view is identified as an option, the RDBMS optimizer compares the estimated cost, or execution time, for each query, and chooses the one that is most efficient.

TIP Materialized views are easily used to implement pre-joined aggregates.

For example, the user may issue the following query:

```
SELECT
  brand,
  sum(order_dollars)
FROM
  order_facts, product, day
WHERE
  order_facts.product_key = product.product_key and
  order_facts.day_key = day.day_key and
  day.full_date = to_date('11/01/2006')
GROUP BY
  Brand
```

Based on the defining query for the materialized view, the RDBMS identifies this table as able to respond to the query. It compares execution cost for a query against the base schema with the execution cost to access the materialized view. The materialized view proves the more efficient responder because it is significantly smaller and the RDBMS will not have to perform any joins. The RDBMS rewrites the query to access the materialized view:

```
SELECT
  brand,
  sum (order_dollars)
FROM
  ord_bwt_day_brand
WHERE
  full_date = to_date('11/1/2006')
GROUP BY
  brand
```

This rewritten query will be executed much more efficiently.

Materialized Views as Aggregate Fact Tables (Without Aggregate Dimensions)

An aggregate star always includes an aggregate fact table. The dimensions associated with the aggregate star may be base dimensions and/or aggregate dimensions. An aggregate dimension is required only when a base dimension is partially summarized.

When the aggregate star includes no aggregate dimensions, a materialized view is easily created. The aggregate fact table can be fully described by a query against the base schema. Its columns will include aggregated facts grouped by keys that reference the surviving dimensions.

> **TIP** Aggregate fact tables that do not reference aggregate dimension tables are easily constructed using a materialized view.

An example of this type of aggregate fact table is shown in Figure 4.11. The base orders schema in the figure includes dimension tables for Product, Day, Salesperson, and Customer. The aggregate ord_agg_day_sls_cst summarizes order_dollars by Day, Salesperson, and Customer across all products.

This aggregate can be created as a materialized view, using the SQL SELECT statement that appears in the figure.

The query rewrite mechanism will evaluate user queries and cost estimates to determine when the aggregate should be substituted. For example, a user may issue the following query:

```
SELECT
  salesperson,
  sum(order_dollars)
FROM
  order_facts, day, salesperson
WHERE
  order_facts.salesperson_key =
    salesperson.salesperson_key and
  order_facts.day_key = day.day_key and
  day.full_date = to_date('11/1/2006')
GROUP BY
  salesperson
```

This query can be rewritten to leverage the materialized view from Figure 4.11 as follows:

```
SELECT
  salesperson,
  sum(order_dollars)
FROM
  ord_agg_day_sls_cst, day, salesperson
```

```
WHERE
  ord_agg_day_sls_cst.salesperson_key =
    salesperson.salesperson_key and
  ord_agg_day_sls_cst.day_key = day.day_key and
  day.full_date = to_date('11/1/2006')
GROUP BY
  salesperson
```

The structure of this query is identical to the original. The only change is that the materialized view has been substituted for the original fact table. Although joins are not avoided, this query will return faster because the materialized view summarizes data across all products. Each row fetched summarizes numerous rows in the base table, greatly reducing the amount of data that must be read by the RDBMS to resolve the query.

Materialized Views and Aggregate Dimension Tables

Earlier, you saw that database objects like materialized views cannot effectively define an aggregate fact table and associated aggregate dimension table. As depicted in Figure 4.12, each can be built, but when queries are rewritten, the RDBMS fails to recognize their relationship to one another.

The Oracle RDBMS provides a solution to this problem. It allows reference to an aggregated dimension and at the same time eliminates the need to build it. After the base dimension table is created, the levels of summarization and their attributes are declared using a CREATE DIMENSION statement. This statement identifies hierarchy levels implicit in the dimension, along with defining and dependent attributes for each level.

A materialized view can reference a column that defines a level of the hierarchy. When a user query references an attribute that is part of a defined hierarchy level, the RDBMS will be able to join back to the dimension table.

> **TIP** Materialized views are not used to construct aggregate dimensions. Instead, dimensional hierarchies are declared through the CREATE DIMENSION statement. A materialized view can reference levels within the hierarchy.

Consider the Orders schema, as shown in the top portion of Figure 4.14. This time, the desired aggregate includes the Day dimension and Brand. Brand is a summarization of the product dimension, which includes the attributes brand_code, brand_name, and brand_manager.

Rather than build a brand dimension, complete with a brand_key, a hierarchy is defined based on the product dimension table. This hierarchy is declared using a dimension statement:

```
CREATE DIMENSION product_dim
   LEVEL product IS (product.product_key)
   LEVEL brand IS (product.brand_code)
   HIERARCHY product_rollup
     ( product CHILD OF brand)
   ATTRIBUTE product DETERMINES (product.sku, product.product)
   ATTRIBUTE brand DETERMINES (product.brand, product.brand_manager)
```

This statement identifies an implicit hierarchy within the Product table. There are two levels: Product and Brand. Each Product is part of a Brand. The attribute product_key uniquely identifies a product, and it has dependent attributes sku and name. Brand_code uniquely identifies a Brand, and it has dependent attributes brand_name and brand_manager. These relationships are declared only by the dimension statement, not enforced. It is up to the ETL process that loads Product to ensure they are enforced.

A materialized view can now be constructed that includes the brand_code, where otherwise a warehouse key for a brand table would have been required. Because the RDBMS has been instructed that brand_code determines brand_name and brand_manager, it will be able to join this materialized view back to the product table to fetch the name or manager of the brand, if needed. As depicted in Figure 4.15, no brand table has been built, but the end result is functionally equivalent.

If a query is submitted that includes a product attribute, such as SKU, the RDBMS will not use the materialized view. SKU is not dependent on the brand_code, and so the RDBMS must use the base schema.

Additional Considerations

Documentation of the aggregate schema design can acknowledge the use of materialized views. As mentioned in Chapter 3, the defining query can be included with the documentation for a pre-joined aggregate or aggregate fact table. The design of aggregate dimensions is reduced to a logical exercise, but their inclusion in system documentation may enhance schema understanding.

Dimensional hierarchies must be documented and defined. Be sure that there is a defining attribute for each level of a hierarchy. If one does not exist, it must be created and managed as part of the base dimension table.

Special care is required when the schema design calls for an aggregate dimension to serve as a base dimension for another star. For example, a planning_facts star may require a Brand dimension. In this case, it is preferable to build a physical Brand dimension. This allows for the creation and management of a brand_key, which will be one of the foreign_keys in the fact table.

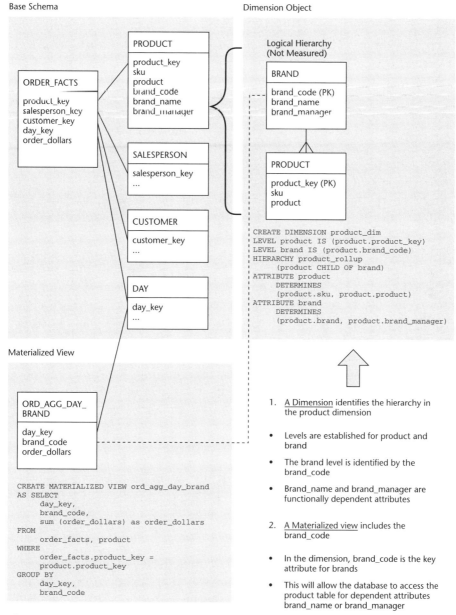

Base Schema

Dimension Object

Materialized View

Logical Hierarchy
(Not Measured)

```
CREATE DIMENSION product_dim
LEVEL product IS (product.product_key)
LEVEL brand IS (product.brand_code)
HIERARCHY product_rollup
        (product CHILD OF brand)
ATTRIBUTE product
    DETERMINES
        (product.sku, product.product)
ATTRIBUTE brand
    DETERMINES
        (product.brand, product.brand_manager)
```

```
CREATE MATERIALIZED VIEW ord_agg_day_brand
AS SELECT
        day_key,
        brand_code,
        sum (order_dollars) as order_dollars
FROM
        order_facts, product
WHERE
        order_facts.product_key =
        product.product_key
GROUP BY
        day_key,
        brand_code
```

1. A Dimension identifies the hierarchy in the product dimension

- Levels are established for product and brand

- The brand level is identified by the brand_code

- Brand_name and brand_manager are functionally dependent attributes

2. A Materialized view includes the brand_code

- In the dimension, brand_code is the key attribute for brands

- This will allow the database to access the product table for dependent attributes brand_name or brand_manager

Figure 4.15 A base schema with a materialized view and a dimension hierarchy.

If Brand is also required as part of an aggregation of order_facts, a dimension can be defined for Product that defines the Brand aggregate. Now, however, the attributes of Brand are defined redundantly, and a correspondence between them is not known to the aggregate navigator. This may be acceptable, as queries against the base planning_facts schema should reference brand directly, whereas queries against the base order_facts should not. It may, however, pose a challenge when creating metadata in business intelligence tools.

Alternatively, Product can be built without brand attributes, save a brand_code, and extended syntax of the CREATE DIMENSION statement can be used to accommodate both tables. This effectively transforms order_facts into a snowflake.

Several additional clauses are used in the CREATE MATERIALIZED VIEW statement that have not been shown here. These specify when the view is to be created, how it is kept in sync with the base table, storage parameters for the table it creates, and whether query rewrite should be enabled. Several database parameters control how the materialized view is leveraged, and packaged procedures provide a means to populate or refresh the view, alter its definition and capabilities, or destroy it.

Clearly, query rewrite should be enabled once the view is populated with data. This allows the database to perform the critical aggregate navigation service so that end users do not need to access the view directly.

The view may be refreshed manually by periodically invoking a command to update it, or kept in sync with the base table in real time. If manual refreshes are selected, the view will become out-of-date when the base table is updated. Database parameters determine whether the outdated materialized view will be used to respond to a query. Given the principle that dimensional aggregates must return the same results as the base table, the database should be configured not to provide results from a stale materialized view. If the view is to be kept in sync with the base schema in real time, additional logs must be associated with the base tables to capture changes and trigger updates to the materialized view.

Living with Materialized Query Tables

The DB2 RDBMS from IBM provides a feature called *materialized query tables*, which can provide aggregate navigation capabilities in a manner similar to Oracle's materialized views. When a materialized query table aggregates data, it is also referred to as a *summary table*. Previous versions of DB2 referred to summary tables as *automatic summary tables*.

Materialized query tables can be used to implement pre-joined aggregates and aggregate fact tables in much the same way that materialized views have been described. The primary difference is one of syntax. This section will briefly look at examples of these applications and then study how DB2 features can be used to build dimensional aggregates that require aggregate dimensions.

Using Materialized Query Tables

A materialized query table is a special type of table that caches the results of a SQL SELECT statement in permanent storage. The SQL SELECT statement may join together data from multiple tables and may aggregate one or more facts. The results of this query are computed and stored in the materialized query table. The database optimizer is aware of this pre-computed aggregation and is able to rewrite queries to access it when appropriate.

This approach is consistent with the one depicted in Figure 4.12. In this case, the aggregate table is a materialized query table. Its defining query is used by the RDBMS to populate it with data, and it is leveraged by the query rewrite mechanism to provide aggregate navigation services.

Materialized Query Tables as Pre-Joined Aggregates

As with materialized views, the simplest application of a materialized query table is a pre-joined aggregate. The defining query for the materialized query table selects the appropriate dimensions and fact aggregations, joining to the necessary dimension tables.

In the previous section, a materialized view was used to implement the pre-joined aggregate depicted in Figure 4.14. Under DB2, this aggregate would be implemented using a materialized query table. Recall that the Orders schema includes dimensions for Product, Day, Salesperson, and Customer. A pre-joined aggregate that aggregates order dollars by Day and Brand is desired. The defining query for the pre-joined aggregate simply selects the desired attributes from the base star:

```
CREATE TABLE ord_bwt_date_brand AS
(SELECT     /* the defining query begins here */
  day.full_date,
  product.brand_name,
  sum( order_facts.order_dollars )as order_dollars
FROM
  order_facts, day, product
WHERE
  order_facts.day_key = day.day_key and
  order_facts.product_key = product.product_key
GROUP BY
  day.full_date,
  product.brand_name )
```

This should look familiar; it is almost identical to the corresponding CREATE MATERIALIZED VIEW statement under Oracle. Like its Oracle counterpart, the statement would also include several options that control the behavior of the materialized query table. The RDBMS uses this query to build the aggregate table.

This statement creates a physical table that contains the results of the defining query. Once this summary table is in place, populated with data, and enabled for query optimization, it will automatically be leveraged as appropriate. The query optimizer compares user queries to the defining query in order to identify potential query rewrites. If the summary table is identified as an option, the RDBMS optimizer compares the estimated cost, or execution time, for each query, and chooses the one that is most efficient.

> **TIP** Materialized query tables can be used to implement pre-joined aggregates.

For example, the user may issue the following query:

```
SELECT
  brand,
  sum(order_dollars)
FROM
  order_facts, product, day
WHERE
  order_facts.product_key = product.product_key and
  order_facts.day_key = day.day_key and
  day.full_date = to_date('11/1/2006')
GROUP BY
  brand
```

Based on the defining query for the summary table, the RDBMS determines that the summary is able to respond to the query. It compares execution cost for a query against the base schema with the execution cost to access the summary table. The summary table proves the more efficient responder because it is significantly smaller and the RDBMS will not have to perform any joins. The RDBMS rewrites the query to access the summary table:

```
SELECT
  brand,
  sum (order_dollars)
FROM
  ord_bwt_day_brand
WHERE
  full_date = to_date('11/1/2006')
GROUP BY
  brand
```

This rewritten query will be executed much more efficiently. This process is almost identical to the one involving materialized views.

Materialized Query Tables as Aggregate Fact Tables (Without Aggregate Dimensions)

As discussed under materialized views, an aggregate star always includes an aggregate fact table. The dimensions associated with the aggregate star may be base dimensions and/or aggregate dimensions. An aggregate dimension is required only when a base dimension is partially summarized.

When the aggregate star includes no aggregate dimensions, a materialized query table is easy to define. The aggregate fact table can be fully described by a query against the base schema. Its columns will include aggregated facts, grouped by keys to the surviving dimensions.

TIP Aggregate fact tables that do not reference aggregate dimension tables can be constructed using a materialized query table.

An example of this type of aggregate fact table was shown in Figure 4.11, and you have already seen that this was easily implemented using materialized views. The same holds true for materialized query tables; the SQL SELECT statement that appears in the figure serves as the defining query for the materialized query table. As with materialized views, the query rewrite mechanism will evaluate user queries and cost estimates to determine when the aggregate should be substituted.

Materialized Query Tables and Aggregate Dimension Tables

Earlier, you saw that database objects like materialized query tables cannot effectively define an aggregate fact table and associated aggregate dimension table. As depicted in Figure 4.12, each can be built, but when queries are rewritten, the RDBMS fails to recognize their relationship to one another.

Like Oracle, DB2 has added functionality that enables the identification of one or more hierarchies within a dimension. This permits the construction of aggregate fact tables that would otherwise require an aggregate dimension table. In the case of DB2, this capability is not provided via declarative SQL. Instead, it is accomplished by establishing a *cube view*.

Cube views are an optional component for DB2 that extend the metadata catalog to include OLAP-oriented information about the schema. They also enable DB2 to provide several services that leverage that information. Using cube views, it is possible to build a materialized query table that partially summarizes a dimension and have the RDBMS engine automatically rewrite queries to access the summary table as appropriate.

Cube views are defined using the OLAP center. This application allows a star or snowflake to be described in explicit dimensional terms. This dimensional representation is known as a *cube*. The cube model is defined in terms of facts and dimensions, which map back to the relational schema. Dimensions are defined in terms of hierarchies and levels. A level contains key attributes and related attributes that are functionally dependent on the key attributes.

Once the cube view has been established for the base schema, the RDBMS is aware of the functional dependencies among attributes in the dimension table. These attributes can be leveraged by a materialized query table. The query rewriter can use this information to join the summary table back to the dimension if a query needs functionally dependent attributes.

TIP Materialized query tables are not used to construct aggregate dimensions. Instead, dimensional hierarchies are declared as part of a cube view. A materialized query table can then reference levels within the hierarchy.

Consider the Orders schema once again. You wish to implement an aggregate that summarizes order facts by Day and Brand. Brand is a summarization of the Product dimension. A cube view is established that describes the facts and dimensions of the base schema. As part of this definition, the hierarchy within the Product dimension is explicitly defined. The Brand level is identified by the brand_code, and brand_name and brand_manager are dependent. Once you have established the cube view, a materialized query table can be defined that uses the day_key and brand_code to define the desired aggregate fact table. This is illustrated in Figure 4.16.

Because the RDBMS is aware of the functional dependency of brand_name and brand_manager on the brand_code attribute, it can join the summary table to Product if these attributes are needed. The result is functionally the same as having a Brand table.

Additional Considerations

Additional considerations are similar to those already discussed for Oracle. Documentation of the aggregate schema design should acknowledge the use of materialized query tables and cube views. As mentioned in Chapter 3, the defining query can be included with the documentation for a pre-joined aggregate or aggregate fact table.

The design of aggregate dimensions is reduced to a logical exercise, but their inclusion in system documentation may enhance schema understanding. Dimensional hierarchies must be documented and defined, as they will become a critical piece of the cube view. Be sure that there is a defining attribute for each level of a hierarchy. If one does not exist, it must be created and managed as part of the base dimension table.

Several additional clauses are used in the CREATE TABLE statement that have not been shown here. These specify when the materialized query table is to be created, how it is kept in sync with the base table, and whether query rewrite should be enabled. Additional commands can enable or disable rewrite based on the summary table, provide a means to populate or refresh it, alter its definition and capabilities, or destroy it.

Working Without an Aggregate Navigator

The option of working without an aggregate navigator is universally available. While not ideal, this approach can provide limited benefit. It is important to understand the limitations of the approach if it is to be used effectively.

Base Schema

Cube View

Materialized Query Table

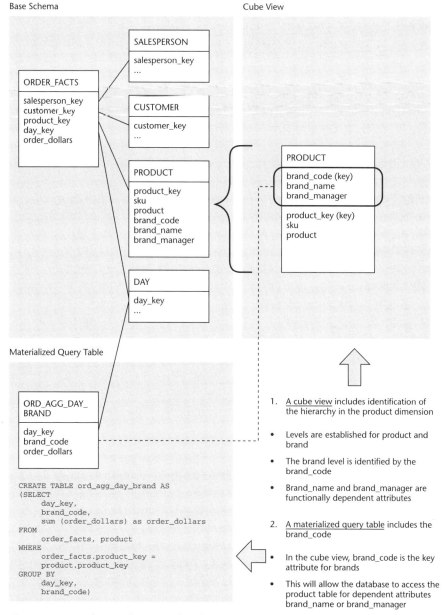

```
CREATE TABLE ord_agg_day_brand AS
(SELECT
     day_key,
     brand_code,
     sum (order_dollars) as order_dollars
FROM
     order_facts, product
WHERE
     order_facts.product_key =
     product.product_key
GROUP BY
     day_key,
     brand_code)
```

1. A cube view includes identification of
    the hierarchy in the product dimension

  • Levels are established for product and
    brand

  • The brand level is identified by the
    brand_code

  • Brand_name and brand_manager are
    functionally dependent attributes

2. A materialized query table includes the
    brand_code

  • In the cube view, brand_code is the key
    attribute for brands

  • This will allow the database to access the
    product table for dependent attributes
    brand_name or brand_manager

Figure 4.16   A base schema with cube view and a materialized query table.

Human Decisions

Because there is no aggregate navigator, the appropriate table for every query must be chosen by someone. As you have already seen, this requires an understanding of the dimensionality of the query, the dimensionality of the aggregate schema design, the relative size of the potential responders, and their availability status. This can be a confusing process for end users, but technical personnel may be able to make these choices. The portfolio of aggregates can be managed with these groups in mind.

> **TIP** With no aggregate navigator, deploy few if any aggregates to end users building ad hoc queries. Technical staff building pre-defined reports can be expected to handle a larger pool.

Users building ad hoc queries should be bothered with very few, if any, aggregates. All should have access to the base schema. For power users who are up to the technical burden, provide access to one or more aggregates. Experience suggests that the number of aggregates made available in this manner should be very small—one to two at the most. This ensures that the most efficient aggregate will be selected, and also reduces the functional dependency of the queries built by these users on aggregates that may be changed in the future. This also minimizes the risk of querying aggregate tables when they are out of sync with the base schema.

Technical personnel building pre-defined parameterized reports can be expected to manage a slightly larger pool of aggregates. Information on available aggregates and their relative size should be available to all developers. Testing the performance benefit of using an aggregate should be incorporated into the process of developing reports.

Maintaining the Aggregate Portfolio

Without the aggregate navigator, every query must be expressed in aggregate-aware SQL. The selection of the appropriate tables is done manually during the report design process, not automatically at execution time. This complicates the process of adding or removing aggregates, and requires that aggregates be kept on-line and in sync at all times.

Changes to the aggregate portfolio will have an impact on existing queries and reports because they contain direct references to aggregates. Removal of an aggregate table will cause any report that references it to fail because the table no longer exists. Addition of an aggregate will not improve query performance without rewriting applicable queries and reports. This dependency between aggregate schema and reports must be incorporated into the processes of building reports maintaining aggregates.

> **TIP** Without an aggregate navigator, changes to the aggregate portfolio will affect queries and reports that have already been built.

The dependency of predefined reports on aggregate tables must be documented as reports are developed. This allows analysis of the impact of changes to the aggregate portfolio on existing information products. When the aggregate portfolio is to be changed, the planning process must include redevelopment of any report that included an aggregate being removed.

Impact on the ETL Process

Because aggregate-aware SQL is hard-coded into queries and reports, the aggregates must remain on-line whenever the data warehouse is available to end users. Otherwise, execution of dependent reports will fail. And because they cannot be taken on- and off-line independently of the base schema, the aggregates must be kept up-to-date whenever the data warehouse is available. Otherwise, they would violate the guiding principle of accuracy.

TIP Without an aggregate navigator, aggregate availability cannot be considered. The base schema and aggregate must be loaded simultaneously, or the warehouse must be taken off-line during the load process.

These restrictions must be accommodated by the ETL process that constructs the aggregates. One way to accommodate this is to load the base schema and aggregate simultaneously. As you will see in the next chapter, this makes changes to the aggregate portfolio difficult. By loading aggregates separately from the base schema, portfolio changes affect a smaller part of the ETL process.

If the base schema and aggregates are loaded in separate processes, the warehouse must be unavailable to users during the entire load process. This prevents users from running a report that references an aggregate that is out of sync with the base schema.

Summary

Using dimensional aggregates introduces new requirements for the data warehouse architecture. The appropriate table to respond to a given query is a function of the dimensionality of the query, the dimensionality of the aggregate schema design, the relative size of the potential responders, and their availability status.

The purpose of an aggregate navigator is to make these decisions at query execution time. This chapter identified a series of requirements for this capability, and used it to evaluate the three most common styles of aggregate navigation. Additionally, this chapter looked at specific implementations from Oracle and IBM. These implementations have the distinct advantage of *building* the aggregates, as well as providing aggregate navigation services. In other cases, aggregate construction will be a manual process.

The next two chapters look at the construction process in detail. Aggregate processing will be placed in the context of the overall ETL process in Chapter 5. The steps required to create and maintain the aggregate tables themselves are identified in Chapter 6.

ETL Part 1:
Incorporating Aggregates

Before aggregates can be used, they must be loaded with summary data. Aggregate processing is therefore a major component of the process that loads the data warehouse, often referred to as *the ETL process* or *the load process*.

This is the first of two chapters that explores the loading of aggregates. It describes the process of loading the base schema of the data warehouse and what considerations arise when aggregates are added to the mix. The next chapter explores in detail the specific processes that load aggregate tables.

This chapter begins with an overview of the ETL process for the base schema. A critical part of any data warehouse implementation, the load process may involve several tools and must solve some difficult problems.

Next, this chapter describes the processes involved in loading the base schema tables. While tool-specific implementations will vary widely, every load must meet certain basic requirements. These requirements will serve as the basis for high-level process flows, illustrating the steps required to load base dimension and fact tables.

Once the base schema load has been described, this chapter looks at how aggregates are incorporated into the process. The presence of aggregates requires that the load process manage the availability of aggregates, taking them off-line during processes that update base tables. The aggregate processing may take two forms: a complete rebuild or an incremental refresh.

Using RDBMS features such as materialized views to implement aggregates eliminates much of the work of building the aggregates, as described in the Chapter 6. But they still require some special attention. You must manage parameters so that the RDBMS knows when aggregates are to be used in rewritten queries, and you must select an approach to their refresh.

Last, this chapter examines a real-time warehouse load process and studies its impact on aggregates.

The Load Process

The development of load process is a critical component of every implementation. It holds the most risk and accounts for the majority of person-hours allocated to the project. The load is constructed using a diverse set of tools collectively known as *ETL tools*. Regardless of the specific tools used, the major processes of any warehouse load can be defined, and each process can be functionally decomposed into smaller processes.

The Importance of the Load

During a data warehouse implementation, the lion's share of project resources is focused on the development of the load process. Logically, this should make sense: The dimensional model has been designed to simplify the reporting process. As you saw in Chapter 1, most data warehouse queries follow a simple pattern. The load process does the difficult work that makes these queries possible, transforming a transaction-oriented schema design into a dimensional design. By performing this work once, when the schema is loaded, it will not be necessary each time an analytic query is performed.

The load process is also the focus of a disproportionate share of project risk. The complexity of transforming the data from a transactional design to an analytic design is one factor. Additionally, it is during the load process that data from multiple systems will be brought together. The load process must deal with the varying definition of similar entities across different systems and produce a standard picture for the data warehouse. This is no small challenge, as the warehouse must produce results that are consistent with the transaction-based systems.

Often during the load process the quality of source system data is discovered to be poor. Important attributes of the source systems may prove to be sparsely populated, or used inconsistently by users. This potentially affects the design of the data warehouse schema, crippling key functionality.

Tools of the Load

The data warehouse load may be developed using a specialized ETL product, or coded using general purpose programming tools. In either case, the development platform of the load will be referred to here as the ETL tool.

A load that is coded without the use of a packaged ETL product is referred to as a *hand-coded* load. This type of load centers on custom programs to extract and transform data. These programs are written using tools available on the source and/or target systems. For example, where a mainframe data source is involved, much of the processing may be hand-coded in COBOL. Where the data sources are primarily relational, much of the processing may be performed through development of stored procedures in the RDBMS.

The hand-coded load is attractive for numerous reasons. First, the tools required are already present in the enterprise. They are used to build and maintain the operational systems. Second, tool-specific training is not required; resources are readily available that are skilled in the use of these tools. These factors are often combined into a cost-based argument for hand coding.

The true price of a hand-coded load must also include maintenance of the data warehouse load. In comparison to loads that are built using packaged ETL tools, the hand-coded load is much more difficult to change. The load consists of lines and lines of code, which must be carefully adjusted when changes are required. This is particularly onerous for an individual who was not involved in developing the initial load. As you will see in Chapter 7, data warehouse development is most successful as an iterative process. The complexity and duration of an iteration loop is also dramatically increased with the hand-coded approach.

Additionally, a hand-coded load does not provide strong metadata about the transactional sources of data, the data warehouse schema, or the load process itself. The maintenance of this information therefore becomes an additional task. This metadata is used to provide end users an understanding of the lineage of the information in the data warehouse, and it is used by I.T. to assess the impact of changes to the design of the transaction and or warehouse systems. It must be managed externally to the load routines, and therefore can become out of sync with the reality.

For these reasons, specialized ETL software is usually implemented. Packaged ETL software typically maintains a repository of information about the source systems and data warehouse schema, as well as the processes that are used to extract, transform and load the data. Graphical tools allow developers to construct these processes without writing code, increasing the understandability and maintainability of the load. ETL software also provides functionality specifically suited to the warehouse load, such as key management capabilities and parallelization of standard processes.

ETL tools generally fall into two categories: code generators and server-based tools. Code-generating ETL tools output programs that will be executed externally to load the data warehouse. This may be mainframe-based code (such as COBOL), RDBMS-based code (such as stored procedures), or code that runs on an application server (such as Java). Server-based ETL tools are more common today. They include their own engines that carry out the load process, interacting with sources and targets directly.

In addition to the ETL software, the load process may involve a variety of additional tools. These may include mainframe extraction utilities, integration and messaging software, data cleansing applications, specialized sorting tools, and automation software. Each of these tools assists the load processing in one way or another, performing specific tasks with unique efficiency.

The workings of the ETL tool and associated tools are unique to each commercial product. But regardless of the implementation, the processing requirements of the load can be broken down into a series of tasks. Information must be extracted from source systems, dimensional attributes must be constructed, warehouse keys must be established, and so forth. The discussion of the load process in this book deals with these logical processes, which are common to every load.

Incremental Loads and Changed Data Identification

The data warehouse load is often described as two processes: the initial load and the incremental load. The initial load is theoretically a one-time-only process in which all existing source data from history to date is placed into the data warehouse. It is followed by periodic incremental loads, in which only new and changed data from the source system is processed and added to the data warehouse tables. The incremental load handles less data, but does more work. It must identify and apply slow-change processing rules. As you will see shortly, these rules dictate how to process data that has changed in the source system.

The reality of data warehouse loads is that every load is an incremental load. The notion of an initial load that can ignore slow-change processing is usually a fallacy. A warehouse that is loaded on a daily basis, for example, may encounter multiple slow changes within a day. Even where this is not the case, the initial load is likely to include historic data as well as current data. The history will be loaded in time slices, starting with the oldest slice. Only the first slice will be a true initial load. The processing of each subsequent slice must account for slow changes.

Given that an incremental load is required, a separate initial load process is superfluous. The incremental load process will suffice. It can be used for the initial population of the warehouse; all records processed the first time it runs are new records.

For these reasons, an initial load that ignores slow-change processing is not usually part of a production data warehouse. An initial load may be a useful prototyping tool, where a quick load of sample data is used to validate a schema design. But as a production capability, its value is probably dubious and certainly redundant.

TIP All processes discussed in this chapter will perform an incremental load; they will not assume that the warehouse tables are empty.

One of the keys to making the incremental load process as efficient as possible is the development of a mechanism that allows it to consider only source data that has changed or is new. This reduces the processing requirements of the data warehouse load significantly. Information that has not changed does not have to be analyzed and processed.

A variety of techniques for the identification of changed data exist, but their enumeration and explanation are beyond the scope of this book. It will be assumed that some sort of changed data identification process is in place. Of course, in some cases, it is determined that it is more efficient to let the warehouse process all data during each incremental load. The processes developed in this chapter and the next will continue to function in such a situation; they simply process more information.

Chapter 6 will, however, develop a process for the identification of changed data for the processing of *aggregates*. As you will see, this is accomplished by adding a date of last update attribute to the base schema. The inclusion of these attributes was first introduced in Chapter 3. Their use will be discovered in Chapter 6.

The Top-Level Process

The discussion of the data warehouse load in this chapter and the next will be broken down into high-level processes. Each high-level process, in turn, will be broken down and discussed in further detail. The top-level processes around which this discussion is organized are depicted in Figure 5.1.

This chapter begins with a discussion of the processes that load the base schema—step 1 in Figure 5.1. This process is broken down into two major steps: loading the base dimension tables (step 1.1), and loading the base fact tables (step 1.2). As you will see, there are good reasons to perform these tasks in distinct processes, and to load dimension tables before the fact tables.

Next, this chapter discusses how aggregates fit into the high-level process (step 2). You will see why the aggregate load should be performed in separate processes, look at different strategies for loading aggregates, and understand their relationship to the base schema load. The detailed processes of loading aggregate dimension and fact tables (steps 2.1 and 2.2) are explored in Chapter 6.

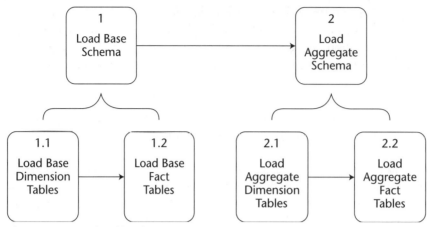

Figure 5.1 Top-level load processes.

The high-level processes and their breakdowns, as described in these chapters, represent distinct categories of tasks. While they are illustrated with dependencies (the arrows in the diagrams), they are really generalizations. The actual load dependencies in a data warehouse are table-level dependencies.

For example, Figure 5.1 breaks down the base schema load into two processes: loading dimension tables and loading fact tables. The line between the two processes indicates that the dimension tables must be loaded before the fact tables. This distinction makes sense at a high level; the dimension tables must be loaded first because fact tables will require their primary keys.

But note that the actual dependencies exist between specific tables. For example, the load of a particular fact table may begin as soon as all its related dimensions have been loaded. There may be other dimensions that are still being loaded; they can continue in parallel. Any fact tables that reference these must continue to wait.

Loading the Base Star Schema

The process of loading the base schema requires that fact tables and dimension tables be loaded. Fact tables bear foreign keys to the dimension tables and are therefore dependent entities. This would suggest that dimension tables be loaded first.

When there is a single source application, it is possible to take one extract or query and process all data in a single load program. The program would scrutinize each record, insert or update each dimension as required, and construct a fact record. This is sometimes favored because of the assumption that it permits a single pass through the incoming data set.

However, several factors may argue for multiple processes. A single process will analyze dimensional information redundantly, once for each fact rather than once for each distinct dimension record. Many dimensions may involve multiple data sources, perhaps best served by creating a staging area for the source data.

The most important reason to develop a separate load process for each table is maintainability. A single load that updates multiple tables can be very difficult to maintain. And as the data warehouse grows in size, maintenance becomes a more important issue. A change to the rule by which a dimension value is decoded would require development and QA on a process that loads that table, along with several other dimension tables and a fact table. As the scope of the warehouse increases, some of these tables may also be referenced by additional fact tables. These fact table loads will have to wait until the first fact table has been loaded because the same load routine includes needed dimensions.

TIP Separate load processes should be dedicated to each warehouse table.

Because the fact tables contain foreign keys that reference dimension tables, the dimension tables must be populated first. An overview of the load process must therefore begin with the dimensions.

Loading Dimension Tables

The dimension table load requires processing incoming data according to rules that were established during the design of the base schema. The dimension load must acquire the source data, assemble dimension values, process new dimension records, process type 1 changes, and process type 2 changes. The way a load meets these requirements can be understood in terms of a process flow diagram.

Attributes of the Dimension Table

Before looking at the load process for the dimension table, you must review the key characteristics of the dimension table. A proper understanding of these characteristics is essential in constructing the load. Recall from Chapter 3 that the design identifies natural keys and surrogate keys. The remaining attributes are classified according to how changes will be handled—through type 1 or type 2 processing. Figure 5.2 illustrates the characteristics of attributes of a product dimension table.

PRODUCT
product_key (sk) sku (nk) product_name (1) product_description (1) unit_of_measure (1) brand_name (1) brand_code (2) brand_manager (2) category_name (1) category_code (2) date_created (hk) date_updated (hk)

Type	Description
Natural Key (NK)	Uniquely identifies a record in the source system
Surrogate Key (SK)	Uniquely identifies a row in the dimension table
Type 1 Attribute (1)	If this attribute changes on the source, update corresponding warehouse records
Type 2 Attribute (2)	If this attribute changes on the source, generate a new warehouse record
Housekeeping (HK)	Column that has no business meaning; used in maintenance of warehouse tables

Figure 5.2   Types of columns in a dimension table.

The natural key is a unique identifier on the source system only. In this example, that natural key is SKU (an acronym for "stock keeping unit"), as indicated by the designation NK. In the Product dimension table, the natural key may have multiple corresponding records because the data warehouse handles changes differently than source systems do. For example, the warehouse will create a new record each time the category of a particular SKU is changed.

The surrogate key is generated specifically for the data warehouse. In Figure 5.2, the surrogate key for the product dimension is product_key, designated by SK. It is a single attribute that uniquely identifies a row in the warehouse table. Surrogate keys are used in the data warehouse because the natural key is insufficient to uniquely identify a record. While a multi-part key is possible, the creation of surrogate keys permits a single column to be used to join the dimension table to fact tables. In the example, a multi-part key would include SKU, brand_code, brand_manager, and category_code. The creation of product_key saves considerable space in the fact table, and improves join performance.

Each of the remaining dimension attributes is categorized as a type 1 or type 2 attribute. These classifications determine what happens when the attribute changes on the source system. Because an incremental load is being designed, the load process must account for potential changes to these attributes.

When a type 2 attribute changes, a new record is generated in the data warehouse. For the product table in Figure 5.2, a change to the category_code, brand_code, or brand_manager of a SKU will require a new record. When a type 1 attribute changes, the value is updated in corresponding dimension records. For the product table in Figure 5.2, a change to the product_name, category_name, or brand_name of a SKU requires existing dimension records for that SKU to be updated. There may be more than one row in the dimension to update for the SKU because type 2 changes may have already occurred.

Housekeeping columns are also created as part of the dimension table. These columns have no business meaning; their primary purpose is to aid the processes that load data. In the diagram, they are labeled HK. As you will see, the date_updated column will prove useful later when building aggregates.

Requirements for the Dimension Load Process

The process of loading a dimension table must incorporate the following major requirements:

- Extraction of the necessary source data
- Assembly of the dimensional attributes
- Warehouse key management
- Processing of new records
- Processing of type 1 changes
- Processing of type 2 changes

The specific means by which these requirements are addressed will depend on a wide number of factors, including the source system platform and design, the ETL toolset being used, and the warehouse design. But the process can be understood at a logical level through a process flow diagram. One logical breakdown of tasks is illustrated in Figure 5.3.

Note that this is one possible breakdown of the major tasks in a load process. Numerous alternative decompositions are possible, and the ETL tool may require defining and sequencing tasks differently. But this illustration captures the essential characteristics of any dimension load and serves as the basis for the discussion to follow.

Extracting and Preparing the Record

The first two major tasks require the acquisition of the necessary source data and the construction of dimensional attributes. Good design documentation should guide these tasks. In Figure 5.3, step 1.1.1 calls for the acquisition of the source data needed to load the dimension. As discussed previously, this may leverage a changed data identification mechanism such that the load process need only consider new and changed data.

The source data may be acquired through a number of means. For example, mainframe data may be extracted programmatically into a file or through specialized utilities. Relational data may be extracted directly via SQL or provided through an export file. Real-time data may arrive through a messaging system or a Web Service. External data may be supplied on-line or through batch extracts. If the source data is relational, it should be extracted with a SELECT DISTINCT to avoid unnecessary processing. If it is non-relational, developers may choose to first bulk-load it into a relational staging area so that SQL operations can be used in this initial step.

A dimension table with multiple sources may require multiple extraction processes, with additional processing to consolidate the information extracted into a single pool of records for processing. Or, separate load processes may be designed for each of the sources.

After the data that has been extracted, it must be organized so that it can be processed one row at a time. This may require that source data be pivoted or transposed so that all the significant attributes that belong together in a dimension record are in a single row. This process is represented by step 1.1.2. In many cases, there is little work to be done, but in other cases this step may call for intensive processing. Hierarchical data structures may require flattening; denormalized data structures may require pivoting, and so forth.

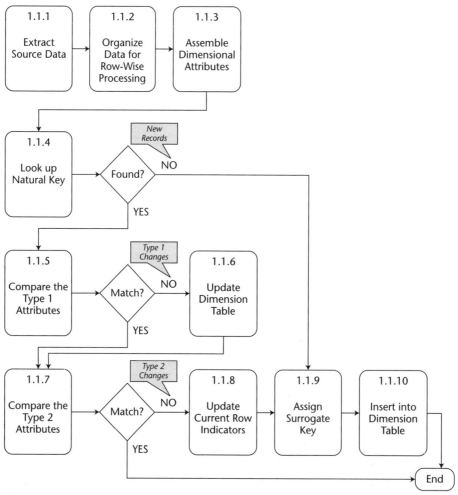

Figure 5.3   Loading a base dimension table.

Once the source data is captured and restructured as a series of rows, step 1.1.3 takes each row of source data and assembles the dimensional attributes. This is a matter of applying transformation rules as spelled out in the design documentation. Codes may be decoded into descriptive values. Fields with multi-part attributes may be split into a series of attributes. Sets of fields may be concatenated together. Null field values may replaced with more understandable text such as "unavailable" or "unknown." The case and format of attributes may be adjusted, and so forth. Some of this task may be pushed back to the process that selects source data. This task might also be broken down to include data cleansing tasks, such as name and address standardization.

Once these first three tasks are completed, a set of *potential* dimension records is now ready for processing. The next several tasks will determine how each of these records is handled. New records, type 1 changes, and type 2 changes must all be processed. Some records may include both type 1 and type 2 changes.

Process New Records

New records are those that have a natural key that has not been encountered in the warehouse before. When a new record is identified, it must be assigned a surrogate key and inserted into the dimension table. In Figure 5.3, these tasks are carried out in steps 1.1.4, 1.1.9, and 1.1.10.

To determine if an incoming record is new, its natural key is searched for in the dimension table. This check, performed in step 1.1.4 is referred to as a *lookup*. If the natural key is not found in the existing table, the record is new. Step 1.1.9 assigns the next available surrogate key to the record, and step 1.1.10 loads it into the product dimension table. If, on the other hand, a record is found during step 1.1.4, it must be further examined to determine if it has undergone type 1 or type 2 changes.

> **TIP** New records are identified by looking up the natural key of a source record in the existing dimension table. If the natural key is not found, a new record has been identified.

An example is shown in Figure 5.4. The top part of the figure shows rows in the existing Product dimension table. The bottom part of the figure shows records being processed as part of an incremental load. The first record is SKU 12B88. In the Product dimension table, check to see if there is already a row for this SKU value. The value is *not found*, so the record is new; the warehouse has never encountered this SKU before. It will be assigned a surrogate key (step 1.1.9) and added to the Product dimension table (step 1.1.10.)

Existing PRODUCT Dimension Table:

	SK	NK	Type 1	Type 2	Type 1	Type 2	
	product_key	sku	product_name	brand_code	brand_name	brand_manager	Additional attributes.... →
	1011	13X22	9x12 Envelope	67A	Bubble Pak	Riley, Wes	
	1022	13X22	9x12 Envelope	67A	Bubble Pak	Johnson, Rena	
	1302	A0322	6x6x6 Box	80B	FlatBox	Jones, Dei	
	1499	B1205	Sur Stik	255	Seal It	Hale, Kay	

Records being processed by Incremental Load:

	sku	product_name	brand_code	brand_name	brand_manager	
1	12B88	9x12 Envelope	67A	Bubble Pak	Johnson, Rena	A new dimension record
2	13X22	9x12 Bubble Envelope	67A	Bubble Pak	Johnson, Rena	Type 1 change affecting two records
3	A0322	6x6x6 Box	80B	FlatBox	Wang, Jay	Type 2 Change
4	B1205	Sure Stick Tape	255	Seal It	Davis, Jon	Type 1 and Type 2 Changes

Figure 5.4 Processing the Product dimension.

Each of the remaining SKUs in the example is already represented in the Product dimension. They must now be examined to determine if they contain any type 1 or type 2 changes. Note that if there had been no change data identification process, there might also be records that contain no changes.

Process Type 1 Changes

Every record that is not new may contain type 1 changes. When a type 1 attribute changes on the source side, it is overwritten in the data warehouse. To identify a type 1 change, an incoming record is compared to a corresponding record in the warehouse. The type 1 attributes are compared. If they do not match, a type 1 change has been identified. In Figure 5.3, this comparison is performed in step 1.1.5.

For the Product table, the product SKU is used to identify a corresponding warehouse record. The type 1 attributes are compared; if they do not match, the SKU has undergone a type 1 change. In the example from Figure 5.4, SKU 13X22 has undergone a change in its product_name, from 9x12 Envelope to 9x12 Bubble Envelope. This is a type 1 attribute, so the dimension table must be updated with this change.

> **TIP** Type 1 changes are identified by comparing the type 1 attributes of an incoming record to those of a record in a dimension that has the same natural key. If any type 1 attributes do not match, a type 1 change has occurred.

Type 1 changes must be applied to all corresponding warehouse records. There may be more than one dimension row corresponding to the source record that has changed because it may already have undergone type 2 changes. In step 1.1.6, the changes are applied to all existing dimension table records that have the same natural key.

This is indeed the case for SKU 13X22. Because this SKU's brand_manager has changed in the past, it has two records in the dimension table. For both records, the product_name must be updated.

> **TIP** Because type 2 changes may have occurred, a type 1 change may need to be applied to multiple rows in the dimension table.

Notice that while all corresponding dimension rows must be updated in step 1.1.6, the comparison in step 1.1.5 need only consider one dimension table record. This is because the application of type 1 changes to all corresponding rows ensures that the corresponding values will be identical for a given SKU that appears multiple times. Like step 1.1.4, this can be accomplished via a lookup in the dimension table; the values being looked up include the natural key and type 1 attributes. If a match is not found, there is a type 1 change.

Process Type 2 Changes

After type 1 changes have been identified and applied, the source record must be checked for type 2 changes. These are identified by looking up the combination of the natural key and all type 2 attributes in the dimension table. In Figure 5.3, this takes place in step 1.1.7. If a match is found, the incoming record is properly represented in the dimension table, and it can be discarded. If it is not found, a type 2 change has occurred. The record is assigned a surrogate key (step 1.1.9) and loaded into the warehouse table (step 1.1.10). Step 1.1.8 is an optimization that helps with fact table loads. It is addressed later in this chapter.

> **TIP** Type 2 changes are identified by looking for the combination of the natural key and type 2 attributes of the record being processed in the dimension table. If not found, a type 2 change has occurred.

For example, the third incoming row in Figure 5.4 contains the SKU A0322. This SKU is represented in the Product dimension table, but its brand_manager has been changed. This requires the insertion of a new row into the Product dimension table.

OPTIMIZING LOOKUPS

The process of looking up information in an existing dimension table is one of the more resource-intensive parts of the load process. Lookups are often optimized by loading the entire lookup table into memory, or at least the columns that are involved in the comparison. This technique is called *caching*. It ensures that the lookup will be executed quickly. During a dimension table load, it is possible that the dimension table will be changed. Updates to the dimension must also be applied to this in-memory copy.

The diagram in Figure 5.3 depicts three distinct lookup processes: one that identifies new records, one that identifies type 1 changes, and one that identifies type 2 changes. Developers sometimes forgo the identification of new records; these records can be processed as if they were type 2 changes. However, this can introduce unnecessary type 1 lookups.

Lookup performance can also suffer if there are a large number of attributes to compare. For example, a table with 22 type 2 attributes would require a large number of comparisons during step 1.1.7. To reduce this difficulty, developers often apply a hash function to the type 2 attributes of each row and store the result in a new column. Now, when an incoming record is being checked for type 2 changes, the same hash function can be applied to the incoming data. The result can be compared to the hash value of the existing row, replacing 22 comparisons with one. A separate hash value can also be constructed for the type 1 attributes of the row. These columns should never be exposed to end users; they are housekeeping columns intended to support the load process only.

Notice that the same record can contain both type 1 and type 2 changes. The next SKU, number B1205, has undergone changes in the product name and the brand_manager. The new product name is a type 1 change, which must be applied to all dimension records for the SKU. The new brand manager is a type 2 change, which requires a new record be inserted for the SKU. For this reason, step 1.1.6 is connected to step 1.1.7, rather than to the end of the process flow.

TIP A source record can contain both type 1 and type 2 changes.

The rules for processing records that combine type 1 and type 2 changes are complicated by the dependencies among attributes in the dimension. A change to a type 1 attribute, for example, may be discarded if that attribute is fully dependent on a natural key or type 2 attribute that has also changed. In the Product example, this would occur if the Brand of a Product were to change. The new record would include changed brand_code and brand_name columns, which are type 1 and type 2 attributes, respectively. However, a type 1 change has not actually occurred; the new brand name is a result of the new brand code. This phenomenon occurs whenever an attribute associated with a hierarchy level within a dimension is designated for type 1 processing. In these situations, the load process in Figure 5.3 must be adapted to scrutinize the defining attributes for the hierarchy level to determine if a type 1 change has actually occurred.

Loading Fact Tables

A fact table can be loaded once all the dimensions upon which it is dependent have been loaded. The major steps include acquisition of the source data, calculation and aggregation of the facts, and identification of surrogate keys.

Requirements for the Fact Table Load Process

Compared to the dimension load, the fact table load may seem simple. Much of the difficult work of loading the base schema is done in the dimension loads, where slow-change processing is performed. The fact table load is governed by the following requirements:

- Extract data from the source systems
- Calculate the facts
- Aggregate the facts to match the grain of the fact table
- Identify surrogate keys for each of the dimensions
- Load the new fact table records into the warehouse

A process supporting these requirements is depicted in Figure 5.5. Once again, this is a logical breakdown, meant to guide the discussion of the load process. The specific tasks and techniques used will vary based on source and target systems and design, the capabilities of the ETL tool being used, and developer preferences.

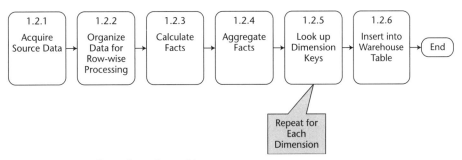

Figure 5.5   Loading a base fact table.

While the process itself may seem simpler, the processing requirements can be more intensive. The volume of transactions processed is likely to be greater than the number of dimension records processed, particularly if a changed data identification mechanism is aiding the dimension load process. And the key identification process will require a lookup into each of the associated dimensions.

Acquire Data and Assemble Facts

The first step is the extraction of the source data, step 1.2.1 in Figure 5.5. As in the dimension table load process, acquisition of source data may take place in a number of different ways, depending on the systems and tools available. The information needed for the fact table load process includes the data elements that will be used to create the facts and natural keys for each of the dimensions. This information should be available as part of the design documentation for the warehouse schema.

After source data has been acquired, it may be necessary to restructure the data so it can be processed one row at a time. For example, some facts may be stored in a series of repeating groups that represent different dimensional qual-ifications of the same fact. This data must be transposed into a format that rep-resents the structure required in the data warehouse. In the top portion of Figure 5.6, sales by each salesperson appear in separate columns. Each record must be transformed into a set of records that correspond to each of the actual days.

In another common situation, source systems provide each fact in a separate row. The records must be combined into a single record that contains each of the facts. In the bottom portion of Figure 5.6, source data provides sales_ dollars, margin_dollars, and quantity_sold in separate rows. The records are consolidated so that they appear as separate measurements. These and other transformations of the source data are represented by step 1.2.2 in Figure 5.5.

Next, facts must be calculated. For example, the star schema calls for an order_dollars fact, while transaction provides unit_price and quantity.

The fact is calculated by multiplying these two source attributes. Calcula-tion of facts can be more complex, especially if the source data is hierarchical, or if each fact is provided in a separate row. In these cases, it will be necessary to flatten the hierarchy or pivot the incoming data in order to compute the nec-essary facts. All this processing is part of step 1.2.3 in Figure 5.5.

If the source data is provided at a finer grain than is required by the data warehouse, it must also be aggregated. If this is the case, the warehouse may be throwing away valuable detail; let's hope the schema designers have con-sidered this move. In any case, the individual transactions are summarized for each set of natural keys to accomplish this aggregation. Care must be taken not to improperly aggregate semi-additive facts; it is assumed that non-additive facts have been broken down into fully additive components in the schema design. In Figure 5.5, aggregation is performed by step 1.2.4.

date	sku	smith	jones	johnson	nguyen	davis	lei
11/4/2007	X2271	2,404.00	9,055.33	7,055.22	1,001.01	877.00	1,200.42
11/4/2007	B1112	108.99	0	244.92	1201.98	755.00	0

date	sku	salesperson	sales
11/4/2007	X2271	Smith	2,404.00
11/4/2007	X2271	Jones	9,055.33
11/4/2007	X2271	Johnson	7,055.22
11/4/2007	X2271	Nguyen	1,001.01
11/4/2007	X2271	Davis	877.00
11/4/2007	X2271	Lei	1,200.42
11/4/2007	B1112	Smith	108.99
11/4/2007	B1112	Johnson	944.92
11/4/2007	B1112	Nguyen	1,201.98
11/4/2007	B1112	Davis	755.00

date	sku	salesrep	type	value
11/4/2007	X2271	1101	Sales Dollars	10,055.22
11/4/2007	X2271	1101	Margin Dollars	2,004.02
11/4/2007	X2271	1101	Quantity Sold	250
11/4/2007	X2271	2200	Sales Dollars	4,505.22
11/4/2007	X2271	2200	Margin Dollars	1,087.02
11/4/2007	X2271	2200	Quantity Sold	129

date	sku	salesrep	sales_dollars	margin_dollars	quantity_sold
11/4/2007	X2271	1101	10,055.22	2,004.02	250
11/4/2007	X2271	2200	4,505.22	1,087.02	129

Figure 5.6 Organizing source data for row-by-row processing.

TIP Fact processing begins by acquiring the source data, transforming it as necessary, computing facts, and aggregating them if needed. This may be repeated for multiple sources.

Where there are multiple source systems, this process may be repeated for each. Alternatively, the initial extractions may be performed separately, with extracted data consolidated into a single staging area. Subsequent tasks are then performed using this consolidated data set.

When the data source for the fact table is relational, these first four steps are often accomplished in a single query. The query selects the relevant natural keys, aggregates, and calculates facts, and groups the results by the appropriate dimensional attributes. In the next chapter, you see that this technique can be used to select data for the construction of aggregate tables.

Identification of Surrogate Keys

For each dimension related to the fact table, it is necessary to include the appropriate surrogate key in the fact table. Because the data being processed has come from a source system, only natural keys are available. The next major step is to use these natural keys to obtain the appropriate surrogate keys. This is step 1.2.5 in Figure 5.5. It must be repeated for each of the dimensions.

Identification of the surrogate keys is a lookup process, similar to the one used to check for existing dimension rows during the dimension table load. The natural key, provided by the source system, is looked for in the dimension table. When the appropriate dimension record is found, the corresponding surrogate key is obtained; this key is used when the fact table record is added to the fact table.

For example, when loading order_facts, it is necessary to assign a product key to each source record before it can be inserted into the fact table. The top portion of Figure 5.7 shows some records that are being processed by the fact table load. In the source system, products are identified by their SKU. This natural key has been acquired by the load process. For the first record to be processed, the SKU is A1011. This value is searched for in the dimension table. The value is found for the dimension row that is highlighted. The product_key for this dimension record contains the value 344. The aggregate fact will be assigned this key.

This process is complicated by the presence of type 2 slowly changing dimensions. If type 2 changes have occurred to the dimension record in question, more than one row may be found in the dimension table. To guarantee the correct dimension key, the lookup must also contain all type 2 attributes. This can be a resource-intensive task if there are a large number of type 2 attributes.

To simplify this process, designers often add a current_record column to the dimension table. This is a simple flag that is set to Current for the most recent version of the record and Not Current for previous versions. When a type 2 change occurs, the previous Current record is changed to Not Current. This allows the fact load to determine dimension keys using only the natural key and the current_record indicator.

Records being processed by Fact Load:

time_key	salesperson_ key	order_ dollars	margin_ dollars	sku		brand_ key
1	1202	1197	1,700.22	643.06	A1011	344
2	1202	1197	984.31	201.64	B3691	

Existing Product Dimension Table:

SK	NK	HK	Type 1	Type 2	Type 2
product_ key	sku	current_ record	product_ name	brand_ code	brand_ manager
22	A33	Current	Flat Box 12"	110	Lei, Michelle
344	A1011	Current	Packing Tape	221	Jones, Paul
1001	B3691	Not Current	TwineSpool	501	Smith, Dei
1201	B3691	Not Current	TwineSpool	501	Klein, Pete
2700	B3691	Current	TwineSpool	702	Jones, Fay

Figure 5.7 Looking up surrogate keys.

For example, in the Product dimension from Figure 5.7 brand_code and brand_manager are type 2 attributes. If either of these attributes changes for a SKU, new records are inserted into the warehouse table. So that fact lookups do not have to include all these attributes, a current_record column is added to the dimension. When a record is inserted into the dimension, the current_record indicator is set to Current. Each time a type 2 change is applied to the dimension, the new row's current_record value is set to Current and previously existing records have their current_record value set to Not Current. This task is performed by step 1.1.8 in the dimension load process from Figure 5.3.

An example of this technique applied to the Product dimension table is shown in Figure 5.7. The second record of data to be processed has a SKU of B3691, and the load program must identify the product_key to insert this transaction into the fact table. The dimension table is scanned for a record where the SKU is B3691 and current_record = "Current". A single record meets these conditions: product_key 2700. Notice that this technique assumes that the same record does not undergo multiple type 2 changes between loads.

> **TIP** New facts are assigned the appropriate surrogate keys through a lookup process. The natural key value is used as an index into the dimension table, and the corresponding surrogate key is retrieved.
>
> Because a single natural key may be represented in the dimension more than once, it is necessary to include type 2 attributes in this lookup or make use of a current_record indicator.

Note that the use of a current_record indicator requires that dimension loads do some additional work. Each time a type 2 change is applied to a dimension table, the previous Current record must be updated to Not Current.

Putting It All Together

A warehouse load consists of a set of processes that perform the tasks described previously. For each star, there will be one process for each of the dimensions and one for the fact table. The dependencies between these processes are determined by the dependencies among the warehouse tables. Each fact table is dependent on the dimension tables for which it holds foreign keys; the fact table load process, therefore, is dependent on the completion of the load processes for each of the dimensions.

These dependencies are taken into account when the load process is automated. Automation of the load may be accomplished using an ETL tool, or through separate enterprise automation tools. In addition to managing the tasks of the warehouse table load, the automation approach performs a number of other tasks, as required by the implementation. These may include locking end users out of the database during the load, dropping indexes or disabling referential integrity, FTP'ing an extract file, loading data into staging areas, paging the warehouse manager if there are load errors, and so forth.

Figure 5.8 illustrates the automation of a simple data warehouse containing two stars: order_facts and inventory_facts. The automation routine initiates the warehouse at a specific time, once necessary source files have been delivered. It then locks end users out of the database and disables referential integrity constraints.

Next, the actual load begins. Load processes are depicted for each table; their dependencies are illustrated using arrows. All the dimension tables can be loaded in parallel. Aware of task completion, the automation routine is able to launch fact table loads once the appropriate dimension tables have been loaded. Each fact table can be loaded only when related dimension loads have finished executing.

Once all tables have been loaded, the automation routine re-enables referential integrity and enables end user access to the warehouse. It may also page the warehouse manager if any errors have occurred.

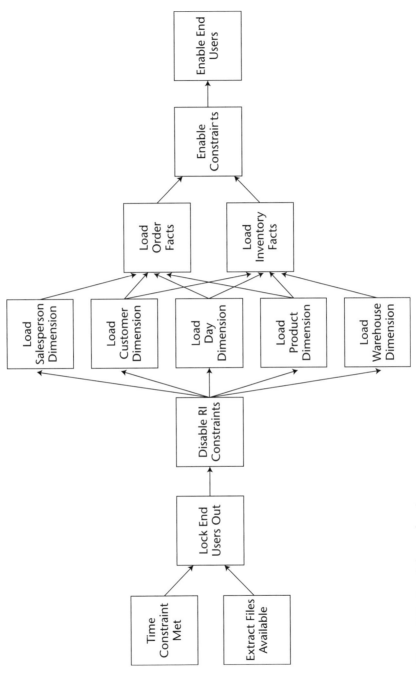

Figure 5.8 Load dependencies.

There are a variety of other topics that concern the load process for the data warehouse. Examples include load automation, contextual dimensions, and integrity checking, to name just a few. But the ETL process has now been covered in sufficient detail for this chapter to turn its focus to the loading of aggregate tables.

Loading the Aggregate Schema

The process of loading the aggregate schema is very similar to the process of loading the base schema. This should come as no surprise; an aggregate star schema is a star schema itself, albeit with a different grain. And pre-joined aggregates share similar properties.

As it turns out, much of the complexity involved in processing the base schema is eliminated during aggregate processing. Examples include multiple-source loads, changed data identification, and the transformation of data for processing one row at a time. Chapter 6 shows how these complexities are eliminated by sourcing the aggregate schema from the base schema.

But before examining the specific processes that load aggregate tables, it is important to consider how aggregate processing fits into the overall load process.

Aggregate loads usually follow the same approach as base schema loads, where a separate program, or process, is developed for each table. The presence of aggregates requires that the load process for the base schema manage the availability of aggregates, taking them off-line during processes that update base tables. This also affects the frequency of aggregate loads. The use of RDBMS features such as materialized views or materialized query tables eliminates the need to design a load process, but availability and load frequency must still be attended to.

Additionally, a choice must be made on the approach to aggregate loads. They may be rebuilt entirely with each load, or refreshed incrementally.

Loading Aggregates Separately from Base Schema Tables

In loading the base schema, separate load processes were designed for each table. This approach isolated the code or routines, localizing the impact of schema design changes. A change to a dimension attribute will have a smaller impact on the modification and testing of the load routine. Separate load routines also permit an overall automation of the load that recognizes dependencies between individual tables. Fact table loads can begin the moment all related dimensions have been loaded; with a single load per star, they might have to wait longer to be processed.

The load processes for aggregate tables should follow this same approach. Separate processes should be used to load aggregate dimension tables and aggregate fact tables. The same reasons apply here; individual routines will be easier to maintain, and discrete processes will permit a more efficient automation of the load. This is especially important for aggregates. Because aggregates are more likely to change over time than the base tables, separate processes are all the more valuable. An aggregate fact table may be discarded, but the aggregate dimensions may be used for new aggregates. And several aggregates fact tables are likely to share the same aggregate dimensions.

TIP Like the base schema tables, each aggregate table should be loaded by a separate process.

Because the processing is similar, developers are sometimes tempted to load base tables and aggregate tables simultaneously. For example, a single program might load a set of dimensions, a fact table, and all related aggregates. But clearly, this program will be far more difficult to maintain than a set of separate programs. And it will introduce new inefficiencies into the load process. Consider a warehouse that is off-limits to end users during the load process. If the base fact table and aggregate fact table are loaded separately, the warehouse can be made available to end users once the base fact table has been loaded. If they are loaded simultaneously, the load process takes longer, and users do not have access to the schema until both tables have been loaded.

There is an exception to this rule. If the data warehouse is loaded in real time, aggregates and the base table must be loaded simultaneously. This is discussed in the section "Real Time Loads" later in this chapter.

Invalid Aggregates

When aggregates are loaded in a separate process from base tables, they become invalid the moment a base table is changed in any way. For example, a base star contains orders by Day, Product, Customer, and Salesperson. An aggregate contains orders by Day, Brand, and Customer. The moment the Product dimension has changed, the Brand dimension is out of sync. Whether a new row has been inserted into a base dimension table, or an existing record has been updated, the aggregate dimension can now provide different query results from the base table.

This dependency has implications for the frequency with which aggregates are loaded and the processes by which they are made available to end users. Off-line loads can leverage the separate processing of aggregates to make the base schema available to users before all processing is complete.

Load Frequency

Given that any change to the base schema tables on which aggregates are based renders them invalid, it follows that the aggregate tables must be loaded on the same frequency as the base tables. Otherwise, the aggregates will remain invalid and useless. For example, if the base schema is loaded daily, the aggregate must be loaded daily. Otherwise, the aggregate schema is invalid when the base schema is updated.

TIP Aggregate tables should be loaded at the same intervals by which the base schema tables are loaded.

This requirement applies even if the aggregate schema summarizes time. For example, consider an aggregate that summarizes transactions by month. If the base schema is loaded daily, the aggregate must also be loaded daily. The summary data for the current month must be updated daily to reflect new transactions that are added to the base schema. It is not appropriate to update the aggregate monthly; to do so would render the summary rows for the current month out of sync with the base table.

Taking Aggregates Off-Line

As you have seen, the moment a base schema table from which an aggregate is derived has been updated, the aggregates can produce different query results. This is a violation of one of the guiding principles of aggregates. This situation must be avoided. This can be accomplished by notifying the aggregate navigator that the aggregate is off-line. In the example, as soon as the Product table is touched by a load process, the Brand table and the aggregate fact table must be taken off-line. Once the aggregate schema is processed, the aggregate tables can be designated as on-line.

This is depicted in Figure 5.9. At the start of the load process, the aggregates are taken off-line. Load processes begin for base dimension tables. After they are loaded, the base fact table load begins, along with aggregate dimension loads. The aggregate fact table load begins when all other loads are complete. After it has been loaded, the aggregates are placed back on-line.

Some aggregate stars do not involve aggregate dimension tables. These aggregates completely summarize one or more dimensions. For example, a base star contains orders by Day, Product, Customer, and Salesperson; the aggregate contains orders by Day and Product. Dimension changes do not render the aggregate invalid because both fact tables reference the identical Product and Day dimensions. However, the moment the base fact table is changed, the aggregate is no longer in sync.

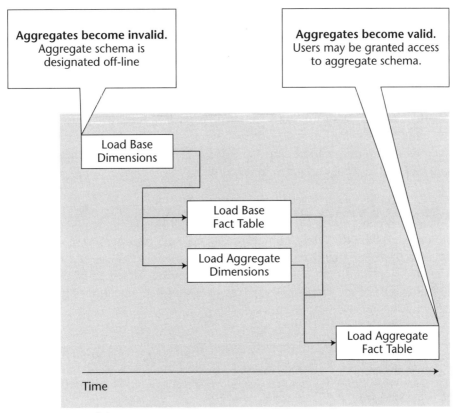

Figure 5.9   Invalid aggregates.

TIP An aggregate dimension and its dependent aggregate fact tables must be taken off-line the moment the base dimension changes.

If not already off-line because of aggregate dimensions, aggregate fact tables must be taken off-line the moment the base fact table changes.

Off-Line Load Processes

Warehouse loads are often designed to take place when end users are not accessing the database. The off-line approach permits load processing to take place without the concurrent demands for transaction consistency generated by user queries. It also permits developers to disable referential integrity constraints or drop indexes during the load process. This off-line load is performed during a *load-window*, often overnight.

In this situation, user access to the base schema is disabled at the beginning of the load process. When the base schema load begins, the aggregates become invalid. This does not matter because users are not able to access the tables anyway. But once the base schema has been loaded, users may be granted access to it. It is therefore important that the aggregates have been designated off-line. This allows the data warehouse to "reopen for business" before all processing has completed. Figure 5.10 depicts this process.

The capability of the aggregate navigator to accommodate the off-line status of aggregates is important in both on-line and off-line load situations. If the aggregate cannot be designated as off-line, the warehouse must remain unavailable to users for the entire load process. Alternatively, the base schema and aggregate schema could be updated at the same time; transactions would update base and aggregates simultaneously.

Materialized Views and Materialized Query Tables

The Oracle and DB2 RDBMS products are capable of building and maintaining aggregates in materialized views or materialized query tables, and rewriting queries to leverage the aggregate as appropriate. As discussed in Chapter 4, these features have the distinct advantage of freeing the warehouse team from developing the aggregate load process.

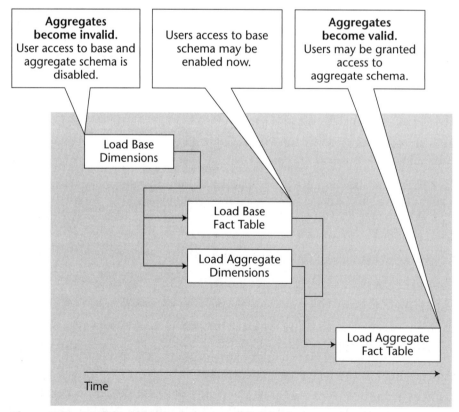

Figure 5.10 Invalid aggregates during an off-line load.

However, these functions must be configured appropriately if the database is to provide these services. An approach must be chosen for their synchronization with the base tables and the aggregates configured so that they are not used by query rewrite mechanisms when they are invalid.

When defining an aggregate using these products, three key characteristics must be specified:

- If the database is to maintain the aggregate in real time, or if the aggregate will be updated on command
- Whether the aggregate will be used in rewritten queries
- Whether an out-of-date aggregate can be used in rewritten queries

The first option determines if the database will automatically keep the aggregate table synchronized with the base tables or if it will be updated on command. By relying on the database to keep the aggregate synchronized in real time, the RDBMS will keep the aggregate in sync with the base table by updating it as the base table is updated. This form of refresh may slow down transactions that update the base table, but may be useful if the warehouse is updated in real time.

If the load process for base tables occurs in batches (nightly, for example), keeping the aggregate in sync in real time may be overkill. Instead, the aggregate can be refreshed manually once the load is completed. This will accelerate load processing, although the aggregate will be unavailable during the load.

It is also important to configure the proper use of aggregates. The RDBMS must be instructed to include the aggregate in rewritten queries, and to do so only when the aggregate is in sync with the base table. Use of an aggregate that is out of sync with the base table, sometimes referred to as a *stale aggregate*, should never be allowed to occur. If permitted, the aggregate would be capable of delivering different results from the base table—violating a guiding principle for dimensional aggregates.

Configured properly, the RDBMS will automatically use the aggregate when it is up-to-date. For example, consider an RDBMS-based aggregate that meets the following criteria:

- Refreshed by a command issued after base schema loads are completed
- Configured to be included in rewritten queries
- Referenced in rewritten queries only when it is up-to-date

In this situation, the warehouse load can proceed without concern for the status of the aggregates. When the load process begins, the aggregate will become out-of-date, and the RDBMS will stop rewriting queries to leverage it. After the base schema is loaded, the RDBMS is instructed to refresh the aggregates. Once the refresh is complete, the RDBMS will resume including the aggregate in rewritten queries. This process is depicted in Figure 5.11.

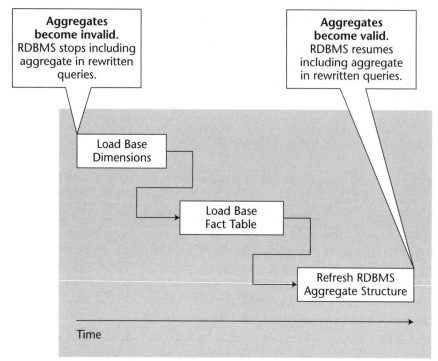

Figure 5.11   The RDBMS managing aggregate status.

Drop and Rebuild Versus Incremental Load

There are two fundamental approaches to the loading of aggregate schema tables. The first is to drop all aggregates at the beginning of each load, and rebuild them from scratch after the load has completed. The second is to construct an incremental load for the aggregate tables. There are merits to each approach.

Drop and Rebuild

The dropping and recreation of aggregate tables during each load permits the construction of a load process that is quite simple in comparison to the alternative. Because the aggregate dimensions are rebuilt from scratch each time, there is no need to perform slow-change processing. All data will be new. *Initial load* style processing, ruled out for the base schema, becomes possible with aggregates.

This type of load may be attractive, if the overall process can be completed within acceptable time limits. For implementations that include large fact tables or dimensions, processing the entire schema repeatedly may not be an option. What is saved in terms of processing complexity is lost because of repeated reprocessing of historic data. Resources may dictate that this approach is ruled out.

When aggregate dimension tables are built, dimension rows are assigned warehouse keys. If the aggregates are dropped and rebuilt during each load, the same aggregate dimension record may receive a different key each time it is loaded. This may occur because of the order in which records are processed and the application of slow changes to the base dimension.

Some types of analysis require that a set of warehouse keys be saved so that the same group of dimension attributes can be examined at a later time. The set of keys is known as a *study group*. Saved to a table, these keys can be joined directly to the fact table's foreign key column to constrain future queries. If the keys can be changed over time, this form of analysis is not possible. Because the aggregate tables are hidden from end users, the consistency of the aggregate dimension key across load process is not likely to be an issue. However, the fact that specific keys can change must be taken into account.

Incremental Loading of Aggregates

For larger data sets, or where the consistency of aggregate dimension keys over time is required, an incremental load is used. The incremental load does not process all base schema data; it processes only new records or records that have changed. While identification of changed data is at times problematic for a base schema load, it is simple for the aggregate load. As is shown in Chapter 6, all that is required is the maintenance of a date_updated column in base dimension tables, and an audit dimension for the base fact tables.

The incremental load process is more complex because slow changes must be processed. As with the base schema, this will require a series of comparisons with already loaded data to determine how each record is processed. However, the incremental load does guarantee that dimension keys are consistent across loads. Figure 5.12 compares and contrasts the two approaches.

An incremental load process for building aggregate dimension tables and aggregate fact tables is developed in Chapter 6. Additionally, Chapter 6 explores how these processes are simplified if the aggregate table is to be dropped and rebuilt with each load.

Drop and Rebuild	Incremental Load
• Processing simplified	• More complex processing
• All data is processed	• Less data is processed
• Aggregate dimension keys are not preserved	• Aggregate dimension keys are preserved
Best for smaller data sets, and where key consistency is not required. *May be best option if aggregate dimension contains a Type 1 attribute not dependent on any other of its attributes. (See Chapter 6.)*	*Use for larger data sets, or where key consistency is required.*

Figure 5.12   Drop and rebuild versus incremental updates.

Real-Time Loads

A growing number of data warehouses are loaded in real time. Instead of updating the fact and dimension tables through periodic batch processes, a real-time warehouse is updated as new transactions occur on the source system. Because of the additional complexity of this style of load process, real-time loads are reserved for situations where there is a clear business benefit to having up-to-the-minute data in warehouse tables. When base tables are updated in real time, the load process for aggregate tables is affected. Effectively, aggregates must be loaded simultaneously with base tables.

Real-Time Load of the Base Schema

A real-time load of the base schema applies changes and inserts records into the schema as a series of transactions, rather than a batch process. In theory, a single transaction could update operational and warehouse tables simultaneously. However, this could affect the performance or availability of the operational system. Instead, transactions that insert or update the source system are logged, or the base tables are fit with triggers that fire as records are added or changed. These mechanisms in turn feed into a process that has been designed to load the transaction into the warehouse tables.

The result is that the warehouse load process receives transactions to process shortly after they have been applied to the source system. Each transaction must be processed according to the same set of requirements identified earlier in this chapter. That is to say, required dimension records must be assembled prior to insertion of a dependent fact; dimension processing must accommodate slow changes; fact processing must include dimension keys. The process developed to meet these requirements may look significantly different in a real-time load, but the same steps are involved.

Real-Time Load and Aggregate Tables

When a schema is loaded in incremental batches, aggregate processing can be performed by a separate process. The aggregate tables are taken off-line while the base tables are processed, and then they are updated and placed back on-line.

With a real-time load, new transactions may be added to the schema constantly. Each time a new transaction arrives for insertion into the base table, the aggregate must be taken off-line, the transaction must be loaded into the base warehouse table, the aggregate must be updated, and the aggregate must be placed back on-line. As the rate of load transactions increases, the effectiveness of taking aggregates off-line for the load dwindles.

A real-time load, therefore, may call for the simultaneous update of base and aggregate tables. This form of processing can be complex, especially where there are several aggregates based on a single base schema. The maintainability of the load routines suffers.

If a back-end database solution is used to implement the aggregates, it can be configured to automatically update the aggregates. This frees developers from attending to the aggregates when the warehouse tables are loaded, but the RDBMS must be able to keep pace with the rate of change to the base schema. The situation calls for careful testing during the design phase of the project, to ensure that the technologies will be able to meet the project requirements.

Partitioning the Schema

To eliminate the requirement to load the base schema and aggregates simultaneously, the warehouse schema can be divided into two partitions: a static partition and a real-time partition. During the day, new transactions are added to the real-time partition. During a periodic window, typically overnight, the contents of the real-time partition are added to the static partition. The static partition can be used for most queries and reports; those that require up-to-date information can be constructed by querying both partitions and creating a union of the results.

Because the contents of the static partition are updated only during the periodic load window, it is similar to a data warehouse that is loaded periodically. Aggregate tables are part of the static schema. These aggregates can be taken off-line when the static partition is being loaded, updated after the base table load is complete, and placed back on-line.

Queries that access the static data achieve the full benefit of these aggregates. Queries that access the real-time partition do not benefit from aggregate acceleration, but this partition is significantly smaller. Figure 5.13 illustrates this process.

Notice that special consideration must be given to how the static and real-time schemas will participate in slow-change processing. The real-time schema must include a complete replica of each dimension so that foreign keys can reference unchanged rows. Changes will be applied in the real-time schema only; they are propagated to the static schema during the batch load process. This means a type 1 slow change may be applied to current transactions during the day, but only applied to previous transactions as part of the nightly load.

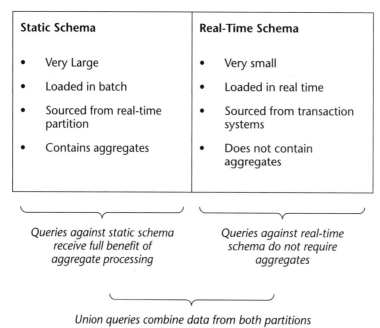

Figure 5.13   Static and real-time partitions for the warehouse schema.

Summary

The data warehouse load is a complex process that must meet several requirements. By dealing with these challenges at load time, the dimensional schema is able to deliver power and performance to applications.

A base schema load consists of dependent processes that load dimension tables and fact tables. Dimension table loads must assemble dimensional data; manage warehouse keys; and process new records, type 1 changes, and type 2 changes. Fact table loads must assemble and aggregate facts, and replace natural keys with the appropriate warehouse keys.

Fitting aggregate processing into this process requires understanding their dependency relationship to the base schema, which will serve as their source. The presence of aggregates requires that the load process manage the availability of aggregates, taking them off-line during processes that update base tables. The aggregate processing may take two forms—a complete rebuild or an incremental refresh.

Using RDBMS features to implement aggregates eliminates much of the work described in the next chapter but still requires some special attention. Parameters must be managed so that the RDBMS knows when aggregates are to be used in rewritten queries, and an approach to their refresh must be selected.

Real-time data warehouse loads complicate aggregate processing because transactions may constantly update the base tables. The effect of this phenomenon on the synchronization of aggregates can be eliminated by breaking the warehouse schema into two partitions—a static partition and a real-time partition.

Having explored the load process for the base schema, and the issues involved in incorporating aggregates, you are now ready to examine aggregate processing in detail. The next chapter looks at the load processes for aggregate dimension tables, aggregate fact tables, and pre-joined aggregates. These processes share much in common with those that load the base tables. In comparison, some aspects of aggregate processing are greatly simplified, while others are more complex.

CHAPTER 6

ETL Part 2:
Loading Aggregates

The previous chapter explored the process that loads the base schema and looked at how the introduction of aggregates would affect that process. This chapter examines the specific tasks required to build the aggregate tables themselves.

Aggregate tables are processed most efficiently when their source is the base schema. This provides a simple mechanism for changed data identification, eliminates redundant processing, and helps ensure conformance. Unless the aggregate is to be updated in real time, there is no reason to reach back to the transaction systems to load them.

As with the base schema, aggregate dimension tables are loaded prior to aggregate fact tables. Each of these processes is explored in turn. Both bear marked similarities to the corresponding processes that load the base schema. In the case of aggregate dimensions, complications will arise if the aggregate contains a type 1 attribute that is not dependent on another of its attributes. In the case of aggregate facts, complications arise when time is summarized.

Instead of loading aggregates incrementally, they may be dropped and rebuilt during each load. While this requires handling much larger volumes of data, the actual processes are greatly simplified, and they avoid some of the potential pitfalls that threaten incremental loads.

The process that loads a pre-joined aggregate looks much different from those that load the tables in an aggregate star. A drop and rebuild can be accomplished by a pair of SQL statements. Incremental loads will require multiple processing passes.

Last, this chapter looks again at database-managed aggregates, such as materialized views or materialized query tables. These aggregates do not require development of a load process. Their definition allows the RDBMS to populate them. But you will see that a tweak to the base schema can improve the efficiency of these aggregates.

The Source Data for Aggregate Tables

In Chapter 5, you saw that the warehouse load is best decomposed into different load programs or processes for each warehouse table. Compartmentalizing the processing limits the impact of changes to the load process and improves manageability.

You also saw that these same guidelines extend to aggregate processing. Attempting to process aggregates in the same program that handles base tables generates complexities that damage the maintainability of the load process and complicates the process of instituting changes to the aggregate portfolio. Unless there is a requirement for real-time loads, these complications are best avoided. Instead, the base schema is processed first; aggregate tables are processed after the base schema has been loaded.

If aggregates are to be loaded through a separate process, they are best loaded from the base schema, rather than from the transaction systems. As hinted in Chapters 3 and 4, this practice greatly simplifies the load process. Changed data identification is greatly simplified, redundant processing is eliminated, and the consistency of the representation of dimensional data is guaranteed. If a real-time load is required, it may be necessary to load aggregates in the same process that loads the base schema.

Changed Data Identification

The efficiency of the ETL process is always a matter of concern. The load must take place within a certain window of time, and hardware resources are not unlimited. One way to improve the efficiency of process is to reduce the amount of data that must be handled. As discussed in Chapter 5, if new and changed data can be identified in source systems, the load process need consider only this data.

Changed data identification is not always effective in improving the efficiency of the base schema load. If there is not an easy way to identify changes on the source system, identification of changed data may require comparing each source record to a snapshot from the previous day. This can prove as resource-intensive as processing all data.

When aggregates are sourced from the base schema, however, a simple method of changed data identification can *always* be instituted. To the base dimension, a column is added indicating the date of last update. This date is updated any time the load process for the base dimension adds or updates a record. For fact tables, an audit dimension is added that contains a column indicating the load date of the fact row. An example of this technique was shown in Figure 3.7.

These simple steps provide a mechanism for changed data identification for the aggregate load processes. When loading an aggregate dimension, it is necessary to consider records only where the date_updated value is later than the most recent load. When loading an aggregate fact table, it is necessary to consider only those base fact table records that have a load_date value that is greater than the most recent load. This greatly reduces the amount of data that would otherwise need to be processed.

> **TIP** Add a date_updated column to base dimension tables and an audit dimension with a date_loaded to base fact tables. Maintain these attributes during the load. They will enable selection of new and changed data when loading aggregates.

Suppose that a Product dimension table contains 200,000 records and serves as a source for a Brand dimension table. Without changed data identification, each of those 200,000 records would have to be processed during each incremental load of Brand. For every product, a set of comparisons or lookups to the existing Brand table will be required in order to identify new records, type 1 changes, and type 2 changes. But only about 1,000 products are new or changed after each load of the base table. These are easily identified by filtering product records based on the date_updated column. This significantly reduces the number of records to be processed.

Elimination of Redundant Processing

In addition to enabling a mechanism for changed data identification, loading aggregate data from the base schema can eliminate redundant processing that might otherwise occur. This is best understood by first considering what would happen if the aggregate schema were loaded from the same source systems as the base schema.

A significant amount of redundant processing is required when separate processes load the base and aggregate schemas from the same transaction systems. Each attribute that is present in both the base dimension and aggregate dimension, for example, will be extracted twice. If there are multiple sources, then any required reconciliation or merge process will be performed twice. If the source system stores data hierarchically or in a denormalized format, then any required transformations, pivots, or normalization will be repeated. In the construction of the dimensional attributes, decodes of values, concatenations of fields, separation of the components of smart codes, and all manner of data transformations will be performed more than once.

> **TIP** When aggregates are loaded in a separate process from the base schema, sourcing aggregates from the base schema avoids redundant processing.

Sourcing the aggregate schema from the base schema eliminates these redundancies. Extraction and preparation of data from the OLTP sources is performed once; dimensional attributes are constructed once. Figure 6.1 contrasts the two approaches. The top portion of the figure illustrates a base dimension and aggregate dimension both loaded from a series of OLTP systems. The shaded area represents processing that is performed redundantly. The bottom portion of the diagram shows a base schema being loaded from the OLTP systems, and the aggregate schema loaded from the base schema. The redundant processing is eliminated.

Similar savings are realized by sourcing aggregate fact tables, or pre-joined aggregates, from the base schema. Again, redundant extraction processes are avoided. This is especially valuable when there are multiple source systems.

Ensuring Conformance

A third benefit of sourcing aggregate dimensions from the base schema concerns the conformance of data values. When the base dimension and aggregate dimension are assembled in redundant processes, the exact same processing rules must be applied to guarantee conformance. The slightest variation in the load processes may result in an attribute that is represented differently in the base dimension and aggregate dimension, violating one of the guiding principles: same results.

Sourcing aggregate tables from the base schema has the benefit of minimizing this risk. Because processes are not performed redundantly, it is easier to ensure conformance. Recall that conformance not only requires proper schema design; it also calls for consistent representation of data values. As discussed in Chapter 3, an aggregate and base dimension conform if:

- The attributes of the aggregate dimension are a strict subset of the base dimension (with the exception of its key).
- Value instances of the common attributes are recorded in an identical manner in both dimensions.
- Of the subset of common attributes: All combinations of values represented in the base dimension are present in the aggregate dimension, and no others.

Redundant processing

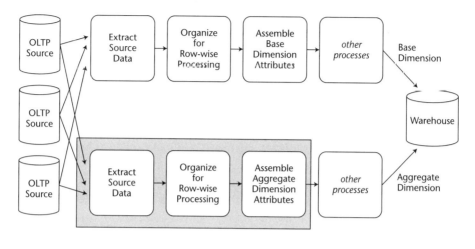

Streamlined processing

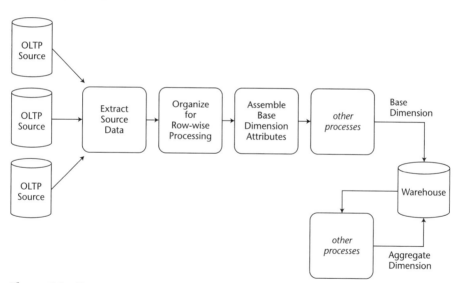

Figure 6.1   Two ways to source an aggregate table.

Consider the second requirement: All value instances must be identical. If a Product dimension and Brand dimension both have a brand_name attribute, the values that appear in the tables must be the same. If "PackIt Deluxe" appears as brand_name in the Product table, it cannot appear as "PACKIT DELUXE" or "Packit Deluxe" in the Brand table. With redundant loads for Product and Brand, the exact same rules must be used to populate the brand_name column. If the aggregate table is sourced from the base schema, there is less concern over the consistent application of transformation rules—they have been applied only once.

> **TIP** When loading aggregate tables in separate processes from the base schema tables, sourcing aggregates from the transaction schema risks the inconsistent application of transformation rules. Sourcing aggregates from the base schema helps ensure conformance.

Similarly, the processing of aggregates from the base schema ensures that the third requirement is met. Combinations of values are more likely to be consistent across both tables if the aggregate is sourced from the base schema. Errors are more easily introduced if the aggregates must go back to the original source system.

Loading the Base Schema and Aggregates Simultaneously

There are situations where it is necessary to load the base and aggregate schemas simultaneously. Clearly, this prevents using the base schema as a source for the aggregate schema. While the simultaneous load will be more complicated, it does avoid some of the problems of redundant loads. Because a single process will load the base and aggregate schemas, processing common to both can be performed only once.

A simultaneous load is called for when the schema is loaded in real time and a partitioning method, as discussed in Chapter 5, is not used. In this case, frequent application of new transactions to the base schema would render the aggregate invalid for a large percentage of time. In a situation like this, the base and aggregate schemas may be loaded simultaneously. Each change is applied in a single transaction to both schemas.

This approach avoids some of the pitfalls described previously because portions of the process that perform the extraction and preparation of data are performed only once, as shown in Figure 6.2. The shaded area shows tasks that are performed once and that benefit both the base schema and aggregate schema.

> **TIP** If a real-time load of the warehouse requires simultaneous aggregate processing, aggregates will be handled by the same load process that handles base schema records.

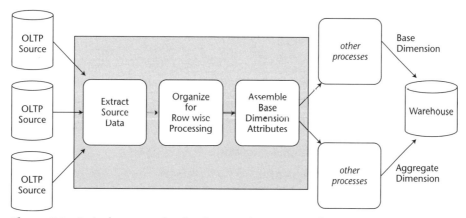

Figure 6.2   A single process loading base and aggregate schemas.

While the loading of the base and aggregate schemas in a single process is possible, the remainder of this chapter breaks the load into separate processes for each table. Bear in mind that the same tasks will be required when developing a single process that loads base and aggregate schemas simultaneously. The overall sequencing of tasks will differ, but the essence of the process is the same. Note that one additional requirement will exist: In addition to performing all processing necessary to populate a base schema record and an aggregate record, all changes must be applied to the data warehouse in transactions that preserve a consistent view of data provided by base and aggregate tables.

Loading Aggregate Dimensions

The process of loading an aggregate dimension table is very similar to that of loading a base dimension table, as described in the previous chapter. An incremental load for the aggregate dimension must extract and prepare records, identify new records and type 1 and type 2 changes, and manage surrogate keys.

As you have seen, many aspects of the load are simplified because the aggregate is sourced from the base schema. The elements that are simplified include identification of changed data and assembly of dimension attributes.

Other aspects can become a serious challenge. Processing a type 1 change to an attribute that is not dependent on any other attribute in the dimension presents numerous difficulties for aggregates.

It is also easy to make the dimension load more complicated than it needs to be. As you will see, the common practice of mapping dimension keys to aggregate dimension keys is not necessary for fact loads.

Requirements for the Aggregate Dimension Load Process

As you have seen, an aggregate dimension table is a dimension table itself. The process that loads an aggregate dimension, then, is subject to the same top-level requirements. As originally presented in Chapter 5, they are:

- Extraction of the necessary source data
- Assembly of the dimensional attributes
- Warehouse key management
- Processing of new records
- Processing of type 1 changes
- Processing of type 2 changes

There is nothing special about an aggregate dimension table that exempts it from these requirements. Source data must be gotten from somewhere and transformed into the appropriate set of dimensional attributes; the aggregate dimension will have its own surrogate key; the load process must accommodate the arrival of new records, and it must also handle slow changes to dimensional attributes.

While the requirements are the same, what happens to a given source record may be different. For example, a new product is added to a system that is the source for an Orders star schema. This causes a new record to be added to the Product dimension. There is an aggregate dimension, Brand, that summarizes the Product dimension. The Brand of the new Product already exists, so there is no change to the aggregate dimension. Similarly, a type 1 or 2 change to the base dimension may or may not involve a corresponding change to the aggregate dimension. And as you will see, a type 1 change can have an unusual effect on both aggregate dimension processing and aggregate fact processing.

As with the base schema load process, the ETL tool will influence how the load is constructed. But once again, the logical process can be understood using a process flow diagram. A logical breakdown of the load process for an aggregate dimension table is shown in Figure 6.3.

This breakdown will frame the discussion of dimensional aggregate processing that follows. While it looks similar to the process that populates a base dimension, there are differences. Some are immediately visible when comparing this process to the one that loads base dimension tables, shown in Figure 5.3. Others will become clear upon examining each step in detail.

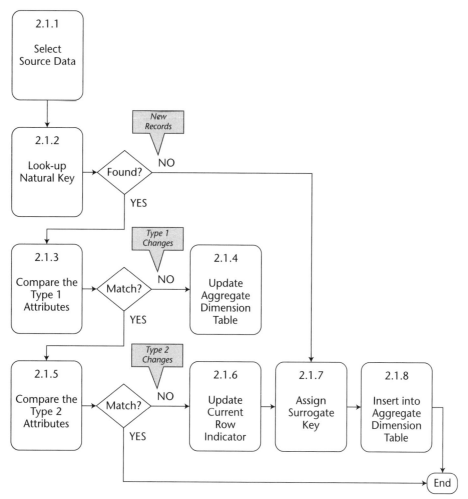

Figure 6.3   Loading an aggregate dimension table.

Extracting and Preparing the Records

Compared to base dimension processing, extracting and preparing the records for loading into the aggregate dimension table is greatly simplified. This simplification results from the sourcing of the aggregate dimension table from the base schema, as discussed earlier. The process will be required to operate on new and changed data only, and there will be no need to assemble dimensional attributes.

The first step in the process flow calls for extraction of the data required to populate the aggregate dimension. This is step 2.1.1 in Figure 6.3. Because the aggregate is based on a single table that is already in the data warehouse, this step can be accomplished using a single query against the base dimension table. For all records that are new or changed since the previous load, a simple query will capture the necessary attributes.

For example, the source for the aggregate dimension tableBrand is the Product dimension table. Most of Brand's attributes come from Product, as shown in Figure 6.4. The only exceptions are the surrogate key, brand_key, which is generated especially for the warehouse, and the housekeeping columns date_created and date_updated, which are generated as part of the load process.

The Product table contains a housekeeping column called date_updated, which indicates when the row was last changed. As discussed in Chapter 3, this column is set to the date the record is first loaded, and updated whenever the record has changed. This column can be used to identify all records that have been inserted or updated since a given point in time, providing a mechanism for changed data identification.

An incremental load of the brand table can begin with the simple query:

```
SELECT DISTINCT
    brand_name,
    brand_code,
    brand_manager,
    category_name,
    category_code
FROM
    product
WHERE
    date_updated > { date of last load } --use actual date of last load
```

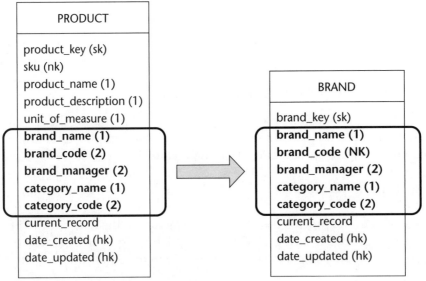

Figure 6.4 Product and Brand.

The SELECT list for this query gathers the attributes needed to construct a Brand record. The Brand attributes are a subset of Product's attributes, so the same combination of values is likely to appear more than once. The DISTINCT operator prevents duplicate rows from being returned. Last, the WHERE clause qualifies the query to consider only rows with a date_updated that is more recent than the last load.

> **TIP** When processing an aggregate dimension, a single table query can be used to identify new and changed data, and to extract it from the source.

For a base dimension, the next steps would have been to organize the data for processing one row at a time and to assemble dimensional attributes. For example, the source system may have stored the data in a hierarchical format, requiring some flattening for the warehouse, and placed the manager's name in separate columns for the first name and last name, requiring concatenation for the warehouse. Similarly, warehouse loads may call for decoding coded values into English language descriptions, adjusting the case for text data, decomposing fields that concatenate separate elements, and so forth.

When processing the aggregate dimension, this is not needed. Because the aggregate table has been sourced from the base dimension table, the information is already organized for processing one row at a time, and no assembly of attributes is required. Each attribute has already been prepared by the process that loaded it into the base table, as depicted in the lower portion of Figure 6.1. The attribute values are already assembled and formatted as required.

> **TIP** When processing an aggregate dimension table, it will not be necessary to transform data for row-by-row processing, or to prepare dimension attributes; these steps have already been handled by the process that loaded the base dimension table.

This simple process stands in sharp contrast to that which is necessary for a base dimension table that comes from multiple source systems, some of which store information in hierarchical or denormalized formats. The savings realized here all result from sourcing from the base schema.

Identifying and Processing New Records

As when processing a base dimension, it is necessary to identify new records for the aggregate dimension. The changed data identification process provides a set of base dimension records that are new or updated; it does not indicate how the information should be handled with respect to the aggregate dimension. A new product that has been inserted into the base dimension, for example, may include brand attributes that are already present in the base dimension. This new record in the base dimension does not generate a new record in the aggregate dimension. And when a new brand record does appear, it may not be a result of a new product record. It can occur as a result of a change to a record in the base dimension.

New aggregate dimension records are identified by a process that takes each incoming base dimension record and uses the natural key to look it up in the aggregate dimension. If it is not found, a new aggregate dimension record has been identified.

In the case of the Brand table from Figure 6.4, the natural key is brand_code. For each record being processed, the Brand dimension is checked for the brand_code value. If a record is being processed that contains the brand_code B507, and that value is not found in the brand_code column of the Brand table, a new record has been found.

> **TIP** New aggregate dimension records are identified by looking up the natural key of each record being processed in the existing aggregate dimension. If not found, a new aggregate dimension record has been identified.

New records are assigned a surrogate key (step 2.1.7 in Figure 6.3) and then loaded into the dimension table (step 2.1.8 in Figure 6.3). When they are loaded, date_created and date_loaded are set to the current date. The current_ record indicator column is set to Current. Recall from Chapter 5 that this will aid in the key assignment process for fact table lookups.

Identifying and Processing Type 1 Changes

The load process for the aggregate dimension table must identify and apply type 1 changes as necessary. Once again, the need for these changes is not indi-cated by the application of a type 1 change to the base dimension table. For example, a type 1 change to the product_name of a record in the Product table from Figure 6.4 will have no effect on the Brand dimension; product_name is not present in Brand.

Type 1 changes are identified by comparing the type 1 attributes of the record being processed with those of one of the records in the dimension table that bears the same natural key value. In Figure 6.3, this takes place in step 2.1.3. If the values do not match, a type 1 change has occurred. The values are updated in the dimension table, as shown in step 2.1.4.

An example is shown in Figure 6.5. The existing aggregate dimension table Brand is shown at the top of the figure. Records being processed by the load process for this table are shown on the bottom. The first record being processed has a natural key (brand_code) of 255. Its type 1 attributes, only brand_name in this example, are compared to those of the corresponding record in the Brand table. The values match, so there is no change.

Existing BRAND Dimension Table:

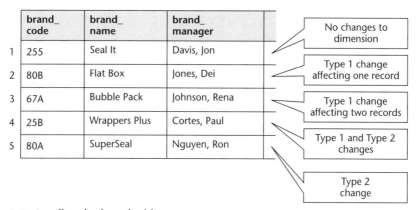

SK	NK	Type 1	Type 2	HK	
brand_key	sku	brand_name	brand_manager	current_record	Additional attributes....
101	67A	Bubble Pack	Riley, Wes	Not Current	
108	67A	Bubble Pack	Johnson, Rena	Current	
112	80B	FlatBox	Jones, Dei	Current	
114	255	Seal It	Davis, John	Current	
119	25B	WrappIt	Smith, Sal	Current	
125	80A	SuperSeal	Jones, Dei	Current	

Records being processed by Incremental Load:

	brand_code	brand_name	brand_manager	
1	255	Seal It	Davis, Jon	No changes to dimension
2	80B	Flat Box	Jones, Dei	Type 1 change affecting one record
3	67A	Bubble Pack	Johnson, Rena	Type 1 change affecting two records
4	25B	Wrappers Plus	Cortes, Paul	Type 1 and Type 2 changes
5	80A	SuperSeal	Nguyen, Ron	Type 2 change

Figure 6.5 Loading the brand table.

The second record being processed has a brand_code of 80B. This is found in the Dimension table, and the type 1 attribute brand_name is compared. This time, the values do not match. The name of the brand has changed from Flat-Box to Flat Box with a space in its name. The record in the aggregate dimension table must be updated.

TIP Type 1 changes are identified by comparing the type 1 attributes of an incoming record to those of a record in the aggregate dimension that has the same natural key. If any type 1 attributes do not match, a type 1 change has occurred.

The third record in the example has a brand_code of 67A. Looking up this natural key in the Brand dimension identifies two records because the brand has undergone a type 2 change in the past—the brand_manager has changed. Either one can be used to compare the type 1 attributes. In this case, the brand_name has changed from Bubble Pak to Bubble Pack spelled with a "ck."

DANGER: TYPE 1 ATTRIBUTES NOT DEPENDENT ON OTHER SURVIVING ATTRIBUTES

Chapter 3 warned that aggregate dimensions should not contain an attribute that is designated as type 1 but not functionally dependent on another attribute in the dimension. The danger of this design is apparent when it is considered in the context of the load process.

Normally, the dimension load process takes the new and changed rows from the base dimension and considers the distinct combinations of attributes that exist in the aggregate dimension. A change to a type 1 attribute is detected by comparison to the existing dimension and handled through an update. Any aggregate facts that had been associated with the old value are now associated with the new value. The aggregate fact table remains in sync with the aggregate fact table.

For example, Figure 6.5 depicted a change to the brand_name associated with the brand_code 80B. The brand_name changed from FlatBox to Flat Box. This change is applied to the existing record for brand_code 80B in the Brand dimension. Aggregate facts that had previously been associated with the old value FlatBox are now associated with the new value Flat Box because they bore the same Brand code.

When the type 1 attribute is not functionally dependent on another attribute in the aggregate dimension, this process breaks down. This situation could occur, for example, if the Product dimension contained a type 1 attribute called product_type, and this attribute was also included in the Brand dimension. Some example data appears in the following table. This time, the brand in question is called FlatPack:

PRODUCT_KEY	SKU	PRODUCT_NAME	PRODUCT_TYPE	BRAND
2001	A-111	6x6x12 Box	Standard Box	FlatPack
3001	B-809	12x12x12 Box	Standard Box	FlatPack
4001	C-229	12x12x12 Box	Standard Box	FlatPack
5001	D-119	6x12x12 Crate	Sturdy Box	FlatPack

If product_type is to be included in the Brand table, Brand will need more than one row for the FlatPack brand—one for Standard Boxes and one for Sturdy Boxes. This can be accommodated by allowing product_type to participate in the natural key of the Brand dimension.

This allows the warehouse to assemble a Brand table with the following values:

BRAND_KEY	PRODUCT_TYPE	BRAND
100	Standard Box	FlatPack
101	Sturdy Box	FlatPack

This may seem to resolve any issues, but consider what would happen if the product designated by SKU B-809 had its product_type changed from Standard Box to Lite Duty Box. A new record could be assigned to the Brand dimension, which would now contain the following rows:

BRAND_KEY	PRODUCT_TYPE	BRAND
100	Standard Box	FlatPack
101	Sturdy Box	FlatPack
200	Lite Duty Box	FlatPack

This seems to resolve any issues in the aggregate dimension, but what about the aggregate fact table? Some of the records attached to brand_key 100 must now be relocated to brand_key 200 because their product_type has changed from Standard Box to Lite Duty Box. Which ones? The only way to know is to go back and scrutinize SKU B-809 to determine that facts with product_key 3001 must be reallocated.

The catch is that neither SKU nor product_key have been considered when performing aggregations—the only attributes selected have been those that will participate in the aggregate dimension table. That is, the load process is not aware that SKU B-809 is the one that underwent the change. In this example, it can be identified by looking in the Product dimension for FlatPack records that include the value Lite Duty Box. Associated facts can be adjusted. That works in this case because Lite Duty Box was a new value. But you won't always be so lucky. Sometimes, the changed value won't be a new one.

Suppose that SKU C-229 subsequently undergoes a change in product_type to Lite Duty Box. In this case, no change is required in the dimension because a Lite Duty Box record already exists in the Brand table for the FlatPack brand.

Because one of the products has been reclassified from Standard Box to Lite Duty Box, the facts associated with brand_key 100 and brand_key 200 all require updates. But no change has been detected in the Brand dimension to alert you to this requirement! Even if you knew that the underlying change occurred, it would be impossible to know how to adjust the facts. It is not sufficient to scan the Product dimension for FlatPack records that are type Standard Box. Some of these existed previously.

(continued)

DANGER: TYPE 1 ATTRIBUTES NOT DEPENDENT ON OTHER SURVIVING ATTRIBUTES *(continued)*

The only way to reallocate facts is to know precisely which records had undergone a type 1 change to the product_type attribute, *and* know the original fact values. This allows the aggregate dimension to be updated as needed, and provides the information necessary to compute the reallocation of aggregate facts.

In the best of all possible worlds, this situation is to be avoided. Type 1 attributes should not be included in an aggregate dimension if they are not functionally dependent on another attribute present in the aggregate dimension table.

If inclusion of such an attribute is an absolute requirement, all hope is not lost. The process that loads the base dimension must audit changes to this attribute, recording the synthetic key, natural keys for the aggregate dimension, and before and after values for the changed type 1 attribute. This information can then be used by an aggregate load process to properly apply the type 1 changes and reallocate aggregate facts. A messy situation, but possible.

By the way, there is still more to worry about. A change to the type 1 attribute may also necessitate deletion of a dimension record. If the SKU associated with product_key 5001 underwent a change in product_type to Standard Box, it may appear that no change is needed in the Brand dimension because there is already a Standard Box record for the FlatPack brand. But the record designated by brand_key 101 must be removed from the aggregate dimension because there is no longer a FlatPack product of type Sturdy Box. If it is not removed from the Brand dimension, a browse of the Brand table may provide different results from a browse of the Product table. Once again, the reallocation of facts must be addressed. All aggregate facts previously associated with the dimension row that has been deleted must be reallocated.

As you will see later in this chapter, the load complexities caused by this type of schema design can be avoided by dropping and rebuilding the aggregates each time they are loaded. In this case, there will be no aggregate facts to reallocate and no aggregate dimension records to purge.

Because brand_code 67A has undergone a type 2 change in the past, this change must be applied to both of the existing records.

TIP Because type 2 changes may have occurred, a type 1 change may need to be applied to multiple rows in the dimension table.

A single record may contain both type 1 and type 2 changes. This is true of the fourth record in Figure 6.5. It contains a type 1 change to the brand_name, and a type 2 change to the brand_manager. All records must be checked for type 2 changes, regardless of whether they presented a type 1 change. For this reason, step 2.1.4 is connected to step 2.1.5 in Figure 6.3, rather than to the end of the process flow.

> **TIP** A source record can contain both type 1 and type 2 changes.

Processing Type 2 Changes

Each source record that has not been identified as a new record for the aggregate dimension must be checked for type 2 changes. This is accomplished by looking in the aggregate dimension for a record that contains the same combination of natural key and type 2 attribute values. This occurs in step 2.1.5 of the process in Figure 6.3. If a match is found, no further processing is required. The source record is properly represented in the aggregate dimension table. If a match is not found, a type 2 change has occurred. The record is assigned a key (step 2.1.7) and inserted into the dimension table (step 2.1.8).

For example, in the first record to be processed in Figure 6.5, the natural key brand_code contains the value 255 and the type 2 attribute brand_manager contains the value Davis, Jon. When these values are looked up in the existing dimension table, a match is found. No type 2 change has occurred.

In the last record to be processed, the natural key brand_code contains the value 80A and the type 2 attribute brand_manager contains the value Nguyen, Ron. When these values are looked up in the existing dimension table, a match is not found. A type 2 change has occurred. In this case, the brand manager has changed. A new record must be inserted into the aggregate dimension table.

> **TIP** Type 2 changes are identified by comparing the natural key and type 2 attribute values with records in the existing dimension. If a match is not found, a type 2 change has occurred.

As discussed in the previous chapter, type 2 slow changes result in the presence of multiple records in a dimension that match a natural key. When facts are loading, obtaining the appropriate surrogate key requires that you determine which of these records to use. This can be accomplished by including the type 2 attributes in the key lookup process. If there are a large number of attributes, developers may choose instead to add a current_record column to the dimension table. This value is set to Current for the most recent version of the record. For previous versions that have subsequently undergone type 2 changes, the value is set to Not Current.

The same technique can be used with aggregate dimensions. In the case of the last record to be processed in Figure 6.5, the brand_manager for brand_code 80A has changed from Jones, Dei to Nguyen, Ron. The current_record indicator for the existing row is changed to Not Current in step 2.1.6. The record being processed is assigned a brand_key in step 2.1.7, and inserted into the dimension with a current_record value of Current in step 2.1.8.

> **TIP** Inclusion of a current_record column in the aggregate dimension table can simplify aggregate fact table key lookups. It can also be used to select a record for comparing type 1 values, as in step 2.1.3 of Figure 6.3.

Key Mapping

In building an aggregate load, developers are often tempted to assemble auxiliary structures that map base dimension keys to associated aggregate dimension keys. These mappings may be contained in a support table for the load process or included directly in the base dimension table. The rationale for this practice is that it eases the load of the aggregate fact tables. The aggregate dimension keys can be selected from the base schema by the process that loads aggregate fact tables.

The technique is usually not necessary. As shown in the next section, the base schema already contains all the data needed to load aggregate facts. The natural keys of the aggregate dimensions are all that is needed. These are used to look up dimension keys during the load process for the aggregate fact table.

A mapping table can simplify the aggregate fact table load by eliminating these lookups, but new complexity is introduced: Other processes must build the mapping table. The construction of a mapping table requires an additional load process or modification of the process that creates the aggregate dimension records. In addition to identifying and processing the new records, type 1 changes, and type 2 changes, the process must now map each record to all related base dimension records.

If the mapping is maintained in the base table, the process that loads the base dimension table will face added complexity. In order to determine the aggregate dimension key value to be assigned to each base record, it must effectively perform all the necessary aggregate processing as well, identifying new records, type 1 changes, and type 2 changes that occur to the aggregate dimension table. If there are more than one aggregate dimension table, this becomes a highly complex process.

> **TIP** Don't bother trying to track the correspondence between base dimension keys and aggregate keys. This will generate a lot of additional work and is not necessary to load the facts.

Last, observe that storing the aggregate dimension keys in the base dimension opens up the possibility that someone might attempt to use them to join to the aggregate dimension. If the query also includes the aggregate fact table, this results in duplication of facts—incorrect results. Alternatively, if the query includes the base fact table, the star schema is being used as a snowflake, and the additional joins are not needed. Unless your front-end tool requires a snowflake design to accommodate aggregates, this should be avoided.

Loading Aggregate Fact Tables

Aggregate fact tables are processed much like their base schema analogs. Because they are sourced from the base schema, several steps in the process are streamlined. A single source query will select the necessary source data, filter out new records only, and aggregate the facts. Lookups are necessary only for surrogate keys that link to aggregate dimensions.

The only complication faced will be processing data that is aggregated over time. Special care must be taken to properly accumulate data for the current period.

Requirements for Loading Aggregate Fact Tables

Like an aggregate dimension, the load requirements for an aggregate fact table are the same as those for its counterpart in the base schema. As stated in Chapter 5, a fact table load must:

- Acquire source data
- Calculate the facts
- Aggregate the facts to match the grain of the fact table
- Identify surrogate keys for each of the dimensions
- Load the new fact table records into the warehouse

A set of sub-tasks that meets these requirements is depicted in Figure 6.6. Not surprisingly, it looks very similar to the process of loading a base fact table, presented in Figure 5.5.

The subsequent sections walk you through each sub-task of the load process.

Acquire Data and Assemble Facts

The first steps in loading an aggregate fact table involve acquiring the source data and assembling the necessary facts. In Figure 6.6, these tasks are accomplished in steps 2.2.1 and 2.2.2.

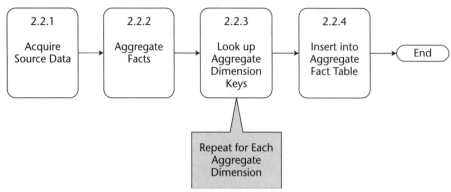

Figure 6.6 Loading an aggregate fact table.

Selecting Source Columns

Because the aggregate fact table is sourced from the base schema, data acquisition is simple. A single relational source will provide all the necessary data: the existing data warehouse. There will be no need to assemble facts from multiple source systems; this has already been done by the process that loaded the base table.

The data selected will include the facts themselves, as well as information needed to associate those facts with the appropriate surrogate keys for all dimensions referenced. This information should be apparent in the load specification, a part of the schema design documentation. Surrogate keys for any dimensions that are not summarized can be selected directly from the base fact table; where the aggregate fact table references an aggregate dimension table, natural keys will be selected from base dimensions.

> **TIP** Regardless of how many sources the base schema had, a single query against the base schema will fetch source data needed to load the aggregate fact table.

An example schema is shown in Figure 6.7. The base schema tracks order facts by Day, Salesperson, Customer, and Product. Brand is an aggregate dimension that summarizes Product. The aggregate fact table summarizes order facts by Day, Salesperson, and Brand. The source data required to build the aggregate fact table is shown in bold type.

The aggregate fact table, ord_agg_day_sls_brand, contains two facts and three foreign keys. The sources for the facts, order_dollars and margin_dollars, are the corresponding columns in the base fact table. Two of the foreign keys reference dimensions that are not summarized: day_key and salesperson_key. These keys can be obtained directly from the base fact table. The foreign key for Brand is not present in the base schema. Instead, it is necessary to select the natural key for this dimension, which is the brand_code column in the Product table.

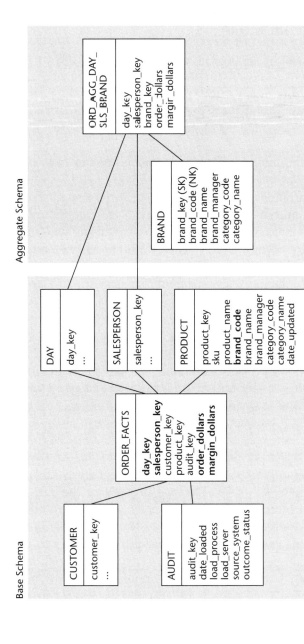

Figure 6.7 Source data for an aggregate fact table.

Processing New Facts Only

The load process can be tailored to handle only new facts by leveraging the load_date column in the Audit dimension table for the base schema. The Audit table provides information about the process that loaded the fact table row, as discussed in Chapter 3. The query that selects the source data will be restricted to records where date_loaded is more recent than the date of the last load.

TIP The Audit dimension table is used to limit processing to new records only.

In the example from Figure 6.7, this will require joining the base fact table to the audit dimension table via its audit_key. New records are identified by selecting records where date_loaded is greater than the date of the last load. The inclusion of this simple audit record in the base schema has provided a free and painless method of changed data capture. Here, it identifies new fact table rows. Some schema designs do call for updates to fact table records; examples are examined in Chapter 8.

Calculating and Aggregating Facts

Compared to the load process for a base fact table, assembling facts for an aggregate fact table is easier. Unlike the load of the base fact table, there is no need to calculate facts. If any transformation or computation of the transaction data were required for storage in the data warehouse, this was done by the process that loaded the base schema. Hence, step 2.2.1 of Figure 6.6 is not followed by a step to calculate facts.

For example, the source system may have recorded sales_dollars and margin_dollars in separate rows of data. The load process for the base fact table will have already transformed the data so that they appear as different columns in a single row. The source system may have stored units_sold and unit_price; the base schema load process will have multiplied these values to compute sales_dollars.

It will, however, be necessary to aggregate the facts. After being extracted from the base schema, they must be rolled up to the level of grain required by the aggregate fact table (step 2.2.2 of Figure 6.6). Non-additive facts should never be aggregated, and semi-additive facts must not be summarized over a dimension across which they are not additive. But there should be no reason to worry about these restrictions now; the schema design will already have incorporated these restrictions.

TIP Aggregate facts should not require transformation or computation, but will require aggregation.

For example, the order_facts table from Figure 6.7 may contain numerous records for a particular Day, Salesperson, and Brand. This would be the case if the salesperson sold to multiple customers that day, or sold multiple products. Each row will include order_dollars and margin_dollars. In the aggregate fact table, these must be summed together and placed in a single row.

One Query Does It All

In order to highlight similarities to the base schema load process, Figure 6.6 has separated the processing discussed thus far into two steps. But in the case of aggregates, a single SQL query will accomplish both of these two steps, as well as identify new records. For the aggregate fact table in Figure 6.7, the following query performs the necessary tasks:

```
SELECT
  day_key,                -- surrogate keys for dimensions not aggregated
  salesperson_key,
  brand_code,             -- natural key for aggregated dimension
  sum (order_dollars),    -- facts, aggregated
  sum (margin_dollars)
FROM
  order_facts,
  product,
  audit
WHERE
  order_facts.product_key
    = product.product_key AND
  order_facts.audit_key
    = audit.audit_key AND
  audit.load_date
    > {date of last load}  -- process new records only
GROUP BY
  day_key,                -- aggregation level for the facts
  salesperson_key,
  brand_code
```

This example provides a template that can be used for most aggregate fact table loads. The SELECT clause captures surrogate keys, natural keys, and facts:

- Surrogate keys are selected for dimensions that are not summarized by the aggregate fact table. In the example, these are the day_key and salesperson_key. They are taken directly from the base fact table; there is no need to join back to base dimension tables to capture these keys.

- Natural keys are selected where the aggregate fact table references an aggregate dimension. In the example, brand_code serves as the natural key for the brand_dimension.

- Facts are selected directly from the base fact table. The facts in the example are order_dollars and margin_dollars.

The query limits data selected to records that have been added since the previous load. This is done through the constraint on `audit.load_date` in the `WHERE` clause. The date of the previous load is substituted for bracketed text.

Aggregation of the facts is achieved by applying the SQL group function `SUM()` to each fact in the select statement. The `GROUP BY` statement indicates the level of aggregation. This aggregation level should match the grain of the aggregate fact table. In the example, the grain is Day, Salesperson, and Brand. The appropriate surrogate keys (day_key, salesperson_key) and natural key (brand_code) are placed in the group by statement to drive this aggregation.

TIP A single query can be used to acquire source data for an aggregate fact table, aggregate the facts, and select only new data.

Identification of Surrogate Keys

Like a base fact table, the aggregate fact table contains a set of foreign keys that reference dimension tables. Some of the tables referenced are base dimension tables; their surrogate keys are present in the base schema and have been fetched by the source query. Others are aggregate dimension tables. Their surrogate keys are not present in the base schema; the source query instead fetches natural keys.

The next step, then, is to use these natural keys to identify surrogate keys for aggregate dimensions referenced. This is analogous to the key lookup process for the base fact table. The difference is that it is necessary only where the fact table references aggregate dimension tables. For each record being processed, the value of the natural key column is looked up in the aggregate dimension table.

TIP In aggregate fact table processing, lookups are used to identify surrogate keys for aggregate dimensions.

An example of this lookup process is shown in Figure 6.8. Two records being processed for an aggregate fact table load are shown at the top of the figure. The first contains the brand_code 80B. This natural key value is looked up in the existing dimension table. The corresponding row, which is shaded in the figure, contains the brand_key 112. This value will be assigned to the record being processed.

Records being processed by Fact Load:

	time_key	salesperson_key	order_dollars	margin_dollars	brand_code		brand_key
1	1202	1197	1,700.22	643.06	80B		112
2	1202	1197	984.31	201.64	67A		

Existing BRAND Dimension Table:

SK	NK	HK	Type 1	Type 2
product_key	sku	current_record	product_name	brand_manager
101	67A	Not Current	Bubble Pack	Riley, Wes
108	67A	Current	Bubble Pack	Johnson, Rena
112	**80B**	Current	Flat Box	Jones, Dei
114	255	Current	Seal It	Davis, Jon
119	25B	Not Current	Wrappers Plus	Smith, Sal
242	25B	Current	Wrappers Plus	Cortes, Paul
125	80A	Not Current	SuperSeal	Jones, Dei
255	80A	Current	SuperSeal	Nguyen, Ron

Figure 6.8   Key lookup.

It is possible that the natural key lookup will match more than one record in the dimension table. This happens when type 2 changes have occurred. To identify the correct key, it would be necessary to include type 2 attributes in the lookup. Earlier, this problem was foreseen. It was avoided by adding a current_record column to the aggregate dimension table. The key lookup process searches for a record where the natural key matches the record being processed, and the current_record contains the value Current.

The second row of data being processed in Figure 6.8 has a natural key of 67A. The dimension table is scanned for a record where the brand_code is 67A and the current_record is Current. This yields one row, which bears the brand_key 108. There is another row in the table for brand_code 67A, but it fails the lookup because its current_record does not read Current.

Aggregating Over Time

The final step is to add the new record to the aggregate fact table. This is represented by step 2.2.4 in Figure 6.6; the record is inserted into the existing table. But the astute reader might observe an apparent flaw in this process. New facts may have arrived that are associated with a combination of dimensional attributes that *already exist* in the aggregate schema.

It would seem that this possibility complicates the process of adding the record to the aggregate fact table. Instead of simply inserting the record, it is necessary to first check if a row already exists for the combination of surrogate keys assembled. If the record exists, it must be updated; if not, a new row is inserted. Fortunately, this conditional processing is not required in every situation and can be avoided in all others.

If the time dimension is not being summarized, the situation is not likely to be encountered. Consider a base schema that includes order facts by Day, Customer, Salesperson, and Product. It is loaded on a daily basis. Each day, new orders occur in the source system. During the load process, they are added to the base schema. Each is assigned the foreign key for the date of the order, which has not been previously encountered. An aggregate schema summarizes orders by Day and Product. Because all the new facts are associated with the new date, there will not be any cases where an existing aggregate fact must be updated. The load process can safely assume all aggregate fact records should be inserted.

But special care must be taken in any situation where the time dimension *is* summarized, or if the load process occurs more than once for each time period (such as hourly loads). Now, new base facts may arrive that correspond to an aggregate fact record that already exists. This can be handled by modifying step 2.2.4 to update the record if it already exists, adding to the existing fact values, or to insert the record it does not exist.

Suppose, again, that a base fact table contains order facts by day, customer, salesperson, and product. New orders are added to this fact table on a daily basis. This time, an aggregate fact table contains order facts by *month* and product. If it is not the beginning of a month, some of the new transactions that arrive may be for a product/month combination that already exists in the aggregate fact table. Table 6.1 shows some of the existing rows that appear in this aggregate fact table. For the sake of simplicity, the sample data has been limited to a single product.

Suppose that it is December 8, 2006, and that December 2006 is represented by month_key 1005. As shown in the last row in the table, some orders have already been taken this month for product 3001. During the day, additional orders are taken for product 3001. When these orders are processed by the incremental load, they must be added to the row for month_key 1005 and product_key 3001 in the aggregate table.

Table 6.1 An Aggregate Fact Table Summarizing Time

MONTH_KEY	PRODUCT_KEY	ORDER_DOLLARS
1002	3001	50,000
1003	3001	49,000
1004	3001	51,000
1005	3001	4,000

TIP When time is aggregated, facts may arrive for key combinations that already exist in the aggregate table. These must be combined with the previously existing facts, if they exist.

This can be accomplished by updating the row for month_key 1005 and product_key 3001. Each day during December, if additional orders are taken from product 3001, this row is updated. The facts for the current period are said to *accumulate*.

The example data included only a single product. But during a given load, numerous aggregate rows may accumulate order_dollars during a given month. Perhaps there are thousands of products that sell on a regular basis. During each incremental load, it will be necessary to check each combination of product_key and month_key to see if it already has associated facts. If so, the existing facts must be updated to include the new orders. If not, a new record is inserted.

Rather than conduct conditional processing that accumulates current month data in existing aggregate rows, some developers choose to delete the current period from the aggregate fact table and reprocess the current period for each load. This allows the load process to assume that every fact loaded into the aggregate is new; it contains a month_key that does not already exist in the aggregate fact table.

TIP Conditional processing of aggregate facts can be avoided by truncating the current period and reprocessing it during each load.

It is not appropriate to handle this situation by loading the aggregate data only at the end of the month. As you have already seen, the aggregate tables must be loaded with the same frequency as the base schema. Failure to do so would render the aggregate schema capable of providing different results from the base schema. In the example, a query against the base schema that summarized product sales by year would provide a different example than the aggregate schema, which would be missing data that has accumulated during December.

The construction of aggregate tables as discussed so far has followed an incremental approach similar to that used for the base schema. As pointed out in Chapter 5, there is another option: dropping and rebuilding aggregates with each load.

Dropping and Rebuilding Aggregates

The aggregate load processes described in the previous sections perform incremental processing. By considering only data that is new or changed in the base schema, the volume of data to be processed is limited. An alternative approach is to drop the aggregate tables at the start of each load and rebuild them in their entirety. As discussed in Chapter 5, this approach increases the volume of data processed and does not guarantee the consistency of keys. But it also simplifies the load process, particularly for dimension tables.

Dropping and Rebuilding Aggregate Dimension Tables

In a drop-and-rebuild scenario, the load process for aggregate dimensions is dramatically simplified. All information being added to the dimension table is new; there will be no need to process slowly changing dimensions. Comparisons that are costly in terms of processing time are eliminated, and all aggregate dimension rows are inserts.

For an incremental load of an aggregate dimension table, much of the processing centered on identifying new and changed records. This was done through numerous comparisons of incoming data to the existing aggregate dimension. In Figure 6.3, these comparisons identified new records (step 2.1.2), type 1 changes (step 2.1.3), and type 2 changes (step 2.1.5). These comparisons are costly in terms of computing resources. Each may require a query against the base schema, or the establishment and use of a cache by the ETL tool. When the table is completely rebuilt with each load, none of these comparisons are necessary.

The incremental load was required to manipulate the aggregate dimension using updates for type 1 changes (step 2.1.4 in Figure 6.3) and inserts for new records and type 2 changes (step 2.1.8). In a drop-and-rebuild process, every record will be treated as an insert. Update processing is eliminated.

A streamlined drop-and-rebuild process is shown in Figure 6.9. The first step removes all data from the existing aggregate dimension. This can be performed by dropping and recreating the table, deleting all rows, or truncating the table. Notice that this requires any dependent aggregate fact tables be purged first.

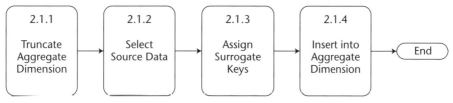

Figure 6.9 Dropping and rebuilding an aggregate dimension.

Once the table is empty, the source data is selected from the base dimension table. This is done through a single SELECT DISTINCT query, which fetches all necessary attributes. There is no need to constrain a date_updated column; all records are new. For the Brand table depicted in Figure 6.4, the WHERE clause can be eliminated. The simplified query becomes:

```
SELECT DISTINCT
    brand_name,
    brand_code,
    brand_manager,
    category_name,
    category_code
FROM
    product
```

There is no need to process this data for slow changes. All necessary combinations of attributes are captured by this query. For example, if a particular brand has undergone a change to its brand_manager, a type 2 attribute, the base dimension will reflect this; products of that brand will be represented by rows containing the old and new values. The preceding query picks up all unique combinations of the attributes.

All data is new, so surrogate keys are assigned to each record retrieved by the query. Each record is then inserted into the dimension table. These steps are performed by the last two steps in Figure 6.9.

For a base dimension table, the load process was optionally enhanced to maintain a current_record column in the dimension. This column aided in the identification of surrogate keys when processing facts. Where type 2 changes occurred, the current_record column allowed the lookup process to identify the most recent version without having to compare all attributes.

In the case of the drop-and-rebuild process, this column proves difficult to maintain. The current_record column of the base dimension cannot be used to identify current_record status for the aggregate dimension. A base dimension may have undergone slow changes to a number of attributes, some of which may appear in the aggregate dimension and some of which may not. While additional processing can be performed to identify current records, the process is probably not worth it. Selection of larger amounts of source data would be required, along with comparison of rows within the source data sets. In the end, it is likely to prove more effective to identify the correct records during fact processing, adding type 2 attributes to the lookups.

Dropping and Rebuilding Aggregate Fact Tables

In a drop-and-rebuild scenario, the process of loading an aggregate fact table is essentially unchanged. The load process is shown in Figure 6.10. This process looks very similar to that which performed an incremental load.

The first step of the process drops or truncates the fact table. In fact, this was likely done prior to processing the aggregate fact table; because it is dependent on aggregate dimensions it may already have been dropped.

Next, source data is selected from the base schema. Because the table is being completely rebuilt, it is not necessary to constrain for new or changed data. For the aggregate fact table depicted in Figure 6.7, the source query is:

```
SELECT
    day_key,                   -- surrogate keys for dimensions not aggregated
    salesperson_key,
    brand_code,                -- natural key for aggregated dimension
    sum (order_dollars),       -- facts, aggregated
    sum (margin_dollars)
FROM
    order_facts,
    product
WHERE
    order_facts.product_key
      = product.product_key
GROUP BY
    day_key,                   -- aggregation level for the facts
    salesperson_key,
    brand_code
```

2.2.1	2.2.2	2.2.3	2.2.4	2.2.5
Truncate Aggregate Fact Table	Acquire Source Data	Aggregate Facts	Look up Aggregate Dimension Keys	Insert into Aggregate Fact Table	→ End

Figure 6.10 Dropping and rebuilding an aggregate fact table.

In comparison to the query for an incremental load, presented earlier, this query eliminates a join to and constraint on the audit table.

Next, aggregate dimension keys are identified through a lookup process, and the records are added to the aggregate fact table. Because all data is new with each load, there is no need to pay special attention to aggregate fact tables that summarize time. Each time the load is performed, the aggregate fact table is empty. All records will therefore be inserted.

The sidebar earlier in this chapter warned that an aggregate dimension containing a type 1 attribute not dependent on another attribute introduces serious complications for the load process. A change to this attribute may necessitate changes to existing records in the aggregate fact table, and identifying and reallocating these changes can be difficult. It may also require that a dimension record be removed from the aggregate schema.

In a drop-and-rebuild scenario, these problems disappear. All records loaded into the aggregate schema are new. This means there will be no aggregate fact records that require adjustment and no dimension records to be deleted. As discussed in the sidebar earlier in the chapter, the drop-and-rebuild approach may be an attractive option when this sort of schema design is required.

Pre-Joined Aggregates

Like aggregate fact and aggregate dimension tables, a pre-joined aggregate can be processed in two ways. It can be dropped and rebuilt during each load process, or it can be incrementally loaded. The drop-and-rebuild approach is simple, requiring a single query to do most of the work. An incremental load does not need to manage any surrogate keys but must still process slow changes to dimension values.

Dropping and Rebuilding a Pre-Joined Aggregate

If a pre-joined aggregate is populated through a drop-and-rebuild approach, the load process is simple. First, the existing table is dropped and recreated, or simply truncated of all data. After this is done, a single SQL statement can do all of the work required to select source data, aggregate it, and insert it into the aggregate table.

The pre-joined aggregate in Figure 6.11 summarizes the facts in the Order table by Date and Brand. Salesperson and Customer have been completely summarized, and do not appear in the aggregate table. The attributes of the base schema present in the aggregated schema are shown in bold type.

Base Schema

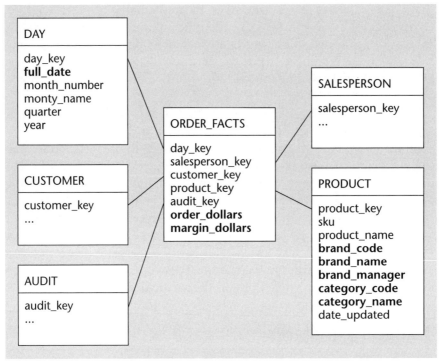

Base Schema

Figure 6.11   A pre-joined aggregate.

In a drop-and-rebuild scenario, the table ord_bwt_day_brand from Figure 6.11 can be loaded by truncating the table and issuing a single SQL statement:

```
INSERT INTO ord_bwt_day_brand
  SELECT
    full_date,
```

```
      brand_code,
      brand_name,
      brand_manager,
      category_code,
      category_name,
      sum(order_dollars) as order_dollars,
      sum (margin_dollars) as margin_dollars
    FROM
      order_facts,
      day,
      product
    WHERE
      order_facts.day_key = day.day_key AND
      order_facts.product_key = products.product_key
    GROUP BY
      full_date,
      brand_code,
      brand_name,
      brand_manager,
      category_code,
      category_name
```

This statement selects all source data from the base schema, aggregates the facts as appropriate, and inserts the data into the aggregate table.

TIP Pre-joined aggregate tables can be populated by truncating the table and issuing a single SQL statement.

Unfortunately, the solution is not this simple if the pre-joined aggregate is to be loaded incrementally.

Incrementally Loading a Pre-Joined Aggregate

Incremental processing of the aggregate is a bit more complex. You might consider modifying the preceding SQL statement to place a constraint on date_loaded. The modified command appears below; new additions appear in shaded lines. Unfortunately, this will not perform all the required incremental processing.

```
    -- WARNING:
    -- This query is insufficient to incrementally load a
    -- pre-joined aggregate table
    INSERT INTO ord_bwt_day_brand
      SELECT
        full_date,
        brand_code,
        brand_name,
```

```
      brand_manager,
      category_code,
      category_name,
      sum(order_dollars) as order_dollars,
      sum (margin_dollars) as margin_dollars
  FROM
      order_facts,
      day,
      product,
      audit
  WHERE
      order_facts.day_key = day.day_key AND
      order_facts.product_key = products.product_key AND
      order_facts.audit_key = audit.audit_key AND
      audit.date_loaded >
          { date of last load }   -- Substitute actual date of last load
  GROUP BY
      full_date,
      brand_code,
      brand_name,
      brand_manager,
      category_code,
      category_name
```

This statement gets you some of what you need, but not everything. Remember that an incremental load must process new records, type 1 changes, and type 2 changes. This new statement will capture new records and type 2 changes, as long as care is taken when time is being summarized. As described previously, the current period must be purged from the aggregate before an incremental load in order to avoid situations where an INSERT is not appropriate.

Unfortunately, the query does not process type 1 changes. For example, the brand_name may be a type 1 attribute. If it changes for a particular brand, the preceding SQL statement will not update existing records in the pre-joined aggregate. In fact, if there are no orders for the product, the change will not appear at all.

One solution to this dilemma is to update the pre-joined aggregate table in a series of passes. First, a pass is made for each dimension that is included in the pre-joined aggregate. Each of these passes uses the date_updated column of the base dimension to locate new records. These records are compared with the corresponding columns of the pre-joined aggregate to identify type 1 changes. Where found, the pre-joined aggregate is updated.

After a pass has been completed for each base dimension represented in the pre-joined aggregate, the preceding query can be issued. It will capture the new records and type 2 changes. If the pre-joined aggregate summarizes time, it must first be purged of all data for the current period.

> **TIP** An incremental load of a pre-joined aggregate requires multiple passes
> that apply type 1 changes for each base dimension represented, followed by an
> insert of new and type 2 changed records.

Needless to say, if the pre-joined aggregate is to be loaded through multiple passes, it is important that it remain off-line until all passes are complete. Only when each pass has completed will it be fully synchronized with the base schema.

Materialized Views and Materialized Query Tables

Back-end database technologies, such as Oracle's materialized views and DB2's materialized query tables, are frequently used to implement aggregate navigation functionality. As discussed in Chapter 4, these technologies can also be used to build and maintain the aggregates.

These capabilities eliminate the need to design an ETL process for the construction of the aggregate tables. As discussed in Chapter 5, it is necessary only to define the aggregate, properly establish the rules that govern when the aggregate will participate in query rewrite, and set up an automated call to the database to refresh the aggregate after base table loads have completed.

While the RDBMS will handle most of the remaining additional work, there are cases where a tweak to the base schema can go a long way toward optimizing performance and keeping down the size of the aggregate table.

Defining Attributes for Aggregate Dimensions

Oracle and IBM provide the capability to define aggregates that partially summarize a dimension, without the need to construct the aggregate dimension table itself. Both products enable this capability by allowing the developer to define hierarchies that exist within the dimension. As discussed in Chapter 4, this is done in Oracle via the declaration of a dimension. In DB2, this is done by establishing a cube view.

Each level of a hierarchy must include a defining attribute or set of attributes. The hierarchy may optionally include attributes that are fully dependent on the defining attributes. These relationships serve as stand-ins for development of physical aggregate dimension tables. An aggregate fact table can be defined as a materialized view (or materialized query table) that includes the defining attribute of a hierarchy level, rather than a foreign key to an aggregate dimension table. The RDBMS uses the known functional dependencies to join back to the base dimension table to retrieve any functionally dependent attributes required by a query.

Optimizing the Hierarchy

This process can be optimized by ensuring that a single attribute exists that can define each level of a hierarchy. Where a hierarchy level is not uniquely identified by a single attribute, a new attribute is added to the base table that serves the purpose. Like a surrogate key, this attribute is warehouse-generated and should be invisible to the end user. In fact, it serves the same role as a surrogate key for an aggregate dimension.

For an example, once again consider the Product table. As shown in Figure 6.12, a hierarchy exists within the table: Category → Brand → Product. Notice that there are three attributes at the Brand level: brand_code, brand_name, and brand_manager. Because the code and manager are both type 2 attributes, this level of the hierarchy can be uniquely identified only by the combination of these two attributes. To reference this hierarchy level in an aggregate, both attributes must be included in its definition.

Although not required by the RDBMS tools, you can add a brand_key to the Product table. This attribute will uniquely define the Brand level within the hierarchy. Aggregate fact tables that are implemented as a materialized view or materialized query table can use this attribute to reference the Brand attributes.

TIP Ensuring that each level in a dimensional hierarchy is defined by a single attribute will minimize the number of attributes that must be included in a database-managed aggregate.

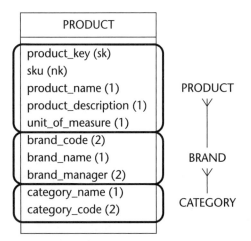

Figure 6.12   A hierarchy within the Product table.

You may have noticed that earlier this chapter suggested not including aggregate keys in base dimension tables. But in those cases, the keys were to be created and managed by a separate process. Locating them in the base dimension table only complicated the process.

Here, the key would not have been maintained elsewhere. It is added to the schema to improve join back performance, providing the RDBMS with a single attribute that defines Brand.

Adding brand_key to the Product table adds additional processing requirements to the process that loads the Product table. Each time a row is added to the Product table, the appropriate key must be assigned for the values of its Brand attributes. These can be obtained by a lookup into the dimension table itself; if not found, a new brand_key is assigned. This is very similar to the process that would be required to load a Brand table, as described earlier.

Summary

Unless the data warehouse is being updated in real time, aggregate tables are processed most efficiently when their source is the base schema. This provides a simple mechanism for changed data identification, eliminates redundant processing, and helps ensure conformance.

The incremental load process for an aggregate dimension table is quite similar to that of a base dimension table. Because it is sourced from the base schema, the process is greatly simplified. Complications arise only when the aggregate contains a type 1 attribute that is not dependent on another of its attributes. In this situation an incremental load will require that changes to the base schema be audited. Alternatively, a drop-and-rebuild approach may be desirable.

The incremental processing of aggregate facts is quite similar to the processing of base facts. Complications arise when the load process is executed multiple times for a given key value within the time dimension. If this occurs, the process must be prepared to handle previously encountered key combinations through an update. This can be avoided by simply truncating and reloading the current period.

While they appear to be a simplified version of an aggregate star, pre-joined aggregates are loaded quite differently. For an incremental load, multiple passes are required for each dimension represented in the aggregate, applying any type 1 changes that occur. A final pass inserts new records and type 2 changes. A drop-and-rebuild can be performed through a single SQL statement.

Last, you saw that database-managed aggregates do not require development of a load process. Their definition allows the RDBMS to populate them. But where a hierarchy level in a base dimension is not defined by a single attribute, creation of such an attribute may improve aggregate performance.

Aggregates and Your Project

The design and implementation of aggregate tables always take place in the context of a project. The project may involve the development of a new warehouse subject area, or be exclusively focused on adding aggregates to an existing schema. Regardless of project nature, aggregates implementation requires a standard set of tasks and deliverables, which mirror those required by the base schema.

This chapter begins with a look at the process of data warehouse implementation. A dimensional data warehouse is most often implemented in parts known as data marts. If organized around a planned framework of conformed dimensions, this incremental approach avoids the dangers of enterprise scope at one extreme, and a departmental focus on the other. It also allows the introduction of aggregates to be delayed until after the first data mart has been constructed, although this is not required.

Next, the specific implementation tasks and deliverables surrounding aggregates are presented in the context of a data mart development project. These tasks are separated into project stages—strategy, design, build, and deployment—but can easily be reorganized to fit any of the popular development methodologies.

Last, this chapter looks at the ongoing maintenance requirements for aggregate tables within a data warehouse, and considers the change management process by which they are modified.

Much of this chapter's discussion of data warehouse implementation has been influenced by the work of my long-time colleague Greg Jones. His practical approach to data warehousing has shaped my own philosophy and work. Here, it serves as the project context for a discussion of aggregates.

Data Warehouse Implementation

Dimensional data warehouses are usually implemented in parts. Known as a *data mart*, each part is organized around a subset of the business processes that constitute the enterprise. Ideally, data marts are implemented according to a master plan, around a set of conformed dimensions. This ensures that as each data mart is brought on-line, it interoperates with the others. However, data marts are sometimes built without consideration for the rest of the enterprise, or as an analytic adjunct to a normalized repository of enterprise data.

Regardless of the overall approach, these dimensional databases are implemented as a series of data marts. This incremental approach provides an opportunity to delay the consideration of aggregates until after the first project. The scope of the initial project is reduced, allowing the business to become familiar with the data warehouse lifecycle. A subsequent project introduces aggregates to the first data mart. Future implementations include plans to incorporate aggregates, which will also be re-evaluated on a periodic basis.

Incremental Implementation of the Data Warehouse

One of the advantages of the dimensional approach to data warehouse design is its ability to scale from a single subject area to the enterprise level. By planning a series of implementations around a framework of conformed dimensions, the data warehouse is delivered incrementally. This avoids the risks associated with a single project of enterprise scope, while also avoiding stovepipe solutions that do not work together. Sometimes, other approaches are chosen. But, in virtually all cases, dimensional solutions are built one subject area, or data mart, at a time.

Planning Data Marts Around Conformed Dimensions

In the best of all possible worlds, a planning process precedes a series of data mart implementations. During this stage, enterprise business processes are identified. For each process, expected fact tables and dimension tables are enumerated. Special care is taken to design a set of conformed dimensions around which these subject areas will integrate. The stars are grouped into a set of data marts, and plans are drawn up for their phased implementation.

The primary objective of this planning process is to form the dimensional framework around which planned data marts will integrate. This allows a balance to be struck between the conflicting extremes of projects of enterprise scope versus departmental focus. The level of effort during this planning stage may vary significantly. For some enterprises, a full detailed schema design and load specification are developed for each schema. In other cases, the business will not tolerate this level of investment in an IT project that does not deliver a system. Instead, a shortened project sketches out anticipated schemas and focuses most of its effort on identifying the conformance points and related source data.

Subsequent to this planning process, individual projects are launched to implement each data mart. These projects may be executed one at a time, or implemented in parallel. By subdividing the enterprise data warehouse into a set of smaller data marts, the problems associated with a single project of enterprise scope are avoided. At the same time, the up-front planning avoids the development of individual solutions that are incompatible with one another.

Avoiding Enterprise-Level Scope

When a data warehouse project incorporates all enterprise requirements into its scope, it becomes a major challenge to fund and manage. The project must address every business process and all user points of view, and touch every transaction system in the enterprise. Its delivery schedule will be measured in years. When it finally goes into production, the project will have consumed vast quantities of resources.

These massive projects suffer several disadvantages. They are often well over a year into their timetable before users start to receive any business benefits. This makes them a difficult sell and can have an adverse effect on the enthusiasm and participation of business users. The large scale of such projects brings with it significant project risk; failure in the face of such investment can be devastating. Last, they require a large, up-front commitment by the business to get underway.

Incremental development of the data warehouse avoids these drawbacks. The most visible advantage is the relative timeframe in which the first business results are perceived. Because the incremental approach subdivides the development of the data warehouse into a series of smaller data mart projects, users can see results in a matter of months rather than years.

For example, a manufacturing company might choose to implement a star schema for the orders process first, and then subsequently add schemas for shipments, inventory, manufacturing, receivables, payables, human resources, and so forth. This series of projects is contrasted with a single project of enterprise scope in Figure 7.1. The incremental approach delivers the orders data mart to users at T1. At this point, a subset of users is receiving business benefits. By contrast, the enterprise-scoped project goes on-line at T2, at which point considerably more time will have passed. The difference between T1 and T2 will be counted in years.

Incremental implementation also reduces project risk. In contrast to a single project of enterprise scope, implementation is divided into a series of smaller projects. Each of these projects requires comparatively fewer resources, smaller budgets, and shorter timeframes. Each is concerned with a limited number of source systems, and generally involves a smaller piece of the overall user community. The projects are therefore easier to control, and potential for failure is dramatically reduced. Notice also that multiple projects can be conducted in parallel; in Figure 7.1, a profitability data mart is in development at the same time as other projects.

From a business perspective, incremental implementation is usually more palatable. Getting started does not require an initial commitment to the complete solution. Projects can be prioritized according to business needs, and each project can be funded separately and by different groups. The early delivery of a production system provides a visible example of the value of analytic solutions and can help sell stakeholders on the value of additional investment.

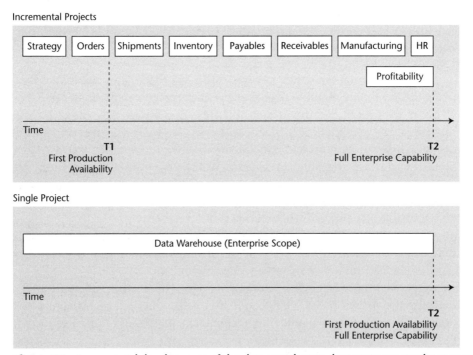

Figure 7.1 Incremental development of the data warehouse demonstrates results sooner.

Avoiding Stovepipe Solutions

Incremental implementation of dimensional solutions can introduce a new type of problem: the *stovepipe* solution. This describes a subject-area implementation that does not integrate with other analytic solutions. Typically built to address the needs of specific groups of users, stovepipes are not able to offer the additional benefits that would otherwise be expected where subject areas meet.

For example, Figure 7.1 includes projects for orders and for inventory. On their own, each of these data marts is able to provide a certain level of value to the enterprise. Together, they can potentially be used to analyze the efficiency of inventory over time, providing additional value over and above that of each data mart. If these systems are not built with an eye toward this higher purpose, they will fail to achieve this synergy, and are referred to as stovepipes. They may involve incompatible technologies, incompatible views of the data, or both. Taken individually, each system may be considered a moderate success. But taken together, they are considered a failure.

While there is sometimes a good business reason to proceed with development of a stovepipe solution, the negative connotations the label has developed are generally warranted. In addition to their failure to allow analysis to cross-business processes, stovepipes result in redundancies and inefficiencies that prove costly. For example, a single dimension may be represented in several stovepipes. Each is loaded through a separately developed process, perhaps even using different ETL tools, and therefore requiring separate skill sets. Worst of all, if two stovepipes provide conflicting data, neither may be trusted by end users.

As you learned in Chapter 1, the points of contact between subject areas are always dimensions. If two subject areas share one or more conformed dimensions, they are compatible. Using the conformed dimensions, a drill-across report can combine queries against each fact table into a single result set, providing cross-functional analysis. Sales and inventory, for example, can be compared by product and date. The comparison is enabled by a consistent view of the common dimensions. This conformance also helps mitigate otherwise incompatible technological platforms. For example, the two data marts may be located on different RDBMS platforms. However, if the same dimensions are implemented on each, and the data values are consistent, it is still possible to drill across.

The key to avoiding stovepipe data marts, then, is to ensure conformance. This is done by performing some up-front analysis across business processes before work begins on the first data mart. This initial planning work identifies the major business processes, the expected fact tables for each, and the dimensions that will be of interest across subject areas. A conformance matrix, similar to the one shown in Figure 2.2, is used to plan for the consistent use of dimensional data across all data marts.

TIP An enterprise data warehouse is planned around a set of conformed dimensions and then implemented one data mart at a time.

This process is still largely neglected or misunderstood. Lack of a common vocabulary is at least partly to blame. The term "data mart," in particular, means different things to different people. While it is used in this book to designate a subject area within a data warehouse, the term is often falsely linked with the stovepipe designation. Stovepipes result from a *process* by which a data mart is implemented, not from their subject-area orientation.

Other Approaches

While best practices suggest incremental implementation of data marts around a set of conformed dimensions, other approaches are often followed. Data marts may be implemented without first planning the overall conformance bus, perhaps because of business priorities or as a departmental effort. These data marts may turn out to be stovepipes. This may occur in the absence of a formal plan, or be the calculated result of a business decision to address a pressing need in a particular area.

Dimensional data marts may also be constructed by extracting data from a data warehouse implementation that is not based on dimensional principles. This may be done to add the analytic flexibility and performance of the dimensional approach to an architecture that is based on different design principles. The data mart itself looks the same as any other dimensional data mart. It comprises fact tables and dimension tables, constructed around the same set of principles discussed in this book. The primary difference is that its source is an enterprise repository of data, rather than a set of transaction systems. It may include aggregated data, rather than granular data. This results from the process by which such data marts are implemented, not from their dimensional focus.

Within a single enterprise, different projects may follow different approaches. Multiple data marts may be implemented serially or in parallel. But all three approaches have one characteristic in common: Each implementation is limited to a single subject area. This means that all three approaches can be extended to incorporate aggregates in much the same way.

Incorporating Aggregates into the Project

Aggregates are an important part of the dimensional data warehouse, providing significant performance improvements without significant hardware investment. In most cases, however, they may be omitted from an enterprise's first dimensional implementation. This constrains project scope, which helps the business become familiar with data warehousing implementation. Aggregates can be incorporated into subsequent projects, and may also be the exclusive focus of mini-projects.

Aggregates and the First Data Mart

For every business, the first data mart implementation is a learning experience. It will mark the first use of dimensional modeling, a design technique that goes against the principles used to design transaction systems. It introduces new software products, including Extract Transform Load (ETL) tools and Business Intelligence software, requiring new skill sets for their implementation and use. In comparison to transaction systems, the process of identifying and documenting requirements is very different; specific analytic requirements are often not known in advance. The enterprise will be learning and refining the roles of the participants and the process itself.

The first project is also an important project. Because it represents something new, it will receive heightened visibility. Although focused on a particular subject area, interested parties across the enterprise will be observing its progress. The impact of success or failure will extend beyond the scope of the project. If it is well received, other implementations will follow. If it is not, a reluctance may develop that prevents implementations in other subject areas.

In the face of challenges like these, it is natural to look for ways to reduce project risk, increasing the likelihood of success. You can reduce risk for the first data mart project in a number of ways. Choose a subject area that minimizes the complexity of the solution, perhaps one that requires a single star schema or has only one source system. You can bring in experienced resources to work with the project team. You can maximize user involvement through an iterative approach to design and development. A methodology can be implemented that carefully controls scope through a partnership between I.T. and the business users.

Every step taken to reduce the complexity of the first project helps improve the potential for a successful data warehouse. Another place project managers may look to make cuts is aggregates. Each aggregate table requires project activities to design it, to develop the processes that load and maintain it, to configure and implement an aggregate navigation capability, and to test all these components. Elimination of these steps reduces risk, allows resources to focus on other aspects of the project, and potentially shortens project length.

TIP Aggregates may be excluded from the implementation of the first data mart. This helps limit project complexity, as the enterprise develops a familiarity with data warehouse implementation.

Initially, end users are likely to accept the performance of a system that does not include aggregates. The information provided by the data warehouse is likely not to have been available in the past, and many users will find it liberating. Just having access to the information wins rave reviews, at least initially.

Needless to say, as users develop a familiarity with the data warehouse and its capabilities, they come to expect increased performance. If aggregates are omitted from the first project, their implementation should be planned to immediately follow it.

Subsequent Subject Areas

After the first data mart has been implemented, a follow-on project can add aggregates to the first data mart. Once any aggregates have been implemented, a performance expectation will have been established that must be met. Subsequent projects, therefore, should incorporate aggregates.

A sequence of data mart projects is illustrated in Figure 7.2. The first data mart project does not include aggregates. Instead, they are added as part of a subsequent project. After aggregates have been implemented for the first data mart, they are included within the scope of each subsequent project.

Data marts will not always require aggregate tables. Some data marts will be smaller in size, and will not require an aggregate portfolio. And the star schema can perform very well, even as it grows large. A myriad of database features contribute to performance, including such things as star-join optimization, clustering, compression, partitioning, and parallelization. Front-end tools may also automate the refresh of standard reports, caching the results so that queries do not need to be run when users access the report.

However, once aggregates have been introduced in the enterprise, a performance standard is set that becomes the baseline for new development. An evaluation of performance based on database size and query patterns must be made for each new data mart. If needed, aggregates must be planned and implemented.

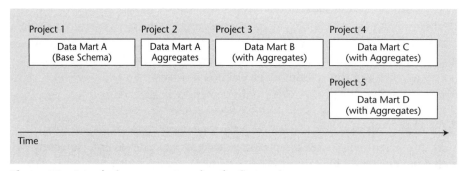

Figure 7.2 Introducing aggregates after the first project.

Implementation of aggregates is not limited to new data mart development projects. The query patterns of an analytic system will evolve and change over time, as discussed in Chapter 2. Answers to business questions lead to new questions. As the number of users grows, the diversity of business questions increases. Over time, the sophistication of users increases. Business strategy and priorities change, which in turn changes the way processes are evaluated. Hence, the best set of aggregates varies over time.

TIP An annual review of aggregate tables in each data mart is well advised. If necessary, a mini-project can be planned to update the aggregate portfolio.

When implementing a new data mart, the necessary aggregates sometimes fall in other subject areas. For example, the new data mart may share one or more conformed dimensions with an existing data mart. Drill-across queries may be aided by aggregates in each of the two data marts that summarize facts at a common grain. These drill-across boundaries are a common source of aggregate requirements, as discussed in Chapter 2.

TIP When identifying aggregates for a new data mart, be prepared to add aggregates to existing data marts that share conformed dimensions.

Whether aggregates are implemented as part of each data mart project, through a series of mini-projects, or both, the specific tasks required are similar. Project steps will be required for their design, construction, testing, and implementation. The next section, then, examines the tasks and deliverables associated with aggregate tables.

The Aggregate Project

Like any software development effort, there are many ways to organize a data warehouse project. The dimensional model lends itself particularly well to an iterative design/build cycle, which fits in with many popular methodologies. Through two or more carefully scoped iterations, the schema design is loaded with data, reviewed, and refined. This allows users to review actual work products against live data, a process that generates valuable feedback on the database design.

Iterative design is not unique to data warehousing. The approach has been employed in software engineering projects for decades. Iterative elements can be found in projects that include prototyping, joint application development (JAD), rapid application development (RAD), or any project approach in which user feedback to working software products is solicited. Iterative design can be incorporated into various project methodologies, including top down, waterfall, and spiral approaches.

Regardless of approach, the inclusion of aggregates in a data warehouse project will always require certain activities. This discussion divides the tasks among a common set of project stages: strategy, design, build, and deploy. The tasks can easily be remapped into any chosen project methodology. They can be used to incorporate aggregates in a larger data mart development project, or to organize a project that adds aggregates to an existing data mart.

In keeping with the approach to incremental deployment described previously, tasks and deliverables associated with the strategy stage are best performed once, and used to plan and organize a series of data mart development projects. Each of these projects will include design, build, and deployment stages. Figure 7.3 illustrates this approach.

This overview organizes tasks around the project stages depicted in Figure 7.3, but you may choose to reorganize the work according to the demands of your business. As mentioned, up-front planning is sometimes skipped. Depending on the business and technical environment, strategy tasks may be redistributed into individual projects or omitted. This risks incompatibility across subject areas, but may fit with business priorities.

Strategy Stage

During a strategy project or stage, the primary strategic task, in terms of aggregates, is the selection of technologies that will be used to perform aggregate navigation. The other major deliverables that touch on aggregates include the development of the conformance bus, and the organization of an implementation plan. Tasks and deliverables are summarized in Figure 7.4.

Technology Selection: Choosing an Aggregate Navigator

The technology that will provide aggregate navigation services is an important component of the data warehouse architecture. The tool chosen will have an impact on the design, implementation, and maintenance of the data warehouse. But these considerations may be subordinated to other concerns during a technology selection process. The tools that offer the capability may offer other services, which are the primary focus of product evaluation. Or, the evaluation may be limited to products that are already part of the warehouse architecture.

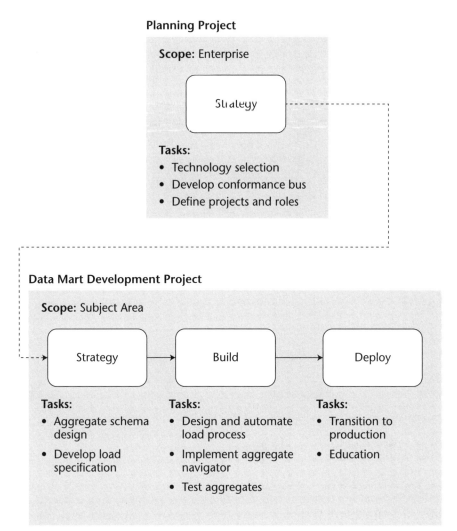

Figure 7.3 Aggregate tasks by project stage.

Whether aggregate navigation capabilities are selected based on an evaluation process, or chosen by default, it is important to fully understand the technology prior to implementing an aggregate, or even planning an implementation. It is important to understand how the technology stacks up against the functional requirements for aggregate navigation, and to understand the workflows that will be required to successfully implement the tool.

Stage	Aggregated-Related Task	Description	Deliverables
Strategy	Technology selection	Select aggregate navigation technology and document its operational profile	• Aggregate navigation component in data warehouse architecture • Documentation of functional profile/procedures for designing, building, and using aggregates
	Develop conformance bus	Design enterprise-wide framework for conformed dimensions	• Documentation of conformance bus • Documentation of rollup dimensions
	Define projects and roles	Divide enterprise model into series of data marts, prioritize projects, and define project roles	• Address inclusion/non-inclusion of aggregates in project scope statements • Indentify roles for design, development, and management of aggregates

Figure 7.4 The strategy stage: aggregate tasks and deliverables.

Constraints on Technology Selection

A variety of products offer aggregate navigation capability, but the ways in which they are configured and managed vary widely. Some are not able to designate aggregates as off-line during a load process. Some tools require extensive reconfiguration when the aggregate portfolio changes. Some tools are easier to use with particular schema designs, such as snowflakes.

The aggregate navigator will therefore have an impact on the design, implementation, and maintenance of the data warehouse. For example, the navigator may dictate that only certain types of aggregate be built, such as pre-joined aggregates. It may require that the entire warehouse be taken off-line while tables are loaded. The aggregate navigation technology will also determine whether the aggregate portfolio can be adjusted on a regular basis, or whether changes are best when batched into a project that revises the aggregate pool.

Because of these impacts, it is logical to assume that aggregate navigation capability will be a key focus in the establishment of the data warehouse architecture. Aggregate capabilities should drive the selection of the software products that comprise the technical architecture of the data warehouse. But there are factors working against this ideal.

Aggregate capabilities are usually bundled with products that perform other functions. In Chapter 4, I mentioned that the capability can be found in business intelligence tools, reporting tools, and RDBMS products. This means that aggregate navigation may be subordinated to other concerns during the selection of technology products. Consider, for example, a business intelligence tool that provides aggregate navigation functionality. An evaluation may reveal that the aggregate navigator is less than ideal because it requires significant rework each time the aggregate portfolio is changed. But the primary function of the business intelligence tool is to perform query and reporting tasks. If the tool excels in these areas, the evaluation must weigh the pros and cons. If tradeoffs must be considered, aggregate navigation capabilities are likely to take a back seat to other features.

When aggregates are to be added to an *existing* data warehouse, the selection of an aggregate navigator will likely be limited to products already on hand. While the existing data warehouse architecture does not have a formally defined aggregate navigation capability, it probably already incorporates one or more products that are capable of performing the service. In this situation, it may be difficult to justify the selection of a new product or replacement of an existing product. Consideration of aggregate technologies may be limited to tools already in place.

Beyond the Requirements

Whether aggregate navigation capabilities are selected based on an evaluation process or chosen by default, it is important to fully understand the technology prior to any implementation project. A list of eight requirements for the aggregate navigator was developed in Chapter 4. Any requirement that is not addressed will have implications on the capabilities that can be delivered. An aggregate navigator that services only one front-end application, for example, cannot improve the performance of a report that is built using a different tool.

It is equally important to understand *how* the tool meets the requirements. A check mark next to each requirement does tell a project manager how to best organize a data mart project that includes aggregates. Use of an aggregate dimension, for example, may require the development of dimensional hierarchies. Similarly, where a tool fails to meet a requirement, its operational profile may provide workarounds. An aggregate navigator that fails to support aggregate dimensions, for example, may still be used to implement pre-joined aggregates.

Evaluation of an aggregate navigator must include the impact of the product on the design, implementation, use, and maintenance of the data warehouse. Specific questions to ask in each of these categories include:

- How does the aggregate navigator affect the design of the data warehouse?

    - Does it require any particular approach to base schema design? If the aggregate navigator requires a snowflake schema, for example, this affects the data mart design process.

    - Which types of aggregates can it support? Support for aggregate fact tables, aggregate dimension tables, and pre-joined aggregates should be reviewed for implications on the aggregate schema. If a tool does not support aggregate dimension tables, for example, then aggregate fact table design must be limited to summaries that completely omit one or more dimensions.

- How does the aggregate navigator affect the construction and operation of the data warehouse?

    - Does the aggregate navigator build the aggregate tables? If so, is this capability mandatory? How are the tables defined and built? The answers to these questions may affect the process of designing the load process. It may be possible to build aggregates using an existing ETL tool, or it may be necessary to allow the aggregate navigator to build the aggregates.

    - Can aggregate tables be placed off-line? Can the aggregate navigator be turned off? If aggregates cannot be taken off-line, the load process is affected. Processing aggregates separately from the base tables will require that the entire schema be unavailable during the load. For a data warehouse that must be on-line at all times, aggregates must be loaded concurrently with the base tables—a sticky proposition, as discussed in Chapter 5.

- How does the aggregate navigator affect the use of the data warehouse?

  - How is the aggregate navigator configured? If the process is painstaking, it may make sense to limit changes to the schema design after implementation.

  - How do front ends take advantage of the aggregate navigator? Some will work transparently, while others will require that queries be explicitly directed to an aggregate navigator. It is also important to know which front ends and back ends are actually supported by the aggregate navigator.

  - How does the aggregate navigator choose which tables to use? Relative table size may not be the only factor. While the smallest fact table typically indicates the best way to respond to a query, some navigators may choose larger fact tables if an aggregate incorporates a smaller dimension table. In addition, many aggregate navigators will require definition or maintenance of database statistics such as table size.

  - Are there restrictions to the queries that are rewritten? The basic query pattern from Chapter 1 should be easily recognized and rewritten. But some aggregate navigators may have problems evaluating database-specific SQL extensions, sub-queries, unions, intersections, or queries involving views. Any advanced SQL techniques used by developers, or generated by BI or reporting tools, should be reviewed. In addition, aggregate navigators that support multiple back ends may not support vendor-specific SQL implementations.

- How does the aggregate navigator affect the change process?

  - How are changes to the base schema incorporated? If the aggregate navigator requires rework each time the base schema is altered, it may be necessary to make small changes less frequently.

  - How are changes to the aggregate schema incorporated? If extensive reconfiguration is required to add or remove an aggregate table, the frequency of changes will also be affected.

The best way to understand the answers to these questions is to test the aggregate navigator, documenting the process required to design, build, use, and change aggregates. These procedures will serve as the basis for incorporating aggregates into the lifecycle processes of the data warehouse.

Testing should involve the construction of several types of aggregates, including aggregate fact tables, aggregate dimension tables, and pre-joined aggregates. Note any design limitations. The load process should be evaluated not only from the perspective of how the data warehouse is loaded today, but also how it may be loaded in the future. The data warehouse may be loaded off-line on a nightly basis, but this may not be the case in the future. Front-end tools must be tested with the aggregate navigator to fully understand its use. It may fail to rewrite queries that it does not understand, limiting the type of query that can be written.

Working through aggregate navigation procedures in these areas will prevent unforeseen complications and enable controlled implementation of aggregates that does not disrupt existing processes. When the aggregate navigation tools are already in-house, this type of evaluation can be performed internally without vendor involvement. This allows the evaluation to be organized as an internal learning process, rather than a criteria-based tool selection process or *shoot-out*, which vendors may attempt to influence or contest.

Additional Strategic Tasks and Deliverables

The other activities that make up the strategy stage do not relate directly to aggregates. Some indirect implications are worth noting, however. These include the development of the conformance bus, the scoping of development projects, and the identification of the roles and responsibilities of data warehouse team members.

The primary focus of the strategy stage is the development of the conformance bus for the data warehouse. Identification of fact tables and conformed dimensions ensures that data marts can be built individually without resulting in stovepipes. Although it addresses only the base schema, the conformance bus is of interest when it comes to aggregates.

First, dimensional conformance provides the basis for drill-across reports that address multiple processes. The conformance bus is therefore fertile ground in the hunt for candidate aggregates, as discussed in Chapter 2. Second, conformed dimensions are not always identical. When one contains a subset of the attributes of another, it is identical to an aggregate dimension, as noted in Chapter 3. This necessitates aggregate load processing, as discussed in Chapter 5, even if no aggregate fact tables are built. The conformance bus, therefore, is an important piece of the aggregate solution.

Once the conformance bus has been identified, an implementation plan is developed. This plan breaks the data warehouse down into a set of data marts, and provides a prioritized development schedule for implementation. Scope definition for each project should stipulate whether aggregates are to be included. As discussed earlier in this chapter, aggregates may be considered out of scope for the first implementation. A follow-on project can be defined to add aggregates to this data mart. From this point forward, each new data mart project should incorporate aggregates.

To the extent that a statement of project scope can enumerate quantifiable factors, tasks, or deliverables, overall project risk can be minimized. For example, stating that the Orders Data Mart Project will include aggregates leaves the scope of the effort vague and subject to risk. Aggregate tables require resources to design and build; the difference between one aggregate star and ten aggregate stars can blow out a project's schedule. Project scope with respect to aggregates can be made more explicit by including a maximum number of aggregate schemas to be built, or by specifying aggregate scope in terms of specific reports or requirements they must support.

Last, it is during the strategy stage that the roles and responsibilities relating to aggregates should be defined. Aggregates often occupy an uncomfortable gray area between schema designers, ETL experts, and DBAs. While there is no requirement that any one of these project roles be assigned exclusive responsibility for aggregates, it is prudent to lay the groundwork for cooperation. The DBA, for example, should be consulted during the design of the aggregate schema. It may be that activation of certain database features may obviate the need for a particular aggregate table. Similarly, it is important to identify who will be responsible for constructing and maintaining aggregates. The technical staff responsible for developing the ETL process may be the logical choice, but database-oriented solutions such as Oracle's materialized views or IBM DB2's materialized query tables may be best administered by a DBA. Whatever the case, the appropriate roles must be defined and activities coordinated.

Design Stage

If you assume that the strategy tasks have been performed as part of a planning project, each data mart development project begins with the design stage. During this project stage, work is focused on designing a dimensional model to support user requirements. The planning project may have produced an initial schema design as part of the overall data warehouse architecture, in which case some of these activities will have been completed.

The dimensional model is developed in conjunction with two information-gathering tasks. One, characterized by a series of interviews with end users, gathers information requirements for the data mart. The other, characterized by interviews with technical personnel, explores the available source data. The design activity involves constructing a dimensional model that reflects the way users view and measure the business process, and the development of the load specification for that model. Additional activities center on identification and design of reports or other front-end products that will draw data from this schema.

In the midst of these tasks, it will be necessary to produce an aggregate design. Two major design tasks focus on aggregates: the design of the aggregate schema, and development of the aggregate load specification. In addition, this stage is often used to develop testing plans for the aggregate tables. These plans will be carried out during the build stage. Tasks and deliverables for the design stage are summarized in Figure 7.5.

Stage	Aggregated-Related Task	Description	Deliverables
Design	Design aggregate schema	Choose aggregates and design aggregate schema	• Aggregate schema design diagrams • Aggregate fact table definition, including grain and dimensionality • Aggregate dimension table definition, including conformance to base dimension • Table characteristics, including size, growth rate, dependencies, load frequency, and source queries • Column characteristics, including column names, data types, attribute types, source columns, and key lookup requirements
	Develop load specification	Identify source data, load frequency, and load volumes	
	Develop test plan	Plan testing of aggregate tables for performance and accuracy, and of aggregate navigator for correctly rewriting queries	• Test procedures for aggregates, including test queries and measurement process

Figure 7.5 The design stage: Aggregate tasks and deliverables.

Design of the Aggregate Schema and Load Specification

Work on the base schema begins after the first interview and continues through the entire design stage. As the project moves forward and more is learned about requirements and available data, the design is adjusted. About halfway through the design stage, most interviews have been completed. The dimensional design becomes relatively stable in terms of grain and dimensionality. Work shifts to documenting its design and developing specifications for reports. Subsequent changes to the dimensional design may occur but are minor refinements.

It is at this point that work begins on the aggregate schema design. With the grain and dimensionality in place, it is possible to begin the identification and evaluation of potential aggregates, as discussed in Chapter 2. By this time, seasoned analysts may already be aware of potential aggregates. During requirements interviews, common patterns and information requests will emerge, suggesting potential aggregates. Chapter 2 enumerates a number of techniques that will help identify and evaluate potential aggregates. The process will be informed by the capability of the aggregate navigator as well. Any unique requirements or limitations should be reflected in the schema design.

In addition to designing the schema, it is necessary to develop specifications for the process that will load it. For the base schema, this involves mapping attributes to source systems, specifying a process for the identification of changed data, and providing strategies for transforming data as required. In the case of aggregates, Chapters 5 has shown that this process is simplified. The source will be the base schema, and housekeeping columns will provide a mechanism for changed data identification. Special concerns may arise where aggregate dimensions contain type 1 attributes that are not dependent on another attribute in the dimension, or where time is to be summarized, as discussed in Chapter 6.

Aggregate processing must be incorporated into the overall plan for ETL processing. As discussed in Chapter 5, most aggregates are loaded separately from the base schema. If this is the case, they must be taken off-line before a base schema load begins. If this is not possible, all users must be locked out of the database during the warehouse load. Real-time loads may eliminate these requirements by dividing the warehouse into static and dynamic partitions.

Design Documentation

The primary deliverables of the aggregate design process are documentation of the aggregate schema and a load specification. These may be combined into a single deliverable, or provided separately. This documentation should take the same form as the design documentation for the base schema.

Specific deliverables that document the aggregate schema design and load process appear in Figure 7.5. The contents of these deliverables are described in detail under "Documenting the Aggregate Schema" in Chapter 3. Specific examples were provided in that chapter, and are reiterated here:

- Aggregate schema design diagrams (refer to Figure 3.10).
- Identification of each aggregate fact table derived from a base fact table, including its dimensional grain (refer to Figure 3.11).
- Identification of aggregate dimensions and their conformance to base dimension tables (refer to Figure 3.12).
- Detailed documentation of aggregate dimension table characteristics, including size, growth rate, dependent aggregate fact tables, load frequency, and source queries (refer to Figures 3.13 and 3.14).
- Column-by-column documentation of aggregate fact and dimension tables, including column names, data types, attribute types, source columns, and key lookup requirements (refer to Figures 3.13 and 3.14).

This documentation may be supplemented by other materials, as required. For example, it may be useful to identify the mechanisms by which the load process will take aggregates off-line. These can be supplemented with illustrations like the one in Figure 5.9. Detailed dependencies between specific load processes may also be included; an example appears in Figure 5.8. Specific technologies may dictate inclusion of additional information. For example, the use of materialized views suggests including declarations for views and dimensions, as included in Figure 4.15.

Developing Test Plans for Aggregates

During the design stage, it will also be necessary to develop plans for testing the aggregate tables. The testing must verify that the aggregate tables deliver the expected performance enhancement, provide the same results as the base schema, and are properly utilized by the aggregate navigator.

Test plans provide a set of test queries and procedures that will be executed and measured or evaluated during the build stage. In the case of performance tests, each test query is run against base and aggregate schemas, and response time is compared. Accuracy is tested by running each query against base and aggregate schemas, and comparing results. Aggregate navigators are tested by comparing original queries to the rewritten queries produced by the aggregate navigator. These techniques are described in more detail in the next section, "Build Stage."

Testing plans are often structured so that the tester of each program or product is not one of the developers who worked on it. In addition to defining the testing approach, the plan should specify how results are to be measured and documented. The plan should explicitly define what constitutes a passing versus failing designation.

Build Stage

During the build stage, the base schema is instantiated and load processes are developed to populate it with data. An iterative approach is often followed, allowing adjustment to the schema design during this stage. This same iterative approach can aid in aggregate development. Major tasks during the build stage, as related to aggregates, begin with the construction and population of the aggregate tables. This may involve developing an ETL process, or utilizing database features to define and initialize aggregate tables. The aggregate navigator is installed or configured, and front-end tools are configured to use it as necessary. All components of the solution are tested and accepted prior to moving into the deployment stage.

Iterative Build and Aggregates

An iterative approach to the build task is often used. The schema is populated through an *initial load* process, which ignores the processing of changed data. This schema serves as the basis for a user review session or process, which captures feedback and identifies in-scope refinements to the schema design. The design is adjusted, and the process is repeated. The iterative nature of this approach is illustrated in Figure 7.6.

This method provides solid user feedback when contrasted to a paper-based design review. In the presence of actual data or actual reports, users are better equipped to evaluate the solution. But the approach also introduces project risk. Without proper controls, it is possible to get stuck in this loop. What constitutes an allowable change must be defined in advance, along with the number of planned iterations. Figure 7.7 illustrates the database build process under a set of controlled iterations. This approach avoids *scope creep* that might otherwise result from interactive design.

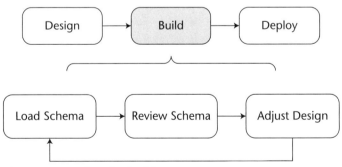

Figure 7.6   An iterative build process.

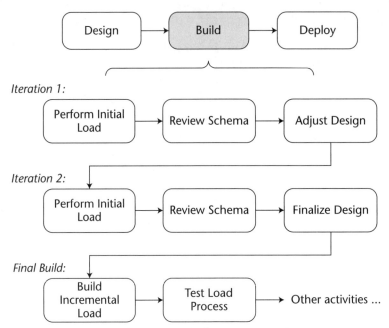

Figure 7.7   Controlled iterations of schema construction.

The design and construction of aggregate tables can benefit from the iterative approach. An initial build may be used to evaluate the aggregate design and configure the aggregate navigator. Evaluation of aggregates does not require user interaction, but does require benchmarking the performance of the aggregates. As a result of this process, refinement to the aggregate design may be deemed necessary. Once final build is completed, the aggregate schema and aggregate navigator must be tested.

Build Tasks and Aggregates

During the build stage of the project, it is necessary to build aggregates and the processes that load them, automate these procedures, implement the aggregate navigator, and test the solution. Build stage tasks and deliverables associated with aggregates are summarized in Figure 7.8.

Regardless of the project's use of iteration, these tasks will need to be conducted. At a high level, they can be grouped into two major categories: construction and testing.

Stage	Aggregated-Related Task	Description	Deliverables
Build	Implement aggregate schema	Implement aggregate tables in development environment	• Empty aggregate tables • Revised design documentation
	Build incremental load process	Design incremental load routines for each table; integrate aggregate load into overall warehouse load process	• Populated aggregate tables • Incremental load process for aggregate schema • Documentation on ETL programs and maintenance procedures
	Implement aggregate navigator	Install and configure aggregate navigation solution	• Functional aggregate navigator configured for data mart schema • Documentation on ETL programs and maintenance procedures
	Test aggregate schema	Benchmark aggregate performance and test for data accuracy	• Benchmark documentation/test results • Sign-off of testers
	Test aggregate navigator	Ensure that aggregate navigator properly rewrites queries from all front-end tools	• Test results • Sign-off of testers

Figure 7.8   The Build stage: aggregate tasks and deliverables.

Building Aggregates and Configuring the Aggregate Navigator

Like the base tables, an initial load of aggregates can omit the processing of changed data. This permits the overall performance of the aggregates to be assessed. Although relative size estimates are produced during design, these remain only estimates. Actual construction of aggregates will reveal the true table size, as determined by the sparsity of the intersection of included dimensions. Other factors, such as storage characteristics and skew, may also offset initial estimates of the performance benefit of an aggregate table.

Results of initial testing may require revision to the aggregate design. Any design refinements must be included in the design documentation. The testing process itself may also be documented, as discussed in the next section. If the iterative approach is used, the initial load process may be added to the project plan as a deliverable. However, it will not be transitioned into the production environment, so detailed documentation is not required.

Once it is determined that the aggregate offers the performance benefits expected, development of the incremental load process begins. This incremental load process will be the one that is used to load the aggregate tables in a production environment. The aggregate loads must also be integrated into the overall load process, and automated. The process must ensure that all dependencies are considered at execution time, and that aggregates are placed offline as required.

At the same time, the aggregate navigator is implemented. Any necessary configuration is completed so that the aggregate navigator can rewrite queries to utilize aggregate tables included with the data mart schema. Front- and back-end tools are configured to work with the aggregate navigator as necessary.

Documentation must be produced for each load process, the load automation, and any day-to-day management or maintenance requirements. This documentation will help warehouse managers monitor the regular load process, and provide procedures to follow should errors occur. The configuration and management of the aggregate navigator must also be documented.

Notice that specific technologies may require re-sequencing or merging some of these tasks, but that the basic requirements remain the same. For example, database aggregate navigators such as materialized views and materialized query tables require a different flow because they provide aggregate navigation and build services. The processes of defining the aggregate table, developing its load process, and configuring the aggregate navigator are accomplished by defining the materialization and setting up parameters that govern its management. If the materializations are to be refreshed after each load, the load automation process must be modified to call the database's refresh function at the appropriate time.

Testing Aggregates

After the aggregates are built and the aggregate navigator is configured, the solution must be fully tested. These tasks are of extreme importance, so much so that many project managers choose to elevate testing to its own formal project stage. Regardless of where testing fits into the project plan, three types of testing are required:

- Aggregate schema must be tested for performance (benchmarking).
- Aggregate schema must be tested for accuracy.
- Aggregate navigator must be tested.

The first form of testing, performance testing, has already been mentioned. The performance test compares the performance of a query against a base table with the performance of the same query against the aggregate table. The aggregate should provide several orders of improvement in response time. When testing these characteristics, it is important to be cognizant of internal database processing techniques. Execution of a query may cause database tables to be cached so that the next time the query is executed, performance is artificially accelerated. It may be necessary to flush the cache in between execution of test queries.

The second set of tests checks the aggregate tables for accuracy. Here, it must be proven that the aggregates adhere to the guiding principle that they always provide the same results as the base schema. This is accomplished by generating a series of flash totals from the base and aggregate schemas at various levels of granularity. Facts are summarized from both tables at different granularities, and compared to ensure that all values match. The aggregate can also be evaluated to determine that it is properly responding to slowly changing dimensions. Changes are introduced to the base schema, the incremental load is executed, and flash totals are checked again. Queries that test for dimension values that have undergone slow changes are carefully scrutinized. Outlying cases such as type 1 attributes not dependent on any other attribute are reviewed as well.

Last, the aggregate navigator must be tested. The goal of this testing is to ensure that queries are actually being rewritten to take advantage of the aggregate tables. The aggregate navigator may have utilities that allow an operator to review rewritten SQL; database products allow this through the analysis of query execution plans. Each front-end tool should also be tested to ensure that it is benefiting from rewritten queries. Depending on the products involved, this may be a simple task, or it may require coordinated scrutiny of database log tables. It is also important to verify that the aggregate navigator responds properly as aggregates are placed on- and off-line. A test query that benefits from each aggregate can be used to verify this capability, executing once with the aggregate on-line and once with the aggregate off-line.

The test results should be documented according to the procedures that are included with the test plan. As previously discussed, this will usually require that each test be carried out by someone who did not work on the development of the item. If any tests fail, developers are notified and the appropriate programs are revised. Once revision is complete, the testing must be carried out again. The testing process ends when all tests earn a *pass* designation and testers submit documentation of the results.

Deployment

At the end of the build stage, all components of the data mart solution have been built, documented, and tested. This includes the schema, the load routines, the front-end applications, and all supporting software. In the deployment stage, these items are all re-deployed in a production environment. Final tests are conducted to ensure the validity of the deployment. Education or user training is conducted as required by the project plan.

For aggregate tables, deployment activities center on their transition to production. If there is no aggregate navigator, the end user education program must include specific instruction on how to leverage aggregates. These tasks and deliverables are summarized in Figure 7.9.

These deployment tasks can be broken down into two major categories: the transition of the solution into a production environment, and the development of any necessary user education.

Transitioning to Production, Final Testing, and Documentation

Most of the deployment tasks center on the transition of aggregates to the production environment. The final deliverables mirror those of the build process; they involve establishing components of the production environment and providing finalized documentation.

Involved in this transition are the aggregate schema itself, the automated incremental load process, and the aggregate navigator. Each of these components, and any supporting software, is redeployed and configured in the production environment. A final series of tests is performed to verify that the migration to production did not introduce new errors.

During this project stage, all documentation is finalized. The schema design documentation should reflect any changes to the design or load specifications for the aggregate tables. Load documentation should reflect the final state of the routine that loads each table, the overall load process as executed on a regular basis, and all required maintenance and contingencies. The final configuration of the aggregate navigator and any required maintenance procedures are also documented.

Stage	Aggregated-Related Task	Description	Deliverables
Deployment	Implement production aggregate schema	Implement aggregate schema in production database	• Aggregate tables • Finalized design documentation
	Implement production load process	Implement production incremental load; populate aggregate tables	• Populated aggregate tables • Finalized load and maintenance documentation
	Configure aggregate navigator	Configure production aggregate navigator to use aggregate tables; configure front-and back-ends as necessary	• Functioning aggregate navigation services • Finalized documentation on configuration and maintenance procedures for aggregate navigator
	Final testing	Validate aggregate performance and accuracy; ensure that aggregate navigator properly rewrites queries from all front-end tools	• Test results • Sign-off of testers
	Education	Develop and conduct training for warehouse staff or users as necessary	• Training materials and resources

Figure 7.9 The deployment stage: aggregate tasks and deliverables.

End User Education

Aggregates do not normally bring new requirements for end user education. The aggregate navigator allows end users and report developers alike to interact exclusively with the base schema, as discussed in Chapter 4. By design, no additional instruction is necessary for the consumers of data warehouse information.

In situations where aggregate tables are deployed without an aggregate navigator, education is required for any individuals who are granted access to the aggregate tables. They must be taught when to use the aggregate schema versus the base schema, and how to decide between options when multiple choices exist. As discussed in Chapter 4, this may be a difficult leap for many end users. Specific users may be singled out to receive this information. Any technical staff developing reports must also be instructed on the proper selection of tables.

Where appropriate, the relevant information on aggregate availability and usage must be incorporated into the data warehouse user education plan. Because the manual use of aggregates is an error prone process, a periodic review with end users is advisable.

Management of Aggregates

An aggregate table is an unusual database construct, designed and developed like a table, but functioning like an index. Table designs are generally managed by data modelers and governed by formal projects; indexes are usually the responsibility of a DBA and subject to less formal change control processes. This can create confusion and uncertainty surrounding the maintenance of aggregates. Who is responsible for managing the aggregates, and how are changes handled?

The primary maintenance responsibilities associated with aggregates must be defined and assigned to individuals to ensure the proper day-to-day management of aggregates. Ad hoc changes to the aggregate portfolio are generally to be avoided in favor of project-centered adjustment. Changes to the aggregate schema are likely to be required more often than changes to the base schema, so smaller, aggregate-focused projects may be necessary.

Maintenance Responsibilities

Specific responsibilities related to aggregates must be acknowledged to ensure the proper maintenance of aggregate tables. These key responsibilities will be incorporated into one or more existing project roles. By assigning these responsibilities to existing roles, any ambiguities are eliminated.

The primary maintenance responsibilities for aggregates include:

- Monitoring of aggregate refresh process
- Correction of aggregate processing errors
- Management of the aggregate navigator

The individual responsible for *monitoring the aggregate refresh process* verifies that incremental updates to aggregates take place as scheduled and without errors. This may require a standard operational procedure, or be included in the load process through an automated notification. Satisfactory completion of aggregate processing must be declared before any changed aggregates are placed on-line.

Any errors identified are immediately turned over to the individual responsible for *corrections to aggregate processing errors*. This individual identifies the source of any error, corrects it, and ensures that the aggregate table is resynchronized with the base schema. The monitor of the refresh process is then notified that the error is corrected and the aggregate can be placed on-line.

The *manager of the aggregate navigator* may be called on to take aggregates on- or off-line in emergency situations. This individual is also responsible for any ongoing configuration required by the aggregate navigator, such as the collection of table statistics.

TIP Assign key responsibilities for aggregate management to existing data warehouse roles.

The products used to build and navigate aggregate tables will help determine how these responsibilities are assigned. In the case of materialized views or materialized query tables, the database administrator will likely be assigned all three roles. This individual will be responsible for monitoring the refresh of the aggregate tables, taking any corrective actions necessitated by errors, and configuring the database query rewrite capability as necessary.

When aggregates are built using an ETL tool, and navigated by a business intelligence product, aggregate responsibilities are distributed across multiple data warehouse roles. Monitoring the load process is best assigned to the same operational manager that monitors the load of the base schema, typically known as *the data warehouse manager*. This role is already responsible for monitoring the load process for base tables and coordinating the resources necessary to respond to errors. Responsibility for corrective actions is best carried out by an *ETL developer*, and management of the aggregate navigator will likely be assigned to the individual responsible for management of the business intelligence product.

Ad Hoc Changes to Aggregate Portfolio

The portfolio of data warehouse aggregates will require periodic changes. These changes will sometimes appear minor, giving rise to an impulse to adjust them on an ad hoc basis. This temptation should be avoided at all costs.

Like an index, the primary purpose of an aggregate table is to improve data warehouse performance. Indexes are frequently changed, added, or removed in production systems by the DBA. Sometimes, these changes are tested prior to implementation, but they are not subjected to the same rigors as a schema change. Because aggregates serve a similar purpose to indexes, it is natural to approach their adjustment the same way. This temptation is particularly strong when database features are used to implement aggregates, such as materialized views or materialized query tables.

But adjustments to the indexing scheme carry significantly less risk than adjustments to the aggregate portfolio. At worst, errors in index definition will degrade system performance. But an improperly defined aggregate can generate inaccurate results, or cause critical reports to stop working. These contingencies are far more serious than a change in system performance, undermining the integrity of the entire data warehouse. Even a materialized view can cause such damage if its query rewrite parameters are not adjusted properly.

Because the cost of a mistake can be serious, aggregate changes should be subject to the same rigors as a full development project. Each aggregate change should undergo the same series of project tasks defined in this chapter, with the same series of deliverables. This may seem onerous, but the risks justify this level of attention. And even when you follow these requirements, changes to a single aggregate table can be made quickly.

TIP All changes to the aggregate portfolio, no matter how small, should incorporate the appropriate design, build, and deployment tasks outlined in this chapter.

The required tasks do not require that a full-blown project be established each time a change is needed. Minor changes can be implemented by following a procedure, or mini-project, that incorporates the required steps. Following this standard procedure, the aggregate design is adjusted and documented, the load process revised and tested, and the solution is migrated into production. In some cases, a single individual may be able to execute all the design, build, and deployment tasks in as little as one hour.

An Ongoing Process

The portfolio of aggregates necessary to maintain performance standards will change over time. These changes are the natural result of several factors, including the increasing sophistication of data warehouse users and the evolution of business priorities. The initial implementation of a data mart usually replaces several information products that were previously compiled through a manual process, and provides new reports or analyses that address previously unmet needs. These information products will be gladly consumed by end users. The newly available information will soon give rise to new questions, and new reports will be developed.

Because the dimensional approach models a business process, rather than a specific information requirement, the design of the star schema remains stable. What changes is the way in which the schema is used. New reports are developed by or for business users, in response to their ever-evolving questions about business processes. This process is a natural part of any data warehouse lifecycle.

As user interaction with the data warehouse evolves, dominant query patterns change. New business priorities may require different ways of analyzing specific processes. As query patterns change, it is possible that the most appropriate set of aggregates will also change. Although the base schema may require adjustment only rarely, the optimal portfolio of aggregates changes with greater frequency.

Changes to the aggregate portfolio should not be exclusively bound to projects involving changes to the base schema. As discussed earlier in this chapter, a periodic review of the aggregate portfolio makes sense. Such reviews can be conducted every 12 to 18 months, unless pressing performance issues present themselves sooner.

TIP Changes to the aggregate portfolio should not be limited to times when the base schema changes.

On the occasions where the base schema does require enhancement, the impact on aggregates must be accommodated by the project plan. The same business requirements that necessitated schema design changes may indicate new query patterns. New aggregates may be in order. Existing aggregates may be affected as well. As base schema attributes are added or changed, corresponding aggregates and their load processes will require adjustment.

Summary

The dimensional data warehouse is usually implemented as a series of data marts. When preceded by a planning project, incremental implementations fit together like the pieces of a puzzle, forming an enterprise data warehouse. When their coordination is not planned in advance, the result is incompatible stovepipes.

Aggregates are commonly excluded from the scope of the first data mart. This allows the team to focus on development of the new set of competencies required by the data warehouse. They can be added to the data mart in the future, once the team has developed a familiarity with the data warehouse life-cycle. Alternatively, every project may include aggregate implementation in its scope.

The process of designing and implementing aggregate tables mirrors that of the base schema. It can be understood as a set of tasks and deliverables in each of four major project stages: strategy, design, build, and deployment.

This chapter has enumerated the specific activities and deliverables necessary at each project stage. These tasks can be reorganized to suit any development methodology. They can be executed for aggregates alone, or incorporated into a larger development effort that includes the base schema.

Attention to aggregates is not limited to development projects. Once placed in production, some maintenance activities are required. As you have seen, specific responsibilities can be assigned to existing data warehouse roles, ensuring that nothing is overlooked.

Last, you saw that aggregate tables must be subject to a change management process that follows the same tasks and deliverables as a development project. Minor changes may be executed by following a procedure or mini-project that incorporates the necessary tasks and deliverables. Periodic reviews of the aggregate portfolio should be planned, and any changes to the base schema are likely to affect aggregates as well.

Advanced
Aggregate Design

Previous chapters have covered all the basics of dimensional aggregates, including their selection, design, usage, construction, and how they factor into software development projects. This chapter returns to the topic of design, exploring the impact of advanced dimensional design techniques and alternative schema design approaches.

The advanced dimensional modeling techniques to be explored fall into two broad categories: those that primarily concern facts or fact tables, and those that primarily concern dimensions or dimension tables. Each base schema design technique brings limitations and implications for aggregate design. Advanced fact table techniques explored include snapshot models, accumulating snapshots, and schema designs in which the fact table contains no facts at all. Dimensional techniques explored include transaction dimensions, bridge tables, and solutions for heterogeneous attributes.

The approach to aggregation detailed in this book can be adapted to other types of schema design. The snowflake schema, in particular, is well suited for dimensional aggregation. A fully normalized schema can also benefit from carefully constructed dimensional aggregates, although their identification and construction may prove more challenging.

Previous chapters have described dimensional design concepts in sufficient detail for the uninitiated reader to understand how a base schema works. For some of the advanced design topics covered here, similar treatment would require multiple chapters of explanation. Those interested in learning more about the advanced dimensional design techniques presented in this chapter are encouraged to consult *The Data Warehouse Toolkit, Second Edition* (Wiley, 2002) by Ralph Kimball and Margy Ross.

Aggregating Facts

Up to this point, all fact table designs discussed have fallen into a single category: the transaction fact table. There are two other types of fact tables to consider: those based on a periodic snapshot design and those based on an accumulating snapshot design. Each bears unique consideration when it comes to the construction of aggregates. In addition, this chapter will consider how to handle base schema designs in which the fact table contains no facts at all.

Periodic Snapshots Designs

The *periodic snapshot* is a fact table design technique that captures the status of a business process at fixed intervals in time. This technique allows analysis of facts that would otherwise be difficult or time consuming to compute. Periodic snapshots typically include at least one fact that is semi-additive; its values cannot be added together across time periods. Dimensional aggregates involving semi-additive facts must not summarize the fact across the non-additive dimension. Schema designs may average the semi-additive fact across periods or sample status at longer intervals, but these derived schemas cannot be further summarized.

Transactions

The base schema designs studied to this point contain transaction fact tables. A transaction fact table models a business process as a series of events or activities. Each time the event occurs, a row is added to the transaction fact table. Dimensions associated with the row provide the contextual detail of the transaction, and facts provide a means of measurement.

The Orders fact table has served as the primary example. It is a transaction fact table that captures order transactions at the lowest level of detail possible—the order line. Additional transaction fact tables might track shipments and returns. Transaction fact tables can be found in other areas of the business as well. Spending, for example, may be modeled by a series of transaction fact tables that track the award of contracts, the issuance of purchase orders, the receipt of invoices, and their payment.

Transaction fact tables are not limited to capturing financial transactions. They may also track such things as the processing of a document, the placement of a phone call, a Web click, the location of a package, a medical test, the filing of an insurance claim. In short, any business process that can be thought of as a series of events, each of which has a set of details associated with it, can be modeled as a transaction fact table.

Snapshots

A transaction fact table of the lowest possible grain supports a wide variety of analytic questions. But this design can be difficult to use when studying the cumulative effect of a series of transactions. It may be possible to compute the status of a process using transaction history, but to do so can be difficult. The transactions that contribute to current status may be numerous. If the transactions stretch very far into the past, the data warehouse might be required to maintain a longer transaction history than would otherwise be desired. And often, the process by which current status is accrued is complex, not lending itself to computation in real time.

Your bank account, for example, can be fully understood as a series of deposits, checks written, interest payments, and fees. But imagine if the bank had to consult the entire history of these transactions, starting from your initial deposit, to determine your account balance at any point in time. And if the bank wanted to look at total deposits, not just yours, it would have to do this for every current account.

Status questions, such as account balances or inventory levels, are better answered using a different type of fact table design. While a transaction model captures the individual events that represent a business process over time, a snapshot model captures the status of a process at fixed points in time.

A periodic snapshot model for product inventory, shown in Figure 8.1, provides inventory status information as of the end of each business day. For each period, inventory level is measured for each product at each warehouse. The fact table, inventory_snapshot_facts, contains foreign keys that reference Product, Warehouse, and Day dimensions. The inventory level is stored as the fact quantity_on_hand. This design may be augmented with other facts that capture the value of the inventory on the date of the snapshot, and the quantity shipped during that day.

The snapshot schema behaves much like any other star. Facts from the fact table can be combined with dimensional attributes and aggregated to perform a variety of meaningful analyses. Inventory can be analyzed without having to compute it from the variety of transactions that affect it. But, as you will see, special care is required.

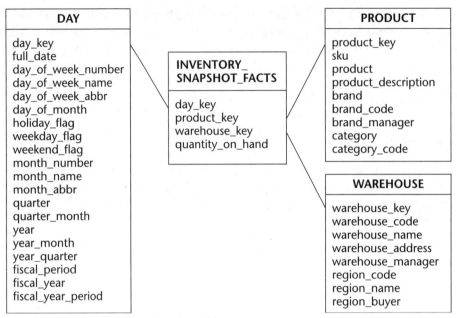

Figure 8.1   A periodic snapshot fact table.

Snapshot models are useful in a variety of situations. In banking, a snapshot star can capture daily balance by account, customer, and branch. In accounting, a snapshot fact table can be used to represent receivables by customer and day. In inventory management, a snapshot fact table represents the quantity of product at a warehouse at a point in time.

Semi-Additivity

While transaction fact tables tend to contain fully additive facts, many of the facts in snapshot fact tables are semi-additive. A fully additive fact can be aggregated across any dimension; a semi-additive fact can be aggregated across some dimensions, but not others. Special care must be taken when working with a semi-additive fact, whether building reports or designing aggregates.

Status tables usually contain semi-additive facts that are not additive across time. These facts usually represent levels of some sort, such as quantities on hand or dollars in an account. Quantity_on_hand from the inventory_snapshot_ facts table in Figure 8.1 is semi-additive. It can be meaningfully summed across Product or Warehouse to produce a valid quantity, but not across Day.

For example, suppose that at the end of yesterday, each of five warehouses had 10 widgets on hand. These values can be added together, across warehouses, for a quantity_on_hand of 50 widgets. But if a warehouse had a quantity_on_hand of 10 yesterday, and a quantity_on_hand of 10 today, you cannot add the quantities up across snapshots and say that it has a quantity_on_hand of 20.

> **TIP** Periodic snapshots are likely to contain facts that are not additive across snapshot periods.

Not all facts contained in a snapshot table are semi-additive. As mentioned previously, a units_shipped fact might be added to the schema in Figure 8.1 to assist in computing the turnover of inventory. This fact represents the quantity shipped during the snapshot period. It is fully additive. It can be meaningfully summed across products, across warehouses, or across days.

In a query or report, semi-additive facts must be used carefully. When summing a semi-additive fact, the query must be constrained by the non-additive dimension, or the sum must be grouped by value instances of the non-additive dimension. Queries that sum the quantity_on_hand fact, for example, must either filter for a specific date, or group totals by date. If the report contains subtotals or grand totals, the same rules must be applied.

A semi-additive fact *can* be aggregated across periods by computing averages, rather than sums; the result is a new fact. For example, assume the quantity_on_hand for a product at a warehouse at the end of each of three periods is 10, 20, and 0, respectively. The average over those three can be computed as the sum of the quantities (10+20+0) divided by the number of periods (3), resulting in the value 10. This result is *not* a quantity on hand, but an *average* quantity on hand. It has a different meaning; it is a new fact.

Invisible Aggregates for Periodic Snapshots

When designing an invisible aggregate schema to summarize a periodic snapshot, the presence of semi-additive facts limits available options. The aggregate schema must include the same period dimension as the base schema. Summation across the period dimension would produce inaccurate results; averaging across the period dimension would produce a new fact, and moreover a table of very limited use.

The inventory snapshot schema from Figure 8.1 measures quantity_on_hand by Product and Warehouse at the end of each Day. The Warehouse dimension includes a geographic region code and name, as well as a buyer responsible for managing region-wide inventory. Regional-level analysis can be supported by an aggregate table that summarizes quantities at the regional level, as shown in Figure 8.2. If each region contains approximately 20 warehouses, this aggregate will provide a good performance boost for regional analysis.

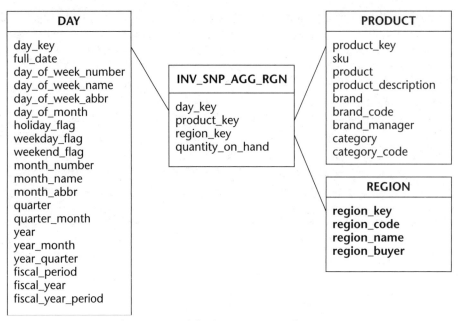

Figure 8.2   A regional aggregate of the inventory snapshot.

This aggregate fact table summarizes the base fact table by adding together quantity_on_hand values for each of the warehouses within a region. This computation makes business sense, and the resulting quantity_on_hand is semantically consistent with that of the base fact table. It represents the same information, but at a different level of detail. Any query against the aggregate schema will provide the same results as the base schema, but will require processing approximately one-twentieth the number of rows. Like its counterpart in the base schema, the quantity_on_hand fact is semi-additive; care must still be taken not to add these values together across snapshot periods.

It is not possible to build an invisible aggregate that summarizes inventory_snapshot_facts over time. The summation of quantity_on_hand across the Day dimension makes no business sense. The resulting fact would fail to meet the business definition for quantity_on_hand.

TIP   Periodic snapshots that contain a semi-additive fact cannot be represented by an invisible aggregate that summarizes across time periods.

A base schema that includes a semi-additive fact may be used to construct new schemas, but the result is not an invisible aggregate. This may occur through averaging the semi-additive fact or by saving the snapshots at the end of longer time intervals. As you will see, these derived schemas may be useful but are not invisible.

Averaging Semi-Additive Facts Produces a Derived Schema

While it is not possible to summarize semi-additive quantities across time periods by computing their sum, it *is* possible to summarize them by computing their *average*. In the case of the inventory snapshot, a monthly summary might compute the average daily quantity on hand. But notice that the resulting fact has a different business meaning. It does not represent a specific quantity that was available at the time of the snapshot, but rather the average quantity available over the course of the snapshot period. It is necessary to give the fact a name that makes this semantic distinction clear. In the schema in Figure 8.3, it is called average_daily_quantity_on_hand.

This schema may be derived from the schema in Figure 8.1, but it is not an invisible aggregate. It does not contain the same facts, immediately failing the conformance test. It is not capable of responding to a SQL statement in the same way as the base schema. While both schemas may be used to figure out an average daily quantity on hand, the syntax required to do so is markedly different.

TIP Summarization of a semi-additive fact across its non-additive dimension by averaging its value may have business use. The result is a derived schema; it is queried differently from the original schema.

The schema from Figure 8.3 is instead considered a derived schema. Queries will access this derived schema directly. The aggregate navigator is not expected to rewrite queries destined for inventory_snapshot_facts to access this schema. The facts carry a different meaning; the SQL syntax required to fetch the same results from each schema contains differences beyond simple table substitutions.

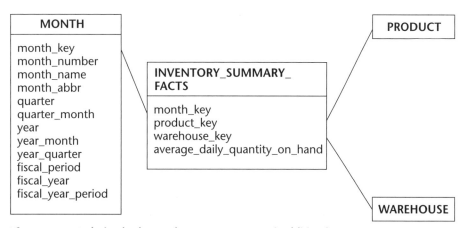

Figure 8.3   A derived schema that averages a semi-additive fact.

Notice that the average_daily_quantity_on_hand is not additive. Its values cannot be meaningfully added together across warehouses, time periods, or any other dimension. Instead, summarization of averages requires revisiting the base data. Unlike quantity_on_hand, it is not possible to summarize these facts through averages; an average of averages will not produce the correct results. The non-additivity of an average severely hampers the utility of the schema but is sometimes desirable for specific types of analysis. For example, banks have many uses for an average daily balance.

Taking Less Frequent Snapshots Does Not Produce an Invisible Aggregate

A periodic snapshot can be used to produce snapshots at broader intervals. For example, the inventory snapshot schema in Figure 8.1 samples inventory levels at the end of each day. By extracting the rows for the last day of each month, a new schema is created that provides snapshots for the end of each month. The result is shown in Figure 8.4. This process would be slightly more complex if the schema also included fully additive facts such as quantity_shipped, but a monthly snapshot could still be derived.

The monthly snapshot schema looks very similar to the daily schema. The only difference is that the Day dimension has been replaced with a Month dimension. Because the end-of-month snapshot is taken on a particular day, some schema designers choose to use a day dimension, connecting the fact table rows only to days that represent the last day of each month. In this case, the schema design would be identical.

Although the original schema and the monthly snapshot contain the same quantity_on_hand fact, the monthly snapshot cannot be treated as an invisible aggregate. Even in the presence of a full-time dimension, it is capable of producing different results from the base schema. For example, it cannot be used to compute averages across months—this would require recourse to the individual daily values.

TIP Dimensional aggregates cannot be constructed by taking less frequent samples of a periodic snapshot.

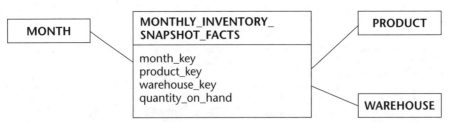

Figure 8.4 Sampling at a different period: a derived schema.

Like a schema that averages the semi-additive facts from a periodic snapshot, this schema may still prove useful. One or more of these techniques is often used to maintain historic data on-line as old data is purged from the snapshot. This form of summarization may prove a useful component of an archiving strategy, as you see in Chapter 9.

Accumulating Snapshots

A third type of schema design is known as the *accumulating snapshot*. This form of design follows something as it undergoes a series of standard steps or events. A summarization that provides significant reduction in row count usually requires elimination of so much dimensional detail that the summary provides little value, and the summary cannot be used to compute lags between process steps. Dimensional aggregates may focus on individual process steps, omitting some of the facts included in the base schema. More likely, however, the underlying process step is already fully understood by a transaction-based schema.

The Accumulating Snapshot

Many business processes can be understood in terms of a series of stages or steps that something must undergo. In made-to-order manufacturing, an individual item is ordered, manufactured, quality assured, packaged, and shipped. In banking, a mortgage application is submitted, reviewed by a loan officer, evaluated by an underwriter, and eventually consummated at a closing.

When the individual items that pass through the process are readily identifiable (an individual item being manufactured, a specific mortgage application), and the processing steps or milestones are predicable (the manufacturing process stages, the mortgage approval phases), its status can be tracked by an accumulating snapshot model. Such a model provides a way to understand the status of an individual item at the detail level, the workload at each processing step, and the efficiency with which items move from one stage to the next.

Consider the process by which a mortgage application moves from initial submission to closing. The process begins when an applicant completes a mortgage application with a mortgage officer. A processor then takes over, ensuring that documentation required to evaluate the loan application is gathered. Next, the application is reviewed by an underwriter, who reviews the application and supporting documentation, evaluates potential risk, and approves or rejects the application. The amount approved for underwriting may be less than the amount of the original application. Finally, the mortgage becomes legally binding at the time of closing.

Figure 8.5 shows an accumulating snapshot for the mortgage application process. The grain of this fact table is an application. Each application will be represented by a single row in the fact table. The major milestones are represented by multiple foreign key references to the Day dimension—the date of submission, the date approved by a mortgage officer, the date all supporting documentation was complete, the date approved by an underwriter, and the date of closing.

Note that it is not necessary to build five date dimension tables. A single date dimension can serve in all these roles; it will simply be aliased at query time or through a series of views. Similarly, the three employees involved in the process are represented by three foreign key references to the Employee dimension—one for the mortgage officer, one for the processor that assembles the supporting materials, and one for the underwriter.

The facts include several dollar amounts. The amount of the original application is the application_amount. The amounts approved and rejected by the mortgage officer and underwriter are recorded as officer_approved_amount and underwritten_amount. The amount actually loaned at closing is the closing_amount. The remaining facts will be discussed shortly.

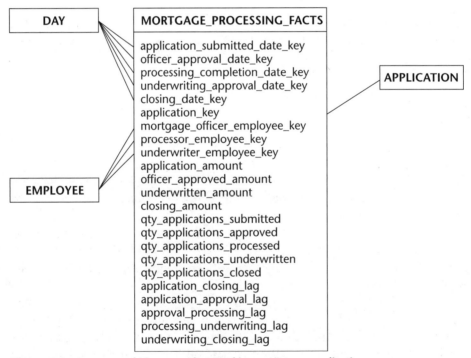

Figure 8.5 An accumulating snapshot tracking mortgage applications.

When the application is first submitted, the only date that is known is the report submission date. The appropriate day_key is assigned to the application_submission_date_key. In order to accommodate the dates that are as yet unknown, the Date dimension must contain a row for *unknown* or *n/a*. The key value for this row will be assigned to the remaining dates. The application_amount is set to the requested mortgage amount from the application. The remaining dollar amounts are initialized to zero.

As the application works its way through the process, the fact table row will be updated. The various date keys are revised as each milestone is reached. The additional facts are filled in as the appropriate milestones are reached. The fact table also contains a series of *lag* columns. These represent the number of days the application spends at each stage. Each lag is a simple calculation based on milestone dates, and is populated once it completes the appropriate stage. They allow measurement of processing time. The fact table also contains a series of quantities, each corresponding to one of the milestones. The value of each count is 0 or 1, depending on whether the application has reached the corresponding milestone. These facilitate workload reporting and will take on other values when aggregated. To make it easier to identify the current status of an application, a status attribute may be added to the application dimension or as a degenerate dimension in the fact table.

Using this schema, it is possible to study the lifecycle of a particular application, the workload at each processing, and the efficiency of the overall process itself.

Aggregating the Accumulating Snapshot

The grain of an accumulating snapshot is an individual entity that undergoes a process. When constructing an aggregate, each row must summarize numerous entities to provide significant performance savings. Because the base fact table represents a series of unique events that have occurred to the item in question, an aggregate may require summarization in many dimensions to prove useful.

For example, suppose an aggregate is to be constructed for the schema in Figure 8.5 that will support monthly analysis of the final milestone—closing payments. Simply summarizing the closing month—one of the several roles for the Day dimension—would provide no savings in rows at all because the application defines the granularity of the fact table. If an aggregate were to summarize across applications, the base schema rows would be aggregated into groups that reached each of the preceding milestones on the same date. Here, minimal summarization may be accomplished. The more milestones there are, the fewer rows are likely to be summarized. To achieve any sort of reduction in row count, it becomes necessary to summarize one or all of the milestone dates.

TIP Summarization of an accumulating snapshot often requires sacrifice of significant dimensional detail to provide a useful reduction in size.

When lags are included in the base schema of an accumulating snapshot, as they were in Figure 8.5, they will need to be omitted from most aggregates. This is because the lag corresponds to the time interval between two milestones for a particular entity that undergoes a process. When the fact table is summarized, each row now represents multiple entities. A lag can be replaced by an average lag, but this is a new fact. The aggregate fails the test of invisibility; it has different meaning, and SQL against it must be written differently. And once stored as an average, the lag cannot be further summarized in any reports.

TIP Lags are not additive. They may be summarized in a report by averaging them. But storing an average lag in a summary table has limited use because averages cannot be further summarized. The averages destroy the invisibility of the aggregate fact table. Aggregates of accumulating snapshots therefore lose much of their utility.

With the dimensional detail significantly reduced, and lags missing from the result, the potential usefulness of an aggregate is diminished. Counts may be included, permitting basic workload analysis at each milestone, but process efficiency cannot be measured in terms of lags.

Some attempts to construct a useful aggregate from an accumulating snapshot result in an aggregate that is a transaction model. This is possible when a particular fact corresponds with one of the milestone dates. An aggregate schema includes this fact in the fact table, and uses the relevant milestone date as a time dimension. Some utility may be provided here, if there is not already a detailed transaction schema surrounding the process. But again, the aggregate may not summarize a significant number of rows.

For example, the mortgage application accumulating snapshot may be summarized across all dates with the exception of the closing date. The fact table contains simply the closing_amount fact. It can be used to track dollars loaned by closing date. If the Application dimension is not summarized, this table will be no smaller than the base schema, which can also provide this analysis. Furthermore, closings may be tracked in more detail elsewhere—a separate schema may track additional characteristics of the loan at closing time, including parties that were involved and a variety of transaction fees.

TIP In general, a transaction schema is best constructed directly from source data, rather than derived from an accumulating snapshot. This ensures that the transaction schema captures the full granularity of the event.

Where a useful aggregate can be designed for an accumulating snapshot, yet another complication arises. Unlike periodic snapshot or transaction schemas, the rows in an accumulating snapshot are frequently updated. The many milestone keys for a row change over time, as will most of the facts. This makes the incremental update of aggregates very difficult; the designers of the load process may find that aggregates are better dropped and recreated at each load.

Factless Fact Tables

Another commonly encountered schema design incorporates a fact table that does not contain any facts. These tables are useful when the sole measurement of an event is its occurrence, or when it is useful to track significant intersections of dimensional values that do not correspond to transactions. In the former case, aggregates construct a fact where none existed before—a count. Symmetry with the base schema can be restored by including this count in the base schema as well. In the latter case, aggregates often destroy the meaning of the coverage relationship captured by the base schema.

Factless Events and Aggregates

Often, there are no facts to associate with an event other than the event itself. In situations like this, a fact table may contain no facts. Each row is simply a set of foreign keys that represent the dimensionality of the event. For example, the fact table in Figure 8.6 tracks student attendance during a school year. The dimensions include Student, Course, Instructor, Date, and School Year. When a student attends class, a row is recorded in the fact table.

Attendance in a class can be determined by selecting the Class dimension and counting fact table records. This process is simplified by adding a fact to the fact table, perhaps called "attendance." This fact will always be populated with the value 1, and it is fully additive. Attendance values can be added together meaningfully across any of the dimensions in a query. The attendance fact can also be summarized in an aggregate table, where it will take on values other than 1.

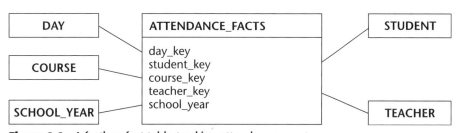

Figure 8.6   A factless fact table tracking attendance events.

Inclusion of the fact in the base schema allows aggregates to be built that will continue to mirror the base schema design. Preserving the symmetry between the base and aggregate schema enables the query rewrite mechanism of an aggregate navigator to function properly. In Figure 8.7, the attendance fact has been added to the factless fact table. Because the attendance fact appears in the base schema and the aggregate, appropriate queries can be rewritten simply by substituting table names, as shown in bold.

TIP To every event-based factless fact table, add a fact that will be populated with the value 1. Besides making the SQL more readable, this fact will allow aggregates to be queried using the same SQL syntax as the base fact table.

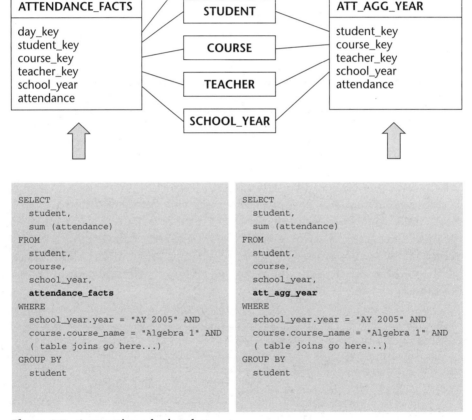

Figure 8.7 Aggregating a factless fact.

Registration and licensing activities are often the subject of factless fact tables; students register for classes, county residents license pets, drivers renew licenses. Regulations frequently require factless fact tables; businesses submit required document types to an authority on a date. Healthcare encounters generate factless fact tables; a diagnostic yields a result for a patient on a date. These event-oriented factless fact tables are transaction tables, like the Orders schema from previous chapters. If you can locate a measurable fact associated with the event, it can be added to the fact table. Fees and costs are the most likely candidates.

Coverage Tables and Aggregates

Another type of factless fact table does not model events, but instead tracks a combination of events that are in effect at a particular time. Called *coverage tables*, they are commonly used to record sales assignments, promotions, or other variable conditions that do not generate transactions of their own. Coverage is tracked in a separate fact table so that the relationship can be recorded even if no transactions are generated. Dimensional aggregates of coverage tables are rare because aggregation destroys the meaning of the base records.

Consider a sales organization in which sales representatives are assigned to named customers. An orders fact table is able to capture the relationship between the salesperson and the customer, but rows are added to this table only when an order is taken. To know who is assigned to which customers at a given time, regardless of performance, a coverage table is required. Figure 8.8 shows a coverage table that tracks the assignment of salespeople to named customers on a monthly basis. This table can be used to track customer assignments, even when an order is not taken.

Usually, a coverage table will be significantly smaller than other fact tables. As such, it may not require any aggregation at all. If it is necessary to aggregate a coverage table, care must be taken to ensure that the aggregation remains appropriate from a business perspective. Dates, in particular, give rise to semantic considerations. If a time period is summarized, the result does not accurately reflect coverage for the period. Instead, it represents a rough approximation; there was coverage at some point during the period covered by the aggregate, but not during the entire period.

Suppose that the coverage table in Figure 8.8 were to serve as the basis for a quarterly summary. If sales assignments vary by month, then there may be as many as three salespeople assigned to a customer during a given quarter. Table 8.1 provides an example. During the first quarter of 2006, three different salespeople were assigned to customer XYZ Ship Co.

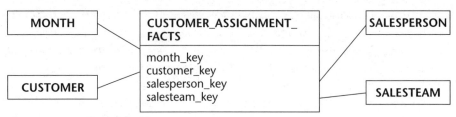

Figure 8.8 A coverage table.

Table 8.1 Monthly Sales Assignments

YEAR	MONTH	CUSTOMER	SALESPERSON
2006	January	XYZ Ship Co.	Robertson
2006	January	XYZ Ship Co.	Reid
2006	March	XYZ Ship Co.	Wong

How would this data be summarized by quarter? You can imagine a quarterly coverage table that includes one row for each salesperson who had been assigned at any time during the period. Aside from the fact that this summary does not reduce the number of rows required, notice that its meaning is different as well. A row in the base table indicated coverage during the period. A row in the summary table would represent coverage for part of the period.

TIP Exercise caution in designing aggregates for coverage tables. Summarization of the time component changes the meaning of a row in the coverage table. Summarization of other dimensions may defeat the purpose of the coverage table.

Other aggregates may be possible that do not introduce new meaning. One aggregate might omit the Salesperson dimension. The coverage table would still indicate that a particular sales team had been assigned to the customer. It would be possible to omit the customer, but this negates the purpose of the coverage table.

Aggregating Dimensions

Advanced techniques for dimension tables may also affect the design of dimensional aggregates. Time-stamped dimensions track slow changes within a dimension regardless of the presence of facts. Bridge tables resolve situations where a dimension attribute can take on multiple values with respect to a fact. Core and custom schemas cope with dimensions where a subset of attributes will vary depending on the specific item described. In each situation, the design possibilities for dimensional aggregates are affected.

Transaction Dimensions

Transaction dimensions track slow changes within a dimension regardless of the presence of facts through timestamps. Summarizing a transaction dimension without eliminating the timestamps often fails to reduce the size of the aggregate by a significant factor. Updates to the expiration timestamp render incremental updates to the aggregate prohibitively complex. In most cases, a transaction dimension is best summarized by eliminating the timestamps.

Timestamping a Dimension

Many business situations call for the careful tracking of changes to dimensional values over time. You have already seen that a type 2 slowly changing dimension can be used to record changes to an attribute by adding a new row to the dimension table when the attribute value associated with a particular natural key value changes. This technique is useful in that it neatly associates transactions with the correct dimensional attribute.

The type 2 approach falls short when it is necessary to be able to identify the status of a dimensional attribute at any point in time. Type 2 changes to an attribute are only associated with a point in time through the fact table; if there is no transaction on a particular day, it is not possible to identify the state of the attribute on that day.

The solution to this design requirement is the construction of a transaction dimension. A pair of dates is added to the dimension record, indicating the effective date and expiration date of the record. When a new record is inserted, the expiration date for the current record is set to a point in time in the future, usually the maximum date supported by the RDBMS. When it undergoes a type 2 change, the expiration is set to the previous date, and a new record is inserted with the effective date set to the current date.

It is now possible to study the state of the dimension at any point in time. A query retrieves records where the effective date is less than or equal to the date in question, and the expiration date is greater than or equal to the date in question. A current_version indicator column may be added to make it easier to identify the current state of affairs. If a series of changes occurring during a single day must be tracked as sequential changes of individual attributes rather than a single change, then effective time and expiration time can also be added as attributes.

The transaction dimension is commonly used in human resources applications, where the many attributes of an employee, including title, base pay, and the like must be carefully tracked over time. It serves as the source for useful analysis on its own, and can also be associated with snapshot or transaction fact tables. This timestamping technique can be used to track changes to other types of things as well; contracts or other documents, for example, may undergo a series of changes in status or assignments that require point-in-time analysis. Government agencies often track contracts in this way.

Aggregating a Timestamped Dimension

A timestamped dimension can be aggregated in much the same way as any other. The effective date/time and expiration date/time may be included in an aggregate dimension, preserving its transaction tracking characteristic. However, inclusion of these attributes may limit the number of rows summarized. It may be necessary to eliminate the effective and expiration dates in order to create an aggregate that will be useful from a performance standpoint.

For example, suppose that a timestamped employee dimension includes the department to which an employee is assigned. A department aggregate is to be constructed in order to support analysis of semi-monthly payroll transactions by department. Table 8.2 shows a small part of the Employee dimension.

Notice that if the transaction dates are included in the department aggregate, the number of rows needed is barely reduced. The only rows that contain the same pair of transaction dates are Wang and Green. Seven rows are reduced to six. A more effective aggregate eliminates the transaction dates; these seven rows are reduced to one, and that one row will serve for many other transactions to employees within the Marketing department as well.

Table 8.2   Values in the Employee Dimension

EFFECTIVE_DATE	EXPIRATION_DATE	DEPARTMENT	EMPLOYEE
1/27/2005	12/31/9999	Marketing	Johnson
1/31/2005	12/31/9999	Marketing	Davies
2/15/2005	12/31/9999	Marketing	Smith
2/16/2005	12/31/9999	Marketing	Wang
2/16/2005	12/31/9999	Marketing	Green
2/17/2005	12/31/9999	Marketing	Samuels
2/28/2005	12/31/9999	Marketing	Rai

> **TIP** In aggregating a transaction dimension, it is usually necessary to exclude timestamps in order to reduce the number of rows in the summary.

If timestamps are included in the aggregate dimension, the load process becomes extremely complex. When a change occurs, the expiration date in the base schema will be updated. For example, employee Green receives a promotion and joins a new department; the expiration date in the preceding table is set to the day before the promotion becomes effective, and a new row is added. However, the aggregate schema contains fact rows associated with Marketing and the dates 2/16/2005 and 12/31/9999. Because Green's expiration date has changed, previously aggregated facts associated with this row must now be reallocated to one with the new expiration date. But how?

The necessary detail to reallocate the aggregate facts is not present in the aggregate schema. This is essentially the same situation discussed in Chapter 6, where a type 1 attribute (the expiration date in this case) has changed, requiring an update to an aggregate fact table. In this case, the base transaction dimension has audited the change to the value in question. It is possible to find the previous value and use it to identify aggregate records that must be updated. This processing will be complicated. The best solution may be to drop and rebuild the aggregate each time the base tables are updated.

> **TIP** If timestamps are present in an aggregate of a transaction dimension, incremental updates will require complex processing to properly update the aggregate fact table.

The same complications do not apply if the timestamps are omitted from the aggregate dimension. In this case, previous transactions remain associated with the old value, and new transactions are associated with the new value.

Bridge Tables

Bridge tables are a design technique used to handle situations where a dimensional attribute takes on one or more values with respect to a fact. The bridge table captures this complex relationship without requiring a change to fact table grain, but comes with restrictions on how it is used.

Bridge tables are used in many ways, and there are several possible approaches to the aggregation of a schema that includes a bridge. In the simplest cases, a derived schema is constructed to eliminate the repeating value, or to allocate it across all facts. Invisible aggregates are built that summarize the derived schema rather than the original schema.

In some cases, the bridge itself may be summarized. However, the presence of an allocation factor can make this approach very difficult to load on an incremental basis. Summarization can be limited to other dimensions within the schema, but again the presence of a weighting factor will produce complications. The most straightforward aggregates of schemas that involve bridge tables simply omit the bridged dimension altogether.

Dealing with Multi-Valued Attributes

In every schema studied thus far, each fact is associated with exactly one value for a particular dimensional attribute. This is reflected by the one-to-many relationship between the dimension table and the fact table. But sometimes it is necessary to associate a single fact table row with multiple values of a dimensional attribute. When this occurs, you have a *multi-valued attribute*.

Multi-valued attributes are an issue in three types of situations:

- When a subset of dimensional attributes repeats an indeterminate number of times
- When the dimension itself is associated with the fact an indeterminate number of times
- When a dimension participates in a hierarchy that has an indeterminate number of levels

In each of these situations, you need to be able to associate a single fact table row with multiple values of a dimension attribute. Each of these dimension values may be associated with many fact table rows. Bridge tables allow you to model these many-to-many relationships, but require that great care be used when the schema is queried. Examples of each type of bridge table appear in Figure 8.9. The first captures the many-to-many relationship between bank accounts and account holders. The second captures the multiple diagnoses that result from a healthcare visit. The third captures the hierarchical relationship between companies to which products are sold. (Notice that the latter two examples bear many-to-many relationships between the fact table and the bridge; these can be resolved by inserting additional intersect tables if desired.)

Queries against these schemas must be appropriately constrained on one of the multiple values in order to eliminate the many-to-many relationship between a dimension and a fact. Otherwise, facts will be counted multiple times—once for each instance of the multi-valued attribute. In the first example, constraining for a particular customer when querying account_balance avoids double counting for accounts that have two account holders. In the second example, you can constrain on a particular diagnosis to count the number of patient encounters with which it is associated. In the third example, you must constrain by a particular parent or subsidiary company in order to avoid double counting.

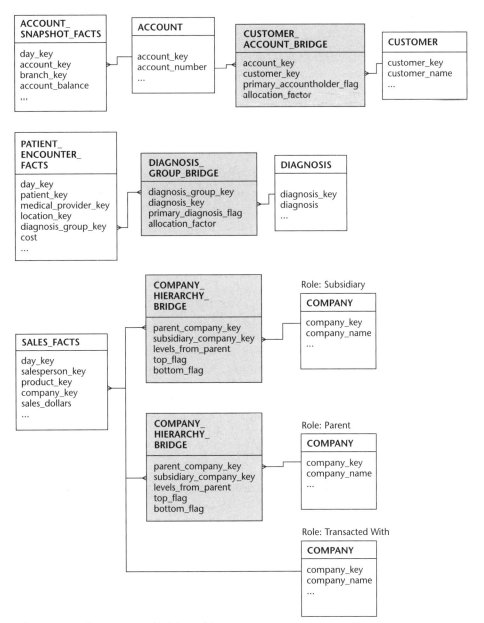

Figure 8.9   Three types of bridge tables.

Sometimes the bridge table carries an allocation factor that can be applied to the fact so that each instance of the multi-valued attribute receives a percentage of the fact value. This allows all values of the multi-valued attribute to participate in the query while avoiding the double counting.

A full discussion on the construction and use of these specialized tables is beyond the scope of this book. For a detailed treatment, see *The Data Warehouse Toolkit, Second Edition* (Wiley, 2002) by Ralph Kimball and Margy Ross.

Aggregates and Bridge Tables

There are several possible approaches to the aggregation of a schema that includes a bridge. The first two approaches involve the creation of a derived schema that eliminates the bridge; invisible aggregates are based on the derived schema. In the first case, the derived schema isolates exactly one role for the repeating attribute. In the second case, it allocates the facts across all values of the repeating attribute.

Direct aggregation of schemas involving a bridge can be somewhat problematic. In some cases, the bridge itself may be summarized, but the presence of an allocation factor can make this approach very difficult to load on an incremental basis. Summarization can be limited to other dimensions within the schema, but again the presence of a weighting factor will produce complications. The most straightforward aggregates of schemas that involve bridge tables simply omit the bridged dimension altogether.

Isolating a Single Role

A bridge table can be used in many ways. Often, the design allows the isolation of one occurrence of the multi-valued attribute, based on a special status or role. By including only this occurrence of the multi-valued attribute, a one-to-many relationship between dimension attributes and facts is restored, and the bridge is no longer required. This may be accomplished by using a view.

The surviving instance of the multi-valued attribute has a more specific business definition than the corresponding attribute in the original schema because it focuses on a particular role. As such, it should be appropriately named, and the result should be considered a new base schema From this interpretation of the base schema, standard aggregates can be constructed.

TIP A bridge can be eliminated by focusing on one occurrence of the multi-valued attribute. This transforms the meaning of the dimensional attributes, so the result is considered a derived schema. This view can serve as the basis for aggregates.

In all of the schemas from Figure 8.9 it is possible to focus on one occurrence of the multi-valued attribute. In the case of the banking schema, the bridge table includes a flag that designates one customer as the primary account holder for an account. The attributes of the primary customer can be merged into the Account dimension by joining the Account and Customer tables via the bridge and qualifying on this flag. The result is shown in Figure 8.10. Each row in the Account dimension now contains a complete set of attributes for a single customer—those representing the primary account holder. These attributes are named as appropriate. This view of the base schema simplifies its use, and can also serve as the basis for an invisible aggregate that includes a subset of attributes from the merged account dimension.

In the case of the patient encounter schema, the same can be accomplished by using the primary_diagnosis flag from the bridge. This isolates a single diagnosis per base fact. As shown in Figure 8.10, this results in a one-to-many relationship between the Diagnosis dimension and the fact table. The view maintains the diagnosis_group_key, so as not to require changes to the fact table. The view allows the diagnosis table to play the role of primary diagnosis. Summaries may be created using any desired subset of attributes from the primary diagnosis; summaries of the primary diagnosis will be symmetrical with this view.

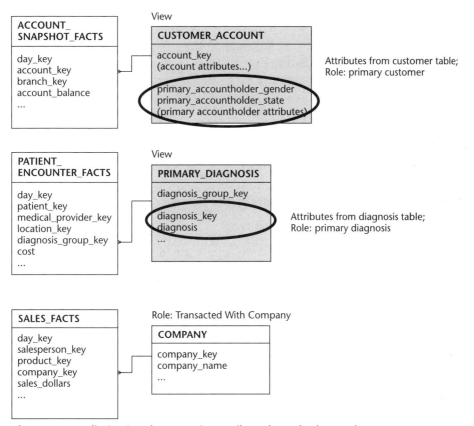

Figure 8.10   Eliminating the repeating attribute from the base schema as a precursor to aggregation.

In the case of the Orders schema, it is possible to eliminate the bridge table altogether by focusing on the company to which the product was sold directly. You do this by joining the company table to the base fact table using the existing company_key, as shown in Figure 8.10. No view is necessary. Aggregation of this configuration is possible using any subset of attributes of the company with whom the transaction occurred.

This approach can also be adapted to allow for a fixed number of instances of the multi-valued attribute. For example, you might be able to identify primary and secondary account holders for each account. Views would establish a derived schema where the Account table holds two copies of the customer attributes, one for the primary account holder and one for the secondary account holder. A similar technique allows the Diagnosis dimension to be joined multiple times to the patient encounter fact table, once for a primary diagnosis and once for a secondary diagnosis.

Allocating the Facts

A similar technique eliminates the bridge while maintaining all instances of the multi-valued attribute. This requires application of the allocation factor against the facts, which gives rise to a fact table or view that is larger than the original base fact table. For an account with two account holders, for example, two fact table rows appear, one for each account holder. The fact values in these rows are allocated according to the allocation factor; the facts now represent allocated balances.

> **TIP** A bridge can be eliminated, and repeating attributes preserved, by allocating the facts for each value. This transforms the grain of the fact table and the meaning of the facts, so the result is considered a derived schema. This schema can serve as the basis for aggregates.

This approach is possible only when the original schema design provides an allocation factor. Without the allocation factor, it is not possible to recalibrate the facts to the refined grain of the derived fact table. The result would involve double counting. In this situation, facts may be omitted from the derived fact table; it becomes a factless fact table, which can be used to track impact of particular dimension values.

Including the Bridge in an Aggregated Dimension

Up until now, the techniques for dealing with aggregation within the bridged dimension have involved first creating a derived schema, and then designing aggregates. The resulting aggregates are symmetrical with the derived schema so that any query rewrite mechanism can take advantage of them through simple substitution of table names. However, the aggregates cannot be substituted for queries against the original schema in this way; they have been constructed by constraining for a particular row.

It is possible to summarize a bridged dimension directly, without elimination of the bridge. This approach requires summarization of the bridge itself because it corresponds to the grain of the base dimension. Preservation of the allocation factor is likely to be prohibitively complex; the alternative may be to exclude facts from the aggregate. Moreover, the result of such aggregation is typically confusing to schema designers and end users alike.

In the banking schema from Figure 8.9, this might be accomplished by producing aggregates of the Account dimension, the bridge table, and the customer table. This would support analysis of summary attributes from account (perhaps an account_type) and customer (perhaps a customer_state.). The allocation factor that bridges the two summarized dimension tables must be revised. This computation is complex; it requires the allocation of the base level facts, their aggregation to two different levels (account summary and account/customer summary), and the computation of the ratio of the detailed summary to the higher summary. Worse, the meaning of this weighting factor becomes difficult to state. In the example, it represents the percentage of a fact associated with a summarization of accounts that is attributable to a summarization of customer.

TIP A bridge table can be summarized in tandem with the dimension tables
to which it relates. Re-computation of an allocation factor may be prohibitively
complex, forcing elimination of facts from the aggregate schema.

Luckily, there are other ways to summarize a schema that involve a bridged dimension. It may be meaningfully summarized in a derived state, as described in the preceding paragraphs, or through complete elimination of the bridged dimension.

Aggregating Within Other Dimensions

If the bridged dimension does not include a weighting factor, it can be included in a schema that aggregates within other dimensions. In this situation, the schema is aggregated in much the same way as a standard schema would be aggregated. Summarized dimensions receive new surrogate keys, and the base facts are aggregated according to surviving dimensionality.

For example, an aggregate of the sales_facts schema in Figure 8.9 summarizes sales_dollars by Company, Salesperson, and Month. The Product dimension is completely summarized; days are summarized by month. The resulting fact table rows are fewer and contain larger values, but still correspond to the same company hierarchy. The bridged dimension is unaffected.

If an allocation factor is present, however, any aggregation of fact table rows will render it invalid. The individual allocation factors operate on base level facts, and cannot be applied to aggregates of those facts. Again, a prohibitively complex re-computation would be necessary.

TIP An allocation factor in a bridge table is destroyed by any aggregation of the facts, even one that does not summarize the dimension that contains the bridge.

Eliminating the Bridged Dimension Altogether

When the bridged dimension is completely omitted from the aggregate, any issues related to multiple values for an attribute are eliminated. These aggregates can be designed and built following the standard techniques covered in pervious chapters. Because the multi-valued attributes do not survive in the aggregate, summarization need not be concerned with isolating roles or re-computing allocations.

TIP When the dimension involving the bridge is completely summarized, invisible aggregates can be designed and built in the same manner as for standard transaction or snapshot schemas.

For example, an aggregate of the sales_facts schema from Figure 8.9 may summarize sales_dollars by Month, Salesperson, and Product. The company dimension is completely omitted from this aggregate, which means you avoid any issues relating to the multiple values for each company's attributes. The fully additive fact is rolled up according to the surviving dimensionality of the aggregate schema; an aggregate navigator can rewrite queries by substituting the names of aggregate tables when appropriate.

The aggregate is still subject to the same concerns as standard snapshot or transaction schemas. For example, semi-additive facts must be respected by the aggregate. This means that an aggregate of the account_snapshot_facts table from Figure 8.9 may not sum account_balance values from multiple snapshot periods. In this respect, it is like any other snapshot table that does not include a bridged dimension.

Core and Custom Stars

The final design configuration to consider involves heterogeneous attributes within a dimension. This situation is modeled by planning a set of schemas: one that captures all common attributes, and one for each set of type-specific attributes. The resulting stars can each be aggregated, but are not considered aggregates of one another.

Often, the possible attributes for a single dimension will vary. Products, for example, may bear distinct attributes depending on what type of product they are. Contracts may bear distinct attributes depending on what type of contract they are. In some cases, the facts will also vary based on dimensional content. You may measure the number of checks written against a checking account, for example, but not against a savings account.

In situations like this, dimensional modelers will provide multiple schemas. One schema, known as the core schema, includes all the facts and dimensional attributes that are present in all cases. Separately, custom versions of the dimension in question are constructed that contain the core attributes plus any that are unique to each particular category or type. This dimension may be joined to the fact table when analysis is to be restricted to the category it represents. If the category has associated facts, a custom fact table is produced as well.

It is not appropriate to consider the core star as an aggregate of the custom stars. Although it may contain the same facts, its scope is broader. Whereas each custom star corresponds to one category within a dimension, the core star carries all data. Instead, the core star can be thought of as derived from the custom stars. Its fact table, for example, represents a union of the common attributes from each of the custom fact tables.

The core and custom schemas can each have their own invisible aggregates. These aggregates are designed and built according to the same rules that govern any other base schemas. Any subset of dimensions may be summarized; partial summarization will require an aggregate dimension with a new surrogate key. The restrictions of semi-additivity must not be violated in the construction of the aggregate.

Other Schema Types

The aggregation techniques presented in previous chapters have focused primarily on star schema designs. Most of these techniques can also be applied to snowflake schemas as well as schema designs in third normal form. The key to understanding the proper application of aggregation techniques is to think dimensionally.

Snowflakes and Aggregates

The snowflake schema is a dimensional model in which dimension tables are normalized. This approach dramatically simplifies the process of building and maintaining aggregates, eliminating the need to build most aggregate dimensions and simplifying the process by which aggregate fact tables are loaded.

The Snowflake Schema

A snowflake schema is a dimensional model of a business process. Like the star schema, it describes the process in terms of facts and dimensions. Facts are stored in a central fact table, along with foreign keys that reference dimensions. It is in the configuration of the dimensions that a snowflake differs from a star. In a snowflake, the dimension tables are normalized.

Chapter 1 examined a snowflaked version of the Orders schema. The snowflake in Figure 1.3 made explicit several hierarchies within the dimensions. In the Customer dimension, for example, attributes that relate the industry of a customer have been moved to a separate table and replaced by a foreign key. In other dimensions, this normalization has resulted in more tables. Product, for example, is normalized to include tables for category and brand.

The normalization of a dimension makes hierarchies among the dimensional attributes explicit. As explained in Chapter 1, a single dimension might contain multiple hierarchies. Figure 8.11 updates the orders snowflake to reflect two hierarchies present in the Day dimension: one that breaks days out according to calendar months, quarter, and years; and another that breaks days out according to fiscal periods and fiscal years. Conceivably, the Day dimension could be further normalized; attributes that represent the intersection of a year and period, for example, might be moved to still other tables.

While it is not the purpose of this book to argue for or against the snowflake design approach, some operational characteristics are worth observing. Although it reduces the size of dimension tables, the snowflake schema does not usually save a significant amount of disk space. This is because the largest tables tend to be fact tables, which contain the same number of facts and foreign keys. Queries will include more joins, which are necessary to relate the numerous tables in the dimensions. This increased complexity may have an impact on performance. Last, note that the ETL process will have more tables to contend with and more surrogate keys to assign.

Aggregating Snowflakes

The added complexity of the snowflake schema can provide some reduction in complexity when it comes to aggregates. For example, an aggregate fact table can partially summarize one or more of the dimensions in the snowflake schema, without requiring construction of an aggregate dimension. Figure 2.1 demonstrated how a dimensional aggregate can be connected to the appropriate nodes of a snowflake schema. This is possible because the snowflake dimension already makes explicit the summary level to which the fact is aggregated.

TIP Aggregate fact tables can often be connected to the normalized dimension tables of the snowflakes, which eliminates the need to design and load aggregate dimensions.

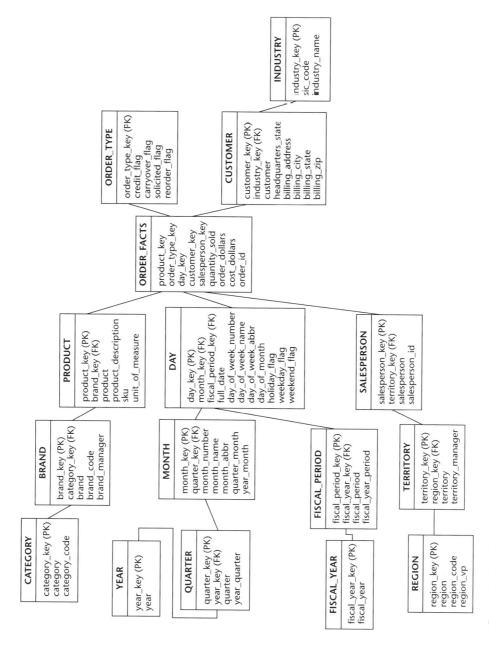

Figure 8.11 The orders snowflake.

The presence of the appropriate dimension in the base schema also simplifies the process by which the aggregate fact table is constructed. Because all necessary surrogate keys are present in the base schema, the aggregate can usually be defined using a single query. There is no need to capture natural keys and perform a lookup process to identify surrogate keys. If an audit dimension is present, it is even possible to perform an incremental update of the aggregate fact table in a single query, simply by qualifying on the date_ loaded attribute. Of course, if time is aggregated, special attention is required to keep the current time period up-to-date. This is discussed in Chapter 6.

TIP When aggregating a snowflake schema, the lack of aggregate dimensions dramatically simplifies the process of loading aggregate fact tables.

Some dimensions contain a set of attributes that are correlated only loosely, or not correlated at all. Junk dimensions, such as the order_type dimension in Figure 8.11, are one example. Another common example is a demographic dimension, each row of which contains a series of demographic attributes. Such dimensions tend not to be broken down into smaller tables in a snowflake schema, but can provide points of aggregation. Where attributes of such a table participate in aggregation, an aggregate dimension is required.

TIP When aggregating a snowflake schema, aggregate dimensions may be required when the base dimension does not isolate the required attributes in a single table.

For example, an aggregate of the orders snowflake may summarize orders by Month, Salesperson, and Credit Flag. This aggregate can be connected to existing dimension tables for Month and Salesperson, but there is no Credit Flag table. An aggregate dimension, complete with surrogate key, must be constructed to support this aggregate. The aggregate facts, in turn, will be assigned the appropriate surrogate key.

Aggregated snowflakes are still subject to the same caveats and complications as a star schema. For example, a type 1 attribute that varies independently of another attribute in a dimension can make maintenance of the aggregates next to impossible, as discussed in Chapter 6. Semi-additive facts must not be aggregated across their non-additive dimension, as discussed earlier in this chapter.

Connection of aggregates to the various dimension tables in a snowflake schema introduces new requirements for the aggregate navigator. When rewriting a query to leverage an aggregate, in addition to substituting the names of appropriate aggregate tables, the aggregate navigator will also be required to remove some joins. This may not be a problem for many aggregate navigators, but it is something that should be carefully tested prior to committing to a project or design approach. This careful validation is part of the establishment of the data warehouse architecture—a strategic task—as described in Chapter 7.

Third Normal Form Schemas and Aggregates

The construction of aggregates for the purpose of improving performance is not limited to dimensional database designs. A third normal form schema design, in fact, often derives greater benefit from aggregates than a dimensional schema design. Useful aggregates are best designed by thinking about the attributes of the schema in dimensional terms.

Normalization is a process by which a relational schema design is adjusted to reduce the possibility of storing data redundantly. As a schema is normalized, attributes that contain repeating values are moved into new tables and replaced by a foreign key. This process requires analyzing and understanding the dependencies among attributes and key columns. There are several degrees of normalization, which formally describe the extent to which redundancies have been removed. For a full explanation, there is no better resource than *An Introduction to Database Systems, Eighth Edition* (Addison Wesley, 2003) by Chris Date.

The optimal relational design for a transaction system is widely accepted to be *third normal form* or 3NF. The predominant transactions of these systems focus on atomic data, such as individual orders or customers. A schema in third normal form supports high performance insert, update, or deletion of this information because the subject data instances occur only once.

> **TIP** The terms *normalized design* and *fully normalized design* are often, and incorrectly, used synonymously with *third normal form*. In fact, there are numerous degrees of normalization. Similarly, *third normal form* is often associated with a diagramming process called entity-relationship modeling (E/R Modeling), although an E/R model can represent other states of normalization.

When a schema in third normal form is subjected to analytic queries, which require recourse to large quantities of transactions, performance can become an issue. These queries require a large number of joins, and the performance cost of this operation accumulates across large sets of transactions.

Figure 8.12 shows part of an order management database design in third normal form. This illustration is incomplete; it includes a small subset of the tables that would be necessary for an order management system, highlights only a few attributes, and labels some of the interesting relationships. (A full E/R diagram would include information on keys, nullability of attributes, optionality of relationships, descriptions of each relationship end, and a complete set of attributes.) Notice that identification of product orders by customer industry will require joining together the seven tables highlighted in the diagram. Even the dollar amount of an individual order line requires joining the order_line table, where quantity is available, with the contract_line table, where the unit price is available.

It is not uncommon for transaction systems to contain *denormalized* replicas of portions of the schema design to be used for reporting purposes. These reporting tables appear similar to the pre-joined aggregates introduced in Chapter 1. They pre-join data that was previously spread across numerous tables, but usually do not aggregate it. Where performance issues remain, aggregation becomes the logical next step.

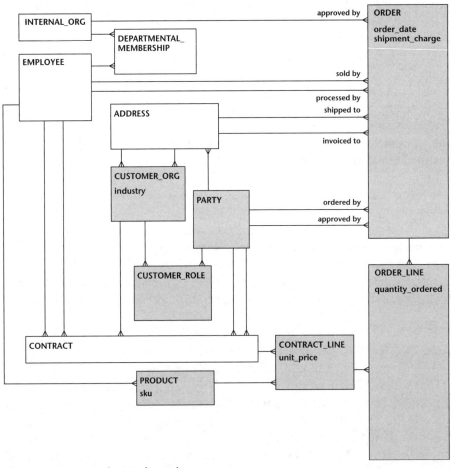

Figure 8.12 Part of an Orders schema.

Designing aggregates for a third normal form schema can be successfully achieved by thinking dimensionally, as discussed in Chapter 2. The data requirements for queries or reports that are exhibiting poor performance can be identified and categorized as facts and dimensions, and then located in the normalized schema. An aggregate table is designed that summarizes the facts used in the reports. The summary table may include foreign keys to existing tables in the database design, in which case it behaves much like an aggregate fact table. The existing tables to which it joins act as dimensions, and their attributes can be used to further summarize the aggregate table as desired.

Alternatively, the aggregate table designed may also include dimensions. In this case, it is more similar to a pre-joined dimensional aggregate. A hybrid approach is common as well; some dimensional attributes may be folded into the aggregate, which also contains foreign keys.

For example, a monthly summary of order dollars by customer can be added to the schema in Figure 8.12. The aggregate is derived by performing all the necessary joins across the shaded tables. Its attributes include the calculation of order dollars (a fact), order month (a dimension), and foreign keys that reference customer_org and Product. Shown in Figure 8.13, orders_agg_month_prod_cust summarizes numerous order lines and dates, and can be further summarized by querying it as you would query a fact table.

> **TIP** Dimensional aggregation techniques can be used to improve the performance of analytic queries directed against schemas in third normal form.

A schema like the one depicted in Figure 8.13 is often referred to as "a poor man's star schema." The summary table can be used like a fact table. However, it does not contain granular data, has not been designed to track the history of dimensional changes, and may not integrate with other applications that contain product data as well. A separate dimensional data warehouse would solve these limitations.

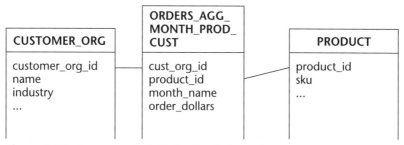

Figure 8.13   An aggregate table for the Orders schema.

Summary

Advanced dimensional design techniques affect the design of dimensional aggregates in a variety of ways:

- The semi-additive facts of periodic snapshots must not be summed across time periods. Invisible aggregates can summarize these facts across other dimensions. Derived schemas may average the semi-additive fact across periods, but cannot be further summarized.

- An accumulating snapshot is generally a poor candidate for aggregation; omission of numerous milestones may be required to produce any savings in size, and the resulting aggregate can include lag times only as averages.

- A factless fact table that models a transaction or event can be aggregated, producing a transaction count. Symmetry with the base schema can be restored by including this fact in the base schema with a constant value of 1.

- Coverage tables are usually poor candidates for aggregation because summarization destroys the business definition of the relationship the table represents.

- Aggregates of transaction dimensions usually omit timestamps. Their presence in an aggregate is likely to limit the number of rows summarized, and updates to the expiration timestamp make incremental loads complex.

- Bridge tables are often the source of derived schemas that eliminate repeating values; these schemas in turn are summarized by invisible aggregates. If the bridge does not include an allocation factor, it may be possible to summarize a bridge table itself, or limit aggregation to other dimensions in the schema.

The snowflake schema design is a variation on the dimensional model in which dimensions are further normalized. Snowflakes dramatically simplify the process of building and maintaining most aggregates. There is usually no need to construct aggregate dimensions and associated surrogate keys; aggregate fact tables can often be incrementally loaded using a simple query.

A fully normalized schema can also benefit from carefully constructed dimensional aggregates. Their identification and construction may prove more challenging, but such aggregates enhance performance by summarizing base rows and eliminating joins.

Related Topics

The previous chapters in this book have organized the discussion of aggregates around fundamental topics: selection, design, use, construction, and the project. This chapter collects together four remaining topics: archives, security, derived schemas, and aggregates that are deployed before detail.

Once added to the data warehouse, aggregate tables are an integral part of its lifecycle. One aspect of the lifecycle that has only been touched upon until now is the archive process, which governs the removal of historic data from the data warehouse. This chapter outlines requirements for the archival process that are introduced by aggregates, and also shows how they can enhance the archival process by summarizing off-line data.

Row-level security is often applied to a star schema by conditionally filtering on specific dimension values based on who is executing a query. This chapter looks at how the introduction of aggregates affects row-based security, and provides guidelines to ensure that aggregate navigation will not disrupt security enforcement. We will also see that aggregates can be deployed as supplemental base schema tables, providing unrestricted access to summarized data.

The aggregates discussed through most of this book have served as invisible summarizations of base schema tables. But not all aggregates are invisible. Next, this chapter looks at three types of derived schemas—merged fact tables, sliced fact tables, and pivoted fact tables—that transform data in such a way that you would no longer expect them to be serviced by an aggregate navigator. Although these derived tables summarize base schema tables, they are also considered part of the base schema themselves, and are accessed by users or applications directly.

Last, this chapter examines decisions that you have to make in the unusual situation where aggregated data is deployed before the associated detail. A tradeoff between level of effort and project risk must be considered, and steps will be required to locate historic detail. Careful planning will help avoid this situation.

Aggregates and the Archive Strategy

Historic data is often removed from a star schema in order to maintain tables of a manageable size. Concurrent with this archival process, corresponding data must be removed from aggregates. This data may be archived itself, or simply discarded. In addition, it may be moved to a separate aggregate table, to serve as an on-line summarization of archived detail.

The Data Warehouse Archive Strategy

The limits of data warehouse size are continuously pushed upward by ongoing improvement in RDBMS technology and a downward trend in the cost of storage hardware. As the upper limits increase, so too does the size at which a business will find the optimal tradeoff between availability of analytic data and the necessary investment to support it. Today, for some data warehouse subject areas, the amount of data generated may not be deemed significant enough to require the purging of older, historic data.

But as the practical limits of database size increase, businesses find new uses for the increased capacity of their data warehouses. High-volume transaction models, once managed at a summary level, can now be stored at the detail level. Streams of data that might once have been considered too large, such as the stream of clicks generated by visits to a website, can be maintained on-line. Thus, even with the increase in the capacity of a well-performing, cost-effective data warehouse, it becomes necessary to take steps to remove older data.

The archive strategy governs the process of removing data from the data warehouse. Usually, this process involves placing data removed from the warehouse table into an off-line storage format, so it can be retrieved in the future. The archive strategy is identified as part of the design process for each star and implemented as part of the ETL process.

During the design process of a star schema, the warehouse architect calculates the size of a row in each fact and dimension table, calculates the initial table size based on the amount of history to be loaded, and estimates the growth rate. The computations indicate how large the initial schema will be at deployment and how quickly it will grow. These results are compared with business objectives and hardware resources to determine if an archival strategy will be required. If it will be necessary to periodically archive data from the schema, the designers will indicate how and when data is to be archived.

The schema design dictates the parameters of the archival process by indicating how much history is to be maintained, and at what frequency aged data is to be archived. The maintenance of historic data in a fact table is usually expressed in relation to the primary time dimension for the schema. For example, the schema design might call for a fact table to maintain "five years of history, archived quarterly" or "eighteen months of history, archived monthly." Based on these parameters, ETL developers design a process for removing historic data from the fact table and into off-line storage.

The archival process for a fact table can be conceptualized by imagining its data segmented into bands corresponding to the archive frequency. The number of bands corresponds to the amount of history to be maintained on-line. "Five years of history archived quarterly" translates into twenty quarters maintained in the fact table. When it becomes time to load data for a twenty-first quarter, the oldest quarter is removed from the fact table. Figure 9.1 illustrates this process. The fact table is divided into twenty logical segments, each corresponding to a quarter, which is the archive period. The fact table is allowed to grow until twenty quarters are filled. When the twenty-first quarter begins, in January 2007, the oldest quarter is archived to tape.

Quarterly or monthly archive frequencies are often rejected because they disrupt the schema's ability to accurately summarize data by year. In the example from Figure 9.1, the removal of Q1 2002 renders the schema unable to report on the complete results for the year 2002. Users and developers alike must understand that the fact table contains incomplete data for this period. For example, a query that is qualified to retrieve data for the year 2002 will only provide partial results for that period. To avoid this situation, schema designers often choose to archive annually.

Even when a fact table is archived on a regular basis, it may not be expected to remain at a constant size. The number of transactions per period may change over time. In the case of steady growth over a period of five years, the most recent period will include significantly more data than the oldest period. Fact table growth, or shrinkage, must be planned for.

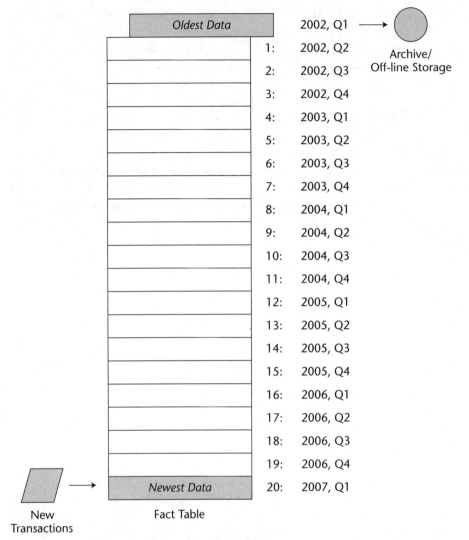

Figure 9.1   Archiving data from a base fact table.

Very large fact tables are often physically partitioned. This provides flexibility in table management, and enables the RDBMS to parallelize the process of responding to user queries. If the physical partitioning is based on the same time attribute as the archival process, the periodic purge involves removing the oldest partition from the table, and creating a new one. If the fact table in Figure 9.1 were partitioned by quarter, for example, each of the segments in the illustration would correspond to one physical partition. At the end of the twentieth quarter, the oldest partition is removed, and new partition is established.

The partitioning scheme is not required to coincide with the archival scheme. As mentioned previously, date partitioning may result in partitions of varying sizes. This imbalance may not efficiently allocate parallelized processing of query results. Further, in the case where a large percentage of queries focus on the most recent period, date partitioning may not enable parallelization at all. Instead, the database administrator may choose to partition the data by some other attribute, or based on a hashing scheme. The archival process still removes historic data as expressed in the schema design, but now requires that ETL programs copy historic rows from the base schema into an archive file and delete them from the fact table.

The process of archiving dimensional data, if necessary, will prove more complex. Except in the case of monster dimensions, dimensional history is often not purged from the star. Archived fact table history, when needed, can be brought back on-line and joined to the existing dimensions as required. When a dimension becomes excessively large, designers may choose to archive dimensional rows that are referenced only by fact table rows that have been archived, and not to any current facts. Alternatively, the schema may seek to identify records that have undergone type 2 changes, or incorporate timestamping in order to identify older records. When dimensional detail is archived, developers must ensure that the surrogate keys are not reused. This ensures that the dimensional data can be brought back into the warehouse if subsequently required.

Aggregates and Archives

When data for the base schema is archived, aggregates must be updated as well. In order to keep aggregates synchronized with the base schema, this rules out aggregations within the time dimension that do not fit neatly into archive periods. Aggregate data may be archived along with the base schema data, or simply purged from aggregate tables. Some designers may choose to move data from the aggregate schema into an on-line summarization of the archived detail; this summary must stand separately from aggregate tables that represent data currently on-line.

Maintaining Aggregates

One of the guiding principles for dimensional aggregates, introduced in Chapter 1, states that when used to answer a query, aggregates must provide the same results as the base schema. This principle requires that when data is archived from the base schema, the corresponding data must be removed from dimensional aggregates as well.

For example, Figure 9.1 shows data from the first quarter of 2002 being removed from a fact table. After this archival process has taken place, a query against the fact in this table not constrained by time will summarize all data available from Q2 of 2002 up to the current period. Any dimensional aggregates based on this fact table must provide the same results; it is therefore necessary to remove data corresponding to Q1 of 2002 from the aggregates as well. If this data is not removed from the aggregate, it will provide a different result for the same query.

TIP Historic data must be removed from invisible aggregates with the same frequency and scope as data from the base schema.

Because summary data must be removed from invisible aggregates when detail data is removed from the base schema, the grain of potential aggregate schemas is limited by the archive strategy. Aggregation within the time dimension must summarize facts within periods that fit perfectly within each archive period.

For example, the schema in Figure 9.1 is archived quarterly. Clearly, a dimensional aggregate that summarizes data by quarter can be purged at the same frequency; when a quarter is removed from the base schema, the same quarter is removed from the aggregates. Monthly aggregates conform as well because each month fits within a quarter; when a quarter is removed from the base schema, the corresponding three months are removed from the aggregate. However, a weekly aggregate will pose a problem. Calendar weeks do not fit neatly into quarters, so quarter is not a part of the time dimension. For a week during which a new quarter begins, rows in the aggregate table would not be associated with a single quarter. This is depicted in Figure 9.2: The first day of the highlighted week falls into Q1 2002, and the remaining days fall into Q2 of 2002.

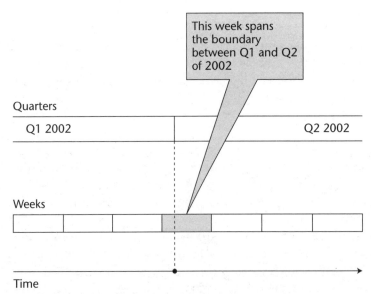

Figure 9.2   A calendar week that spans calendar quarters.

It is possible to build and maintain aggregate tables that summarize data by time periods that are incompatible with the archive cycle. However, these aggregates will require partial reconstruction at archive time. Aggregate rows that span the boundaries of the period to be archived must be removed and then new aggregate rows added for the portion of the base schema that remains. For example, if Q1 2002 ends mid-week, then all data for that week must be removed from the weekly aggregate. Then, the base schema must be consulted to identify data from the week that belongs to Q2 2002, and that data must be added back into the aggregate. In addition, users and developers must be aware that the week in question is not completely represented by the aggregate table.

Archive Versus Purge

While it is necessary to *remove* data from an aggregate when the base schema is archived, it is not necessary to *archive* it. Off-line storage of the *base* rows is sufficient to maintain a record of transactions in case a restore is ever necessary. Queries that require access to the archived data will suffer a performance hit as archived data is moved on-line. This performance hit becomes the primary determinant of query response; the availability of an aggregate in off-line storage may provide negligible benefits.

TIP Historic data purged from aggregate schemas does not require archival. Archived detail data from the base schema is sufficient to maintain history.

If relatively frequent access to archived data is anticipated, it may be useful to archive the aggregate data along with the detail data. Highly summarized queries of historic data, for example, may require moving significantly less data to on-line storage in order to complete query execution. The presence of archived aggregate data can aid in reducing the time and resources required to complete these queries.

Summarizing Off-Line Data

Another potential use of data removed from an aggregate schema at archive time is the construction of an on-line summarization of the archived data. Figure 9.3 shows a base fact table in the upper left, and Aggregate Table A just beneath it. Aggregate Table A is an invisible aggregate; the aggregate navigator substitutes it for the base fact table in application SQL when appropriate. When data is archived from the base schema, corresponding data is removed from Aggregate A. Instead of disposing of this aggregate data, it is placed in Aggregate B. Just as Aggregate A summarizes the on-line fact table, Aggregate B summarizes the off-line facts.

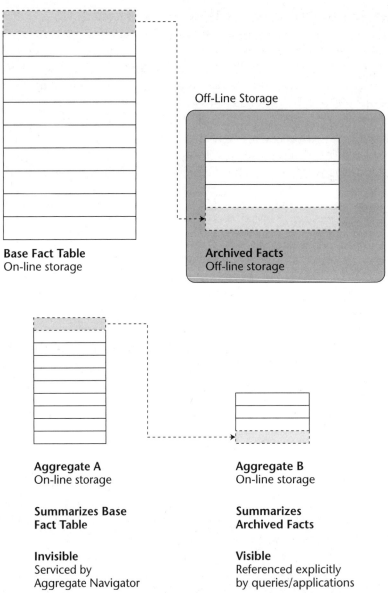

Base Fact Table
On-line storage

Archived Facts
Off-line storage

Off-Line Storage

Aggregate A
On-line storage

**Summarizes Base
Fact Table**

Invisible
Serviced by
Aggregate Navigator

Aggregate B
On-line storage

**Summarizes
Archived Facts**

Visible
Referenced explicitly
by queries/applications

Figure 9.3 Summarizing off-line data.

It is necessary for the summarization of off-line data to be maintained in a separate table from the original dimensional aggregate. Otherwise, the aggregate would contain more historic data than the base table for which it is a summary. The same query issued against the base table and the aggregate table could provide different results.

TIP Data removed from dimensional aggregates during the archive process may be placed in a table that summarizes off-line data.

The data summarized by Aggregate Table B is off-line. Aggregate table B, is not serviced by the aggregate navigator. Instead, users and developers must access it explicitly. Because it is directly referenced by application SQL, it is not considered an invisible aggregate.

Notice that a view can be constructed that performs a union of the two aggregates. This provides another useful derived table: one that summarizes all facts, both on- and off-line.

Aggregates and Security

Security requirements may dictate that not all users are permitted access to all data in a fact table. Dimensionally driven security enforcement is often used to constrain access to fact table detail. When the aggregate navigator is properly considered in the implementation of such a scheme, dimensional aggregates will continue to preserve restrictions. Restricted access to detailed data is often accompanied by unrestricted access to summary data. In this case, an aggregate can be implemented as derived schema to present summary data. This aggregate must be designed so that it does not expose performance at the detailed level.

Dimensionally Driven Security and Aggregates

Often, information contained in a fact table is provided on a need-to-know basis. An individual user may be authorized to access only a subset of the facts. When such a limitation can be expressed dimensionally, the warehouse architects develop a plan that limits access based on data in the star schema. Applied to transaction systems, this technique is often referred to as *row-level security*. Applied to a dimensional schema, it can be described as *dimensionally driven security*.

A dimensionally driven security scheme automatically constrains queries against a fact table for specific dimensional values associated with the user. This enforcement is most often applied directly to fact table keys. For example, business rules may dictate that a salesperson is allowed to access only their own orders and not those of their fellow salespeople. User A is a salesperson subject to this restriction. In the Salesperson dimension table, the surrogate key associated with User A is 1022. A view is constructed that includes the constraint `where salesperson_key=1022` on the appropriate foreign key in the fact table, and User A is configured to access the fact table through this view. Figure 9.4 depicts the view.

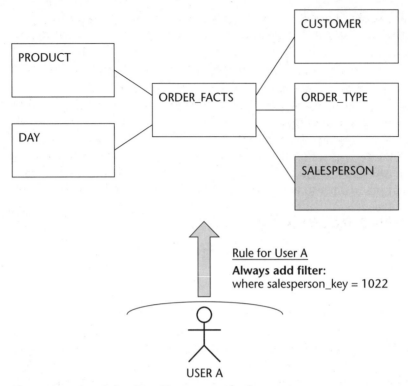

Figure 9.4 Restricting User A's access to the facts.

From the perspective of the user, this approach replaces the fact table with a band or partition containing only records the user is permitted to access. It is effectively a *sliced fact table*, as discussed later in this chapter, but is not physically instantiated. Any query, even one with no constraints, will return only information that the user is authorized to view.

Alternative means for implementation of this scheme may be offered by the RDBMS or by reporting tools that achieve the same result. Each time User A queries the fact table, a qualification on the appropriate salesperson_key is automatically enforced. The scheme may also be extended to involve session parameters and/or a stored list of constraints, generalizing the solution so that it is not necessary to construct a separate view or restriction for each user. If the dimension that is the source of the constraint undergoes type 2 changes, the key constraints will require updates as well. It is not necessary for the user to appear in the dimensional data. For example, a user may be restricted to specific products or customers by constraining on the appropriate keys.

In the presence of aggregates, the insertion of the dimensional constraint should take place before the aggregate navigator receives the SQL query. This enables the aggregate navigator to include the constrained column when identifying dimensional aggregates for which the query can be rewritten. Aggregates that contain the constrained column are considered for query redirection; aggregates that do not include the constrained attribute are not considered. The dimensionally driven constraint therefore survives the query rewrite process.

TIP Be sure the configuration of the aggregate navigator will enforce dimensionally driven security.

Suppose that an aggregate for the schema in Figure 9.4 summarizes order_facts by Salesperson, Product, and Month. When User A queries the base schema, a filter on salesperson_key is automatically inserted into the query. The aggregate navigator searches for possible aggregates that can resolve the query, which includes the constrained key column. The Salesperson-Product-Month aggregate includes the necessary key and will be considered by the aggregate navigator. Similarly, an aggregate that excludes the Salesperson dimension will not be considered. Dimensionally driven security remains enforced. Notice that if there are users for whom no dimensional restrictions are inserted, aggregates that exclude Salesperson may participate in rewritten queries.

If the dimensional constraint is a summary level attribute, it may be necessary to constrain on the attribute itself rather than fact table keys. This ensures that summarizations of the dimension in which the attribute survives will still benefit from rewritten queries, even though the surrogate key has been replaced by one for the aggregate dimension.

In all cases, it is necessary to verify that the enforcement of dimensionally driven security is compatible with the aggregate navigator. The aggregate navigator must receive SQL into which the constraint has been inserted; if views are used to implement the security scheme, it must be able to substitute underlying tables as appropriate.

Unrestricted Access to Summary Data

Often, restrictions that apply to granular data are relaxed for summarized data. When this is the case, an aggregation of the base schema may be made available without enforcement of dimensional restrictions. Accessed explicitly when summary data is requested, this aggregation serves as a derived schema. The aggregate must be designed so that granular performance cannot be deduced though comparison to base schema data.

For example, salespeople may be restricted to viewing their own order detail, but are also allowed to look at summaries of corporate performance. The Order Facts table of Figure 9.4 is made available, subject to dimensionally driven security constraints, to provide salespeople access to their order detail. An aggregate table is constructed that summarizes all orders by Product and Month; this table is made available for unrestricted access to summarized data.

Because the unrestricted aggregation provides different results than the base table—corporate totals rather than salesperson totals—it is a derived schema. It is not serviced by the aggregate navigator, but instead accessed directly by application SQL. In combination with the base schema, it can be used by an individual salesperson to compare their performance with that of the company as a whole.

> **TIP** When a dimensionally driven security scheme is in place, use a derived schema to provide unrestricted access to summarized data.

When a derived schema will provide unrestricted access to summarized data, it must be designed to prevent users from deducing the performance of a restricted value. Known relationships between dimensional attributes may circumvent some attempts to protect detailed data through summarization. In other cases, the skew of data values may make it possible to deduce the performance of a particular individual or group.

For example, if salespeople are assigned to specific customers, summarizing order facts from Figure 9.4 by Day, Product, and Customer does not sufficiently obscure the performance of individual salespeople. Anyone who understands the assignment of salespeople to customers can infer the performance of individual representatives by looking at customer data.

Skew can lead to less obvious breaches of security restrictions on detailed data. Suppose that salespeople operate within sales regions. If the average region contains 20 salespeople, an aggregate of Order Facts by Month, Product, and Region may appear to sufficiently hide the performance of individual salespeople. But if there is one region in which there are only one or two salespeople, the performance of those individuals is exposed by the aggregate.

> **TIP** Verify that a derived schema design will not reveal restricted detail, either through inference or by providing summarization of a very small group.

Derived Tables

The dimensional aggregates on which much of this book is focused are invisible to end users. As anonymous stand-ins for base schema tables, they are chosen when appropriate by the aggregate navigator. Not all dimensional schemas constructed from base schemas fit this profile. A derived schema, as introduced in Chapter 1, transforms the schema or alters its content. Some aggregation may be performed in this process, but the derived schema will be used in a different manner from the base schema.

You have already seen several examples of derived schemas. In Chapter 8, you saw that averaging the semi-additive fact of a snapshot schema resulted in a derived schema. Earlier in this chapter, you saw that the summarization of a dimensionally constrained fact table is a derived schema. In both cases, the new fact table provides different information from the base schema.

Derived tables can be powerful additions to the data warehouse, often used in the development of second level data marts that provide cross-functional analysis. A merged fact table combines information from multiple fact tables at a common grain. A pivoted fact table provides multiple facts in place of a single fact with a fact type attribute (or vice versa). A sliced fact table contains a dimensionally partitioned subset of base fact table data. In each case, the derived schema alters the base schema in design or content; the result will be accessed directly by application SQL.

The Merged Fact Table

Drill-across reports combine information from multiple fact tables based on common dimensionality. When the grains of the two fact tables are different, the lowest level of common dimensionality corresponds to an aggregation of at least one of the fact tables. Chapter 2 observed that if such an aggregation provides significant reduction in fact table size, it is a good candidate for an aggregate table. Because it will be accessed in drill-across reports, you know the aggregation will be used.

For example, the base schema in Figure 9.5 contains fact tables that contain sales goals (annual_plan_facts) and actual orders (order_facts). The sales plan is constructed at a high level of summarization, with quarterly targets by category and sales region. Orders are captured at a significantly finer grain. The two schemas conform at the Quarter, Category, and Region levels. An aggregate of order_facts at this level would summarize a significant number of rows, and be leveraged any time a drill-across report was constructed to compare the plan dollars with actual order dollars. (This aggregate is shown in the top portion of Figure 9.6.)

Execution of a drill-across report requires separate queries against each of the fact tables. Results are then merged together by performing a full outer join on the common dimensional attributes. The fact tables must not be joined in a single query, as this would cause facts to be replicated in a Cartesian relationship. The process by which these steps are carried out varies with the query or reporting tool to be used. The first two queries may be performed separately with results stored in temporary tables, and then joined by a third query; the tool may execute two queries and perform the join itself; or the tool may perform the entire task in a single SQL statement when the required syntax is supported by the RDBMS.

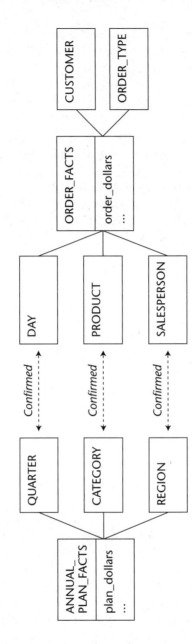

Figure 9.5 Plan versus Actual.

Some query and reporting tools do not support drilling across multiple fact tables. In these cases, a derived table can be constructed to support the drill-across requirement. A single fact table is constructed that merges facts from both base fact tables. This merged fact table must be constructed using the same process as a drill-across report; its contents must represent a full outer join of the data from the two fact tables based on their common dimensionality.

A comparison of planned versus actual orders can be supported by a merged fact table, which is derived from the two fact tables in Figure 9.5. Shown in the bottom portion of Figure 9.6, the merged fact table supports comparison reports for reporting tools that cannot generate drill-across reports. The drill-across operation has been performed in the construction of the fact table, rather than the construction of the report.

Chapter 2 cautioned that a merged drill-across fact table is not an invisible aggregate. It appears to present the same content as the base fact tables, albeit in a pre-joined manner and at a higher level of summarization. But there is a major difference: It may be necessary to store a fact with the value zero in the merged table, even if there was no transaction in the base fact table.

This difference is a result of the full outer-join used to merge data from the two base fact tables. Where a combination of dimensions is represented in one table but not the other, a row must be recorded. For the fact that did not contain a row in the base schema, a value must be recorded.

For example, the annual plan may include targets for a product category that the business decides to eliminate part way through the year. As a result, no orders appear for this category during the fourth quarter. The order_facts table will not contain any rows for these products, nor will order_facts_aggregate in the top of Figure 9.6. But the merged fact table in the bottom of Figure 9.6 contains plan_dollars for the fourth quarter for the product category that was eliminated. For these rows, order_dollars must be set to zero.

This merged fact table can provide different information than the base fact table. A query against the base fact table that sums order_dollars by category for the fourth quarter will not include the product that was eliminated. The same query, directed at the merged fact table, will return the product category in question, with an order_dollars value of zero.

Because of its different behavior, the drill-across fact table should not be substituted by an aggregate navigator in queries that address only one of the fact tables. Instead, this table should be accessed explicitly by application SQL, and only when both facts are required.

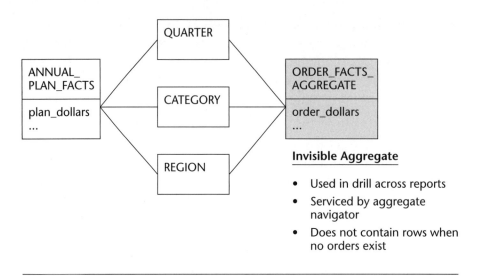

Invisible Aggregate

- Used in drill across reports
- Serviced by aggregate navigator
- Does not contain rows when no orders exist

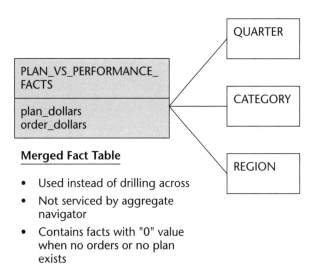

Merged Fact Table

- Used instead of drilling across
- Not serviced by aggregate navigator
- Contains facts with "0" value when no orders or no plan exists

Figure 9.6 Drilling across an aggregate versus using a merged fact table.

> **TIP** A merged fact table is a derived table, capable of providing slightly different results than the base fact tables. It is accessed explicitly by application SQL, and only when facts from all base fact tables are required.

Developers and users should be aware that the merged fact table must not be used for reports that require only one of the facts; these should be directed at the appropriate base fact table. Otherwise, the inexplicable presence of zero values will clutter the report. These values will be further confusing if there are combinations of dimensions not referenced by either fact table. These combinations will not appear at all. For example, there may be another product category for which no plan and no sales existed. This product category will not show up on the report at all, even with a value of zero.

The Pivoted Fact Table

The pivoted fact table is another type of derived fact table. Although it summarizes information from another fact table, the information is restructured in such a way that queries against the two tables must take different forms. Pivoted fact tables are constructed when different types of report benefit from slightly different schema designs.

Financial data marts often require this type of solution. The star schema at the top of Figure 9.7 shows a fact table that summarizes transactions in the general ledger on a daily basis by account, department, project, and transaction type. In this example, there are two transaction types: credits and debits. Credits are positively signed, and debits are negatively signed.

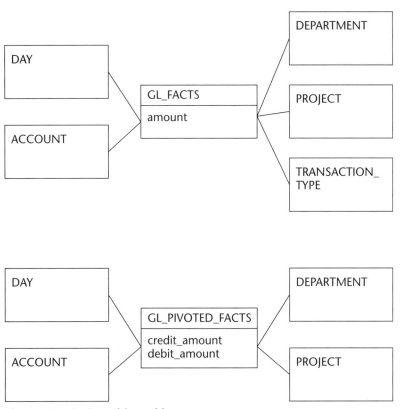

Figure 9.7 A pivoted fact table.

This arrangement allows the net effect of various transactions to be analyzed simply by summing them together across any dimension. For example, Table 9.1 shows a credit of $3,000 and a debit of $2,500 applied on the same day to account 1000, department 47, project 901. The transaction amounts can be summed together to produce a net change of $500 to account 1000, department 47, project 901.

While useful for reports that aggregate across transaction types, many financial reports require that data be structured differently. In these reports, credit amounts and debit amounts must appear in separate columns. Unfortunately, the fact table stores these amounts in different rows. A new fact table, like the one at the bottom of Figure 9.7, can be constructed to support these reports. The transactions that appeared in different rows are now summarized in a single row. Table 9.2 shows the effect on the sample rows.

This arrangement makes it easier to produce financial reports where credits and debits appear in separate columns. Although it contains fewer rows than the previous fact table, this pivoted schema cannot be substituted for the first by an aggregate navigator. The facts have different meanings than the one in the original schema—they are tied to specific transaction types. It may be possible to fetch the same information from these tables, but the SQL syntax will be quite different. And like the drill-across table, the pivoted fact table must include new zero values if a transaction of one type appears but not the other. For example, the account was credited but not debited on a particular day. The original fact table contains no debit amount; the pivoted fact table contains a debit amount of zero.

TIP Pivoted fact tables contain different facts, are queried differently, and may include facts even when no transactions occurred. They are therefore considered derived tables. They will not be serviced by aggregate navigators; instead they are accessed explicitly.

Table 9.1 Transaction Type

DATE	ACCOUNT	DEPT	PROJECT	TRANS_TYPE	AMOUNT
2/1/05	1000	047	901	CREDIT	3,000.00
2/1/05	1000	047	901	DEBIT	(2,500.00)

Table 9.2   Separate Facts for Each Transaction Type

DATE	ACCOUNT	DEPT	PROJECT	CREDIT_AMT	DEBIT_AMT
2/1/05	1000	047	901	3,000.00	2,500.00

Notice that you could just as easily derive the fact table with a transaction type dimension from the fact table with separate facts for each transaction type. Each one represents a pivot of the other. It can be left up to ETL developers to determine which one shall be derived from the other; from the perspective of end users, both are base schemas representing the same information in different formats.

The Sliced Fact Table

The last type of derived table to consider is the sliced fact table. A sliced fact table contains all the attributes of the base fact table but contains only a subset of rows. Unlike merged or pivoted fact tables, the sliced fact table looks identical to the table from which it has been derived.

Sliced fact tables are often used in situations where relevant data is to be replicated from a central data warehouse to a separate geographic location where it will be heavily used, or where data that is collected locally is migrated to a central location and *unioned*. This is illustrated in Figure 9.8. Slices may also be used to relocate *hot* data to an alternative storage technology, such as an OLAP server. The security scheme earlier in this chapter that dimensionally constrained a fact table results in a sliced fact table, although it may not be physically instantiated.

Sliced fact tables may be derived from a base fact table, but should not be considered invisible aggregates of that fact table. Because they are limited in scope to a particular dimension value, such as a geographic range, they are not able to provide the same results as a full fact table. The sliced fact table is not able to answer queries that span slices.

> **TIP**   Sliced fact tables belong to the base schema, and will be accessed explicitly via application SQL.

Like the relationship between pivoted fact tables, a sliced fact table may be derived from the complete fact table, or the complete fact table may be derived from the slices. Which tables are actually derived will be determined by the business use and load process.

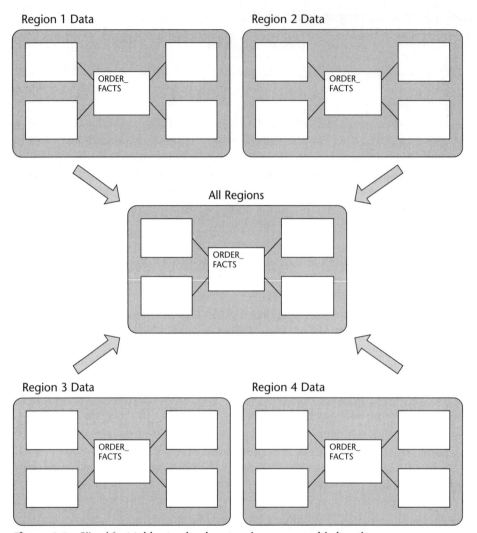

Figure 9.8 Sliced fact tables track sales at various geographic locations.

When Rollups Are Deployed Before Detail

In most situations, detail data is made available before any summarizations are put in place. As a best practice for fact tables, this ensures that transactions are captured at the lowest possible grain. As you saw in Chapters 5 and 6, this also allows for the most efficient load process. Base tables are loaded from operational sources, while aggregates are loaded from the base tables.

In the case of dimension tables, what is considered a summary table may also serve as a base schema table. In Chapter 2, you saw an example where Brand and Month dimension tables were part of the sales forecast star schema, a base star. These dimensions were conformed rollups of Day and Product dimensions, respectively, which are referenced by other base schema tables such as order facts.

Occasionally, the incremental development of data marts leads to an unusual situation in which the rollup table is needed before the base dimension. If sales forecast data is to be implemented before orders, for example, you will need Month and Brand before you need Day and Product. Similarly, financial data marts frequently call for a corporate_organization dimension that will be needed in other subject areas at a more detailed level. The same is often true of account dimensions.

If a conformance bus has been developed for the data warehouse, the implementation team will know in advance when a dimension table being deployed summarizes a detail table needed in the future. The project can incorporate the construction of the more granular dimension, and use it as a source for the rollup. In the absence of advanced planning, the rollup may be built without consideration for the future need of additional detail. In this case, some rework may be well advised.

Building the Base Table First

This book has emphasized the importance of planning the incremental development of a dimensional data warehouse around a set of conformed dimensions. Planning a warehouse bus, or conformance matrix, ensures the consistent use of dimensional data across subject areas. The compatibility of schema designs across subject areas is guaranteed.

When this upfront planning has taken place, developers will be aware of situations in which summary data is required before detail data. Consider the conformance bus depicted in Figure 2.2, which includes a sales forecast subject area and an orders subject area. If the sales forecast data mart is to be built first, the matrix reveals that it will require several dimensions—Month, Brand, and Sales Region—which are rollups of more detailed tables to be constructed later.

When developers know in advance that the initial data mart calls for summarized data, they can plan to build the detail table first. It is then possible to follow the best practices, as outlined in Chapters 5 and 6, to produce summary tables directly from the detail. The additional work required to build the detail table will not be wasted; it will be ready to use when a subsequent data mart calls for it.

This approach avoids a future situation in which it becomes necessary to build a detailed table for which a summary already exists. Because the summary table does not contain the data necessary to build the detail table, the detail table must be constructed from transaction sources. Developers must then choose between the risk of maintaining parallel load processes, or redeveloping the load process for the summary table while preserving its existing key values.

Building the Rollup First

In the absence of a plan that organizes data mart implementation around a set of conformed dimensions, the need for summarized data in advance of detail may be unanticipated or ignored. If the load process for the table in question does not first construct the detailed dimension, future projects that require the detail will face a dilemma. A parallel load process can be developed for the detail data, or the existing summary can be rebuilt. Both approaches have associated risks. And in both cases, it will be necessary to backfill the detail table with historic data corresponding to data already present in the rollup.

Parallel Load Processes

When a detailed table must be built for which a summary already exists, developers may choose to build the detail table and leave the summary untouched. While this approach is possible, it suffers from redundant processing, and risks inconsistent application of transformation rules. For these reasons, Chapter 6 suggested that aggregates should be sourced from base warehouse tables. Now, examine the consequences of the alternative. At best, maintenance becomes more complex; at worst, there is a failure in conformance.

TIP The development of a redundant load process for a detail table associated with an existing summary leads to inefficient load processing and maintenance, and risks conformance failure.

Figure 9.9 depicts parallel load processes developed for Product and Brand tables. These are conformed dimensions; all attributes of the Brand table are present in the Product table, attribute values will be identical, and all combinations of summary attributes present in the base table will appear in the summary table. Only under these conditions can stars that involve these tables be compared in drill-across queries.

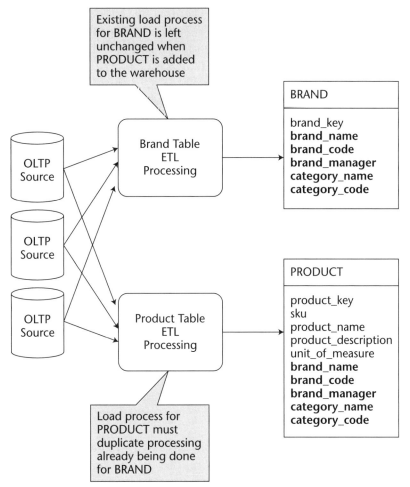

Figure 9.9 Parallel load processes for summary and detail data.

If the load process for the summary table is built first, and left unchanged when the detail table is implemented, redundant processing will be required for the detail table. A separate changed data identification process will be needed. It must identify changes in attributes that are not part of the rollup table. In the example, this includes product attributes SKU, product_name, product_description, and unit_of_measure. In contrast, when a summary is loaded from the base table, only one changed data identification process is needed. As you saw in Chapter 6, a simple update_date on the base dimension table eliminates the need to identify changed source records for summary processing.

All work done to process attributes in the detail table that already exist in the summary table will be performed redundantly. In Figure 9.9, the five attributes of Product that appear in bold type are also present in the Brand table. Identical application logic constructs these data elements in both load processes. When a summary is loaded from the base table, this redundant processing does not take place; the attributes are selected directly from the base table.

Redundant processes for changed data identification and attribute transformation affect the efficiency and maintainability of the ETL process. Because the same work is being done multiple times, system resources are consumed inefficiently. The load process may take longer, require additional resources, and involve multiple error handling contingencies. The implications for maintenance of the warehouse are also significant. New attributes in the dimensional model, changes to the source system design, or updated business rules will require that both load processes be updated, rather than just one.

The inefficiencies of redundant load processes may be acknowledged and accepted by the warehouse team, but this does not eliminate the associated risks. Understanding the implications of maintaining two processes allows for allocation of appropriate resources for the load process. But it does not safeguard against inconsistent application of transformation or processing rules. Any differences in the way source data is selected or transformed by the two processes may result in dimensions that fail to conform. In this case, they will fail to provide accurate results in drill-across situations or where the summary table is used in a dimensional aggregate.

Redeveloping the Load

When a detail table must be built for a summary that already exists, the warehouse team may choose to rework the load process for the summary after building the load process for the detail table. This avoids the inefficiencies and conformance risk associated with maintaining parallel processes. Developers must preserve the surrogate keys assigned to existing summary records; otherwise the referential integrity of the existing schema will be destroyed.

Returning to the example, let's assume that the project team chooses to rebuild the load process for Brand after adding Product to the warehouse. Product is loaded from the operational source systems. The existing load process for Brand is discarded; a new one is created that extracts data from the Product table. The result, shown in Figure 9.10, avoids redundant processing.

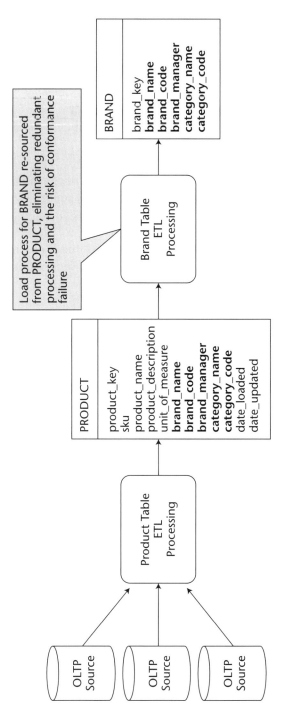

Figure 9.10 Avoiding redundant loads.

This scenario avoids the inefficiencies and dangers associated with the redundant processing option. A single changed data identification process is applied to source system data and used to assemble the product table. The date_updated attribute of Product will be used to identify changed data when loading Brand. All the dimension attributes in the Brand table are assembled only once, during the Product load. Because transformation rules are applied only once, values of conformed attributes will be identical. The danger of conformance failure is eliminated.

> **TIP** When adding a dimension table for which a summary already exists, redevelopment of the rollup's load routine will eliminate processing inefficiencies and reduce the risk of conformance failure.

During the renovation of the load process for the rollup dimension, the existing surrogate keys must be preserved. Existing fact tables contain these values in foreign key columns. Their alteration will destroy the referential integrity of the schema, and require the existing fact table history to be reloaded.

For example, assume the Brand table has been constructed for a sales_forecast fact table. In production for a year, the Brand table now contains several hundred records, each of which has a surrogate key. The brand Redi-Pack, for example, has a brand_key of 2167, which is referenced by many rows in the sales_forecast fact table. It now becomes necessary to add a product table to the data warehouse, to support an order_facts star. After the load process for Product has been developed, the load process for the Brand table is reconstructed. The existing rows in the Brand dimension table must remain unchanged so that sales_forecast facts that reference brand_key 2167 must still point to Redi-Pack because sales_forecast rows contain the brand_key.

> **TIP** When replacing the load routine for an existing dimension table, previously assigned surrogate key values must be preserved.

Historic Detail

When a detail table is built for a rollup that already exists, the new table must be backfilled with historic detail that corresponds to existing summary data. This historic data is needed to ensure conformance, whether the previously existing load routine is left alone, or replaced. Without it, the rollup table will contain information not present in the base table.

In this section's example, a Product table is added to a schema that already contains a Brand table. Product is a new table, whereas Brand contains existing data. If some brands have been purged or updated in the source system, these values will not be represented in the Product table unless steps are taken to load historic data. Without this history, the Brand and Product tables will be capable of providing different results.

TIP When a detail table is built for a rollup that already exists, it is loaded with historic data going as far back in time as the data in the existing table. Without this historic data, the new detail table will not conform to the existing rollup table.

Product and Brand must conform, whether to support drill-across reports or the development of dimensional aggregates. The presence of brands in the rollup table that do not appear in the detail table violates the rule of conformance. While drill-across reports may function, the presence of brands in one schema that are missing in another will confuse users. In the case of a dimensional aggregate, browses against the Product dimension will produce different results depending on the inclusion or exclusion of product attributes.

If historic data is not available for the attributes of the new, detailed dimension table, the existing summary data may be combined with "not available" values for the new detail attributes. This ensures that the summary attribute values are present in both tables so that all queries will return the same results. For example, if Product is constructed after Brand, a Brand that is no longer in use may be inserted with the product_name of Not Available. This ensures that all data present in Brand is present in Product. Be advised; this workaround is one step away from creating a level field. As advised in Chapter 3, be sure that this structure is not exploited to store multiple levels of aggregation in a single fact table.

Summary

The data warehouse may include an archive process by which historic data is removed from database tables and placed in offline storage. To preserve the conformance of aggregates with the base schema, this process must remove aggregate data as well. Aggregations within the time dimension that do not fit neatly into archive periods will confound this process, and should be avoided. Aggregate data need not be archived with the base schema data; instead it may be purged. Aggregate data may also be moved into an on-line summarization of the archived detail; this summary must stand separately from aggregate tables that represent data currently on-line.

Dimensionally driven security enforcement is used to constrain access to fact table detail based on a user's identity. When the aggregate navigator is properly considered in the implementation of such a scheme, dimensional aggregates will continue to preserve restrictions. The requirement for restricted access to detailed data is often accompanied by one of unrestricted access to summary data. An aggregate, implemented as derived schema, can meet this requirement. This aggregate must be designed so that it does not expose performance at the detailed level.

While aggregates are almost always derived from other warehouse tables, not all meet our definition of invisible aggregates. Although not serviced by an aggregate navigator, three types of derived tables provide increased accessibility and performance by simplifying the query or reporting process.

- A merged fact table combines information from multiple fact tables at a common grain, which eliminates the need to access multiple fact tables in a drill across configuration.

- A pivoted fact table provides multiple facts in place of a single fact with a fact type attribute (or vice versa), which eliminates the need to transform rows into columns or columns into rows.

- A sliced fact table contains a dimensionally partitioned subset of base fact table data, supporting partitioned access to data as required by business rules, data distribution needs, or collection requirements.

In each case, the derived schema alters the base schema in design or content; the result will be accessed directly by application SQL.

The incremental deployment of a data warehouse may require the introduction of aggregated dimensional data prior to the detail. If a conformance bus has been developed, this requirement will be identified in advance, and detail data can be loaded along with the rollup summary.

In the absence of advance planning, the rollup might be built without consideration for the future need for detail. Once the detail is called for and its load process created, the team must decide what to do about the process that loads the rollup. Leaving it as-is minimizes work but introduces inefficiency and risks conformance failure; replacing it reduces risk but adds work. In either case, the team must ensure that the detail data covers the same historic period as the rollup, and that keys are preserved. Otherwise, the rollup fails the test of conformance.

Glossary

accumulating snapshot   A fact table design that models an item as it undergoes a uniform series of events or milestones. Aggregation of an accumulating snapshot usually destroys a significant portion of its analytic value, removing multiple milestones and eliminating its ability to support lag calculations.

aggregate dimension table   A stored summary of base schema information that contains dimensional attributes. An aggregate dimension table must conform to a base dimension table. Aggregate dimension tables are typically invisible. An aggregate navigator rewrites queries to access aggregate dimension tables as appropriate; the end user need not know they exist.

aggregate fact table   A stored summary of base schema information that contains facts and foreign key references to one or more dimensions and/or aggregate dimensions. An aggregate fact table stores data from a base fact table at a coarser grain. An aggregate fact table may be invisible to end users if it adheres to fundamental principles outlined in Chapter 1. An aggregate navigator hides its presence from end users. Some aggregate fact tables transform the base data in some way; these derived fact tables do not meet the requirements of an invisible aggregate but may provide benefits as additions to the base schema.

aggregate navigator   A component of the data warehouse architecture that rewrites application queries to leverage aggregate tables. The aggregate navigator maintains all information needed to rewrite queries, so that users and developers need only interact with the base schema.

aggregate schema   Summary tables in a dimensional data warehouse. Those that can stand in for base tables in a SQL query through substitution of table names are known as invisible aggregates. The invisible aggregate schema must provide the same results as the base schema and be composed entirely of attributes present in the base schema. It is invisible to the end users. See also *base schema*.

aggregate star   An aggregate fact table and the dimensions referenced by its foreign keys. An aggregate star summarizes the information from a base star schema at a coarser grain.

aggregation point   A notional level within a dimension to which information may be aggregated. May correspond to a hierarchy level, but hierarchies are not required. For example, product_type is a potential aggregation point within the Product dimension.

audit dimension   A dimension table containing information about the process that loaded fact table rows. Attributes of an audit dimension might include the date of the load, the name of the program that executed the load, and the server on which it was executed. When processing an aggregate fact table load, the audit dimension can be used to identify base schema rows that have been added since the last time the aggregate was updated.

base schema   Fact and dimension tables within a dimensional data warehouse that do not summarize other fact and dimension tables; fact and dimension tables that are not aggregates. Base schema tables are typically built first and loaded from operational systems.

B.I. tool   See *business intelligence tool*.

bridge table   A table added to a star schema that resolves hierarchical relationships between dimensions, or multi-valued attributes that would otherwise require a many-to-many relationship between fact and dimension. The presence of a bridge table will require careful review of proposed aggregations.

browse   The process of querying data in dimension tables. Dimension browse queries are often used to identify constraints that will be used to query the fact table.

bus   See *data warehouse bus.*

business intelligence tool   A packaged software product that enables end users to develop or access queries and reports.

cardinality (of an attribute)   The number of distinct values taken on by an attribute.

conformance bus or matrix   A planning tool that represents graphically how multiple business processes or fact tables reference a set of common dimensions. This tool helps ensure that identical dimensional data is referenced consistently throughout the data warehouse so that implementation of individual data marts does not result in stovepipe solutions. The conformance bus may also be used to identify potentially useful aggregates.

conformed dimensions   Dimension tables that are the same, or where one dimension table contains a perfect subset of the attributes of another. Conformance requires that data values be identical, and that the same combination of attribute values is present in each table.

core and custom fact tables   A schema design that addresses the varying dimensionality of a business process. A core schema includes all attributes that are common for the entire process; a custom schema includes additional attributes common to a dimensional subset. Both the core and custom fact table are considered base schema components, even if one is derived from the other. Dimensional aggregates can be built for each.

coverage table   A factless fact table that tracks the coincidence of dimensional information in the absence of any event or transaction. Coverage tables are used to identify things that do not happen. Aggregates of coverage tables are usually meaningless. Not all factless fact tables are coverage tables.

data mart   A database that contains a copy of operational data, organized to support analysis of a business process. A data mart may be a subject area within an enterprise data warehouse, or an analytic database that is departmentally focused. When not planned as part of an enterprise data warehouse, a data mart may become a stovepipe. When deployed as an adjunct to a normalized data warehouse, a data mart may contain aggregated data. When built around a conformance bus, the data mart is neither a stovepipe nor an aggregation.

data warehouse   A database containing a copy of operational data that is organized for analytic purposes.

data warehouse bus   The relationship between a set of shared, conformed dimensions with the fact tables in a data warehouse. The data warehouse bus is an enterprise-wide dimensional framework that ensures cross-functional compatibility. A data warehouse bus design enables the incremental development of subject area–focused data marts that will not become stovepipes. See also *conformance bus*.

database administrator   An individual responsible for management of an RDBMS. Responsibilities may include user management, indexing, tuning, and backup and recovery.

DBA   See *database administrator*.

derived table   A warehouse aggregate table, constructed from another warehouse table, that alters the schema design or content. Derived tables are considered part of the base schema and are not serviced by an aggregate navigator. They are accessed directly via application SQL. Examples of derived tables include the merged fact table, the pivoted fact table, and the sliced fact table.

dimension   A shorthand term that is used to refer to a dimension table or a dimension attribute.

dimension attribute   Any data element that is used to filter, break down, or roll up facts. Dimension attributes provide context for facts.

dimension table   A table in a star schema design that contains dimensional attributes and a surrogate key.

dimensional aggregate   A table in an aggregate schema.

dimensionally driven security   A scheme that filters the fact table based on one or more dimensional attribute values associated with the profile of the user or group. Dimensionally driven security schemes create a virtual fact table slice for each user. Aggregates of the base schema should work with a dimensionally driven security scheme if the dimensional constraint is added to a query before it reaches the aggregate navigator. A dimensional aggregate may be provided as a base schema object if unrestricted access to summary data is required.

drill across   The process of combining information from multiple fact tables. A drill-across report requires relevant data from each fact table to be combined via a full outer join on common dimensional attributes. When the result is stored in a new fact table, the result is a type of derived table called a merged fact table.

drill-across fact table   See *merged fact table*.

enterprise data warehouse   A database that contains a copy of enterprise data, reorganized for analytic purposes. Subject areas within the enterprise data warehouse are called data marts.

enterprise reporting tool   See *reporting tool*.

ETL   See *extract, transform, load*.

ETL tool   A commercial software product that is used to develop the warehouse load process. Most ETL tools are server-based and contain a metadata repository. In comparison to a hand-coded load process, an ETL tool improves the maintainability of the warehouse load process. The ETL tool may also be used to construct aggregate tables.

extract, transform, load (ETL)   The process by which data is taken from operational systems, restructured to suit the data warehouse design, and placed in data warehouse tables. The ETL process may be developed using custom code, or using a packaged ETL tool. Aggregate tables may also be built as part of the ETL process.

fact   A metric by which a business process is evaluated. Part of a dimensional model, facts are rolled up or filtered based on dimensional attributes, which give them context. In a star schema, facts are stored in a central fact table, which also contains foreign keys referencing dimension tables.

fact table   A table in a star schema that contains facts and foreign keys that reference dimension tables. Fact tables may also contain degenerate dimensions.

factless fact table   A fact table that contains foreign keys but no facts. Factless fact tables may track the occurrence of events, such as student attendance, for which no additional metrics are available. Aggregates for these tables create new facts that count the number of records summarized. Factless fact tables may also track dimensional relationships in the absence of events, in which case they are known as *coverage tables*.

front-end tool   Any software product that provides end users with information from the data warehouse. Front-end tools include reporting tools, charting tools, and OLAP tools. See also *business intelligence tool*.

grain statement   The meaning of a fact table row. Grain statements may be declared dimensionally, as in "orders by date, salesperson, product and customer," or in relation to a business artifact, as in "orders by order_line." The grain of aggregate fact tables is usually expressed dimensionally.

hand-coded load   An ETL process that is built without the use of a specialized ETL tool. Hand-coded loads are built using existing development platforms such as COBOL or procedural SQL.

heterogeneous dimension   A dimension whose attributes vary depending on its type. When a dimension potentially contains heterogeneous attributes, schema designers may choose to include all common attributes in a core schema and add type-specific attributes in a custom schema.

hierarchy   A series of master-detail relationships within a dimension. Many front-end tools require hierarchy definitions in order to support *drilling* features. Some aggregate navigation and construction tools, such as Oracle's materialized views, require explicit declaration of a hierarchy if a dimension is to be partially summarized by an aggregate fact table.

invisible aggregate   Summary tables in a dimensional data warehouse that can stand in for base tables in a SQL query through substitution of table names. The invisible aggregate schema must provide the same results as the base schema, and be composed entirely of attributes present in the base schema. It is invisible to the end users.

junk dimension   A dimension table that contains a group of attributes that are not correlated with one another, usually left over after all remaining dimensional attributes have been assigned to other dimension tables.

key lookup   During fact table loads, the process of using the natural key from source data to identify and assign the appropriate surrogate key in the data warehouse. A key lookup may also be used in the construction of aggregate fact tables. See also *lookup.*

lookup   The process of searching a table for a row or rows that contain one or more attribute values. When performing the incremental load of a dimension table, lookups are used to determine if a dimension record already exists for a source record, or if slow changes have occurred. See also *key lookup.*

merged fact table   A derived fact table that includes facts from two or more fact tables, stored at a common grain. A merged fact table eliminates the need to drill across multiple fact tables, and is often part of a second-level data mart that provides cross-process analysis. Merged fact tables may require the storage of a fact with the value zero where the base fact table contained no rows. Merged fact tables are not serviced by the aggregate navigator; they are accessed directly via application SQL. Invisible aggregates may be built that summarize merged fact tables.

natural key   An attribute or group of attributes that uniquely identify the source data corresponding to a row in a dimension table. These attributes usually do not uniquely identify a row in the dimension and do not serve as its primary key. See also *surrogate key.*

normalization   A process by which a relational schema design is adjusted to reduce the possibility of storing data redundantly. As a schema is normalized, attributes that contain repeating values are moved into new tables and replaced by a foreign key. This process requires analyzing and understanding the dependencies among attributes and key columns. There are several degrees of normalization, which formally describe the extent to which redundancies have been removed. Third normal form (3NF) is widely accepted as the optimal relational design for a transaction system. A star schema design is often referred to as *denormalized,* although it is actually in second normal form.

operational system   A database system that supports execution of a business process. Operational systems capture transactions and associated detail, usually storing this information in third normal form. For the data warehouse, operational systems serve as authoritative sources for enterprise data. Data warehouse practitioners often refer to operational systems as *transaction systems* or *source systems*.

periodic snapshot   See *snapshot*.

pivot fact table   A fact table that replaces a single fact and transaction type dimension with a series of facts, or vice versa. A fact table with a single fact and transaction type dimension will contain rows only for transaction types that occur at the specified grain. A fact table with a series of facts will contain a row if any one of the transaction types occurs. The two fact tables are queried differently, enabling different types of reports. They are not serviced by the aggregate navigator; each is accessed directly by application SQL. Invisible aggregate tables can be built to summarize pivoted fact tables.

pre-joined aggregate   A dimensional aggregate that combines aggregated facts with dimensional attributes. The pre-joined aggregate eliminates the need to join an aggregate fact table to a dimension or aggregate dimension. Pre-joined aggregates are often referred to as *big wide tables*. The redundant storage of dimensional data makes them larger than an aggregate star schema.

reporting tool   A commercial software product that is used to present information from the data warehouse to end users. See also *front-end tool*.

role   An occurrence of a dimension table that appears more than once in a single star schema. For example, a Date dimension appears in multiple roles in an accumulating snapshot. Roles do not require that the dimension be built more than once; views or SQL aliasing may be used to access the occurrences of dimensional data individually.

rollup dimension   A conforming dimension that contains a subset of another dimension's attributes, referenced directly by a base schema fact table. See also *aggregate dimension*.

SCD   See *slowly changing dimension*.

schema family   A base star schema and any aggregates that summarize it.

skew The uneven distribution of attribute values. Skew can result in aggregates that perform well for some queries but not for others.

sliced fact table A derived fact table containing a subset of base fact table data, derived by constraining on a dimensional attribute. Sometimes referred to as a *horizontal partition*. Sliced fact tables are identical to the base schema in structure but not in content. They are not serviced by the aggregate navigator; they are accessed directly by application SQL. Invisible aggregate tables may summarize a sliced fact table. Dimension-driven security schemes create a set of virtual sliced fact tables.

slowly changing dimension The process by which changes to operational data are translated into new or changed rows in the dimension tables of a star schema. See also *type 1 change* and *type 2 change*.

snowflake schema A variation on dimensional schema design in which dimension tables are further normalized, split into multiple tables based on hierarchies in the data.

star schema The instantiation of a dimensional model in a relational database. A star schema consists of a fact table and the dimension tables that it references. The fact table contains facts and foreign keys; the dimension tables contain dimensional attributes by which the facts will be filtered, rolled up, or grouped.

stovepipe data mart A departmentally focused data warehouse implementation that does not interoperate with other subject areas. Stovepipes are avoided through the design of a data warehouse bus—a set of conformed dimensions used consistently across subject areas.

surrogate key The primary key column of a dimension table. The surrogate key is unique to the data warehouse. Key values have no intrinsic meaning, and are assigned as part of the ETL process. By avoiding the use of a natural key, the data warehouse is able to handle changes to operational data in a different manner from transaction systems. The use of a surrogate key also eliminates the need to join fact and dimension tables via multi-part keys.

third normal form (3NF) A level of normalization in which all attributes in a table are fully dependent on its entire key. Third normal form is widely accepted as the optimal design for a transaction system. A schema in third normal form is often referred to as *fully normalized*, although there are actually additional degrees of normalization possible.

transaction dimension   A dimension table that is time-stamped with effective and expiration dates. A transaction dimension allows history of the dimension to be tracked in the absence of transactions, and facilitates point-in-time analysis of dimensional attributes. Aggregations of a transaction dimension usually omit the timestamps.

transaction system   See *operational system.*

type 1 change   A warehouse response to a change in source data in which corresponding dimension data is updated. A type 1 change effectively rewrites the history of facts that have already been associated with the dimension table row.

type 2 change   A warehouse response to a change in source data in which a new dimension row is created. A type 2 change allows the dimensional context of previously existing facts to remain unchanged, while new facts will be associated with the changed value.

warehouse bus   See *data warehouse bus.*

Index